Text Copyright © [Amanda Chamberlain]

All rights reserved. No part of this guide may be reproduced in any form without permission in writing from the publisher except in the case of brief quotations embodied in critical articles or reviews.

Legal & Disclaimer

The information contained in this book and its contents is not designed to replace or take the place of any form of medical or professional advice; and is not meant to replace the need for independent medical, financial, legal or other professional advice or services, as may be required. The content and information in this book has been provided for educational and entertainment purposes only.

The content and information contained in this book has been compiled from sources deemed reliable, and it is accurate to the best of the Author's knowledge, information and belief. However, the Author cannot guarantee its accuracy and validity and cannot be held liable for any errors and/or omissions. Further, changes are periodically made to this book as and when needed. Where appropriate and/or necessary, you must consult a professional (including but not limited to your doctor, attorney, financial advisor or such other professional advisor) before using any of the suggested remedies, techniques, or information in this book.

Upon using the contents and information contained in this book, you agree to hold harmless the Author from and against any damages, costs, and expenses, including any legal fees potentially resulting from the application of any of the information provided by this book. This disclaimer applies to any loss, damages or injury caused by the use and application, whether directly or indirectly, of any advice or information presented, whether for breach of contract, tort, negligence, personal injury, criminal intent, or under any other cause of action.

You agree to accept all risks of using the information presented inside this book.

You agree that by continuing to read this book, where appropriate and/or necessary, you shall consult a professional (including but

not limited to your doctor, attorney, or financial advisor or such

other advisor as needed) before using any of the suggested remedies, techniques, or information in this book.

Table of Contents

ABOUT AMANDA CHAMBERLAIN 9

INTRODUCTION 10

BOOK 1: INTRO, THE WICCAN RELIGION 12

CHAPTER 1: WHAT IS WICCA? 13
    1.1 What's the Difference Between Wicca and Witchcraft? 18
    1.2 What's the Difference Between a Witch and a Wiccan? 18
    1.3 What Does Wicca Have to Do with Magic? 19
    1.4 Wiccan Traditions 19
    1.5 Wiccan Beliefs 21
CHAPTER 2: HISTORY OF WICCA 25
CHAPTER 3: A QUICK INTRO TO WICCAN ALTAR 30
CHAPTER 4: GODDESS IN WICCA 32
    4.1 Origins of the Goddess and the God 32
    4.2 Goddess 36
    4.3 The Triple Goddess 37
CHAPTER 5: OTHER BELIEFS 39
    5.1 Reincarnation 39
    5.2 The Afterlife 40
    5.3 Animism 40

BOOK 2: WICCA WHEEL OF THE YEAR 42

CHAPTER 1: WHAT IS WICCA WHEEL OF THE YEAR 43
CHAPTER 2: VARIOUS SEASONS 46
    2.1 Samhain 46
    2.2 Yule 50
    2.3 Imbolc 56
    2.4 Ostara 60
    2.5 Beltane 67
    2.6 Mabon 71

BOOK 3: WICCA FOR BEGINNERS - STARTER KIT 76

CHAPTER 1: BASIC WICCAN PRINCIPLES AND ETHICS 77
CHAPTER 2: FUNDAMENTAL WICCA TOOLS 81
    2.1 Broom 81
    2.2 Baguette 82
    2.3 Censer 82
    2.4 Boiler 83
    2.5 Athame 83
    2.6 White Knife for the Handle 83
    2.7 Crystal Ball 83
    2.8 Herbs 86
    2.9 Essential Oils 90
    2.10 Cup / Cup 93

2.11 Bell 93
CHAPTER 3: THE WICCA CIRCLE 94
   3.1 The Magick Circle 95
   3.2 Creating a Circle 96
      3.2.1 Step 1 97
      3.2.2 Step 2 97
      3.2.3 Step 3 97
      3.2.4 Step 4 97
      3.2.5 Step 5 98
      3.2.6 Step 6 98
   3.3 Magical Techniques Like Astrology, Tarot, Runes, and More. 99
CHAPTER 4: WICCAN BEGINNER'S RITUAL 102
   4.1 Preparing Your Toolkit 102
   4.2 Making an Altar 105
   4.3 Intentions and Support 107
CHAPTER 5: MAGICKAL WORKINGS 109
   5.1 The Modern Witchcraft Journey 109
   5.2 Focus and Concentration 109
   5.3 Visualization 110
   5.4 Sacred Space 110
   5.5 Cleansing, Consecrating, and Charging 111

BOOK 4: WICCA BOOK OF SPELLS 113
   CHAPTER 1: AN INTRO TO WICCAN SPELLS 114
   CHAPTER 2: SOME PRACTICAL SPELLS 120
      2.1 Spells for Friendship 120
      2.2 Spells for Relationships 121
      2.3 Spell for Better Relationships 122
      2.4 Self-Love Ritual 123
      2.4.2 Working for Others 124
      2.5 Working with Sex & Orgasms 125
      2.6 Spell to Let Go of Old Love 126
      2.7 Soulmate Spell 127
      2.9 Herb and Candle Spell 131
   CHAPTER 3: MORE SPELLS FOR LIFE ENHANCEMENT 134
      3.1 Good Luck Spell 134
      3.2 Courage Spell 135
      3.3 Helpful Answers Spell 136
      3.4 Psychic Attack Reversal Spell 137
   CHAPTER 4: TOP TIPS FOR SPELLS 139

BOOK 5: WICCA BOOK OF THE SHADOWS 142
   CHAPTER 1: HISTORY OF BOOK OF SHADOWS 143
   CHAPTER 2: CREATING A PERSONAL BOOK OF SHADOWS 148
   CHAPTER 3: USING OUR BOOK OF SHADOWS 150
      3.1 Starting Out 150
      3.2 Magic Alphabets 152
      3.3 Keeping Your Book of Shadows Safe and Secure 154

3.3.1 A Spell to Protect Your Book of Shadows from Prying Eyes 155
CHAPTER 4: THE WHYS AND WAYS WICCANS USE THEIR BOOK OF SHADOWS 159
CHAPTER 5: MODERN DAY WITCHCRAFT AND THE BOOK OF SHADOWS 161
CONCLUSION 163

BOOK 6: WICCA CANDLE, CRYSTAL AND HERBAL MAGIC 165

INTRODUCTION 166
CHAPTER 1: WICCA CANDLE MAGIC 167
  1.1 The History of Candle Magic 168
  1.2 A Beginners Guide to Candle Magic 169
  1.3 Elemental Balance 170
  1.4 Beginners' "Luck" in Candle Magic 170
CHAPTER 2: WICCA CRYSTAL MAGIC 175
  2.1 Earthly Magic, Spiritual Energy 175
  2.2 Traditional Uses, Purposeful Practice 178
  2.3 Cleansing Crystals 180
  2.4 Crystals and Intention Setting 183
CHAPTER 3: WICCA HERBAL MAGIC 186
  3.1 An Introduction to Herbalism 186
  3.2 The Importance of the Nature in Wiccan Religion 186
  Wiccan Practices 188
  Ethics 189
CHAPTER 3: MORE 190
  The Pentacle 190
  The Athame 191
  The Goblet 191
  The Wand 192
  The Cauldron 192
  The Besom 192
  Mortar and Pestle 193

BOOK 7: WICCA MOON MAGIC 194

CHAPTER 1: THE WICCAN MOON 195
  1.1 An Introduction to Wiccan Moon 195
  1.2 The History of Modern Wicca 197
CHAPTER 2: RHYTHMS OF THE MOON 199
  2.1 Lunar Energy and Magic 199
  2.2 Tracking the Moon 199
  2.3 Magical Timing and the Lunar Cycle 202
CHAPTER 3: LUNAR PHASES 208
  3.1 Phases of the Moon 208
  3.2 Phase: Waning Crescent 209
CHAPTER 4: THE TRIPLE GODDESS 216
  The Maiden 219
  The Mother 219
  The Crone 219
CHAPTER 5: MORE 221
  Ankh 221

Aura... 221
Bat... 221
Bonfire... 221
Cats... 222
Circle... 222
Cloak.. 222
Crone.. 222
Divination.. 223
Dogs.. 223
Dowsing... 223
Energy.. 223
Evil Eye.. 223
Familiars.. 224
Feather... 224
Frogs.. 224
Ghost.. 224
Goddess.. 224
Grove.. 225
Herbs.. 225
Incense... 225
Menstruation.. 225
Midwife.. 225

BOOK 8: WICCA VS VOODOO 227

CHAPTER 1: UNDERSTANDING ESSENCE OF VOODOO 228
CHAPTER 2: PREPARING YOURSELF FOR SPELLS AND PROTECTION 230
CHAPTER 3: LEARNING BASIC VOODOO SPELLS 234
3.1 Healing Stone 234
3.2 Spell for Healing Sorrows 235
3.3 Money Magic Ritual 236
3.4 Banishing Spell 237
CHAPTER 4: DIFFERENCE BETWEEN WICCA AND VOODOO 240
4,1 Wicca 240
4.2 Wiccan Beliefs 243
4.3 Voodoo 245
4.4 Voodoo Beliefs and Practices 247
CHAPTER 5: ELEMENTS OF VOODOO 250
5.1 Belief in a Divine Creator 250
5.2 Vodoo Spirits, Animism, and Ancestor Worship 251
5.3 Belief in a Soul 251
5.4 Rituals, Priests and Priestesses 252
5.5 Talismans and Fetishes 252
5.6 Sabbats and Esbats 253
5.7 The Wiccan Elements 256

BOOK 9: PAGANISM 259

CHAPTER 1: WHAT IS PAGANISM 260
1.1 Sub-Religions of Paganism 262

 1.2 Neopaganism Beliefs 263
 1.3 The 'Old Religion' Beliefs 264
CHAPTER 2: PAGAN SYMBOLS 266
 2.1 Pentagram 267
 2.2 Triquatra 268
 2.3 Chalice 269
 2.4 Triskele 270
 2.5 Four Elements 271
 2.6 Triple Moon 271
 2.7 Caring for Your Pagan Symbols 272
CHAPTER 3: SIMPLE RITUALS FOR STARTERS 274
 3.1 Understanding the Pagan Ritual 274
 3.2 Pagan Rites of Passage 275
 3.3 Pagan Prayers 278
CHAPTER 4: MYTHS ABOUT PAGANISM 281
 4.1 Paganism Does Not Mean Materialism. 281
 4.2 Paganism Does Not Advocate Black Magic or Animal Sacrifice 281
 4.3 What Do Wiccans Believe? 282
 4.4 Gods and Goddesses 284
 4.5 Wiccan Holidays and Rituals 285

BOOK 10: TAROTS FOR BEGINNERS **287**

CHAPTER 1: WHAT IS TAROT 288
 1.1 Other Theories 289
 1.2 Archetypes and Their Effect on Culture and Society 290
CHAPTER 2: TAROT MECHANICS 292
 2.1 Quantum Physics, Synchronicity, and the Tarot 292
CHAPTER 3: INTRODUCTION TO CARDS 298
CHAPTER 4: THE MINOR ARCANA 302
 4.1 Reading with Minor Arcana Cards 302
 4.2 Tarot Spreads 306
CONCLUSION 316

CAN I ASK YOU A FAVOR? **318**

About Amanda Chamberlain

When it comes to knowledge and writings regarding Wicca, her name is one of the most recognizable names. She has several years of experience in practicing Wicca and has great knowledge in her field as well. There are several books that she has written on the subject. Her books are a complete compilation about Wicca and help the reader to discard all the misbeliefs and myths about the practice of the subject Wicca. Her books can help the reader to strengthen their belief in religion and can also help to change their views about this particular religion. This is not something which you can learn solely through reading books and searching up facts and figures on the internet, but requires a complete command over Wicca and how is it being practiced or how should it be implemented for the daily use. Amanda Chamberlain is a person who fulfills all these criteria hence having a well-known reputation in this field as an author as well as a practitioner.

She makes things easy and convenient for the learners, beginners and all those in need through her work and experience. She always has clear ideas about what she wants to learn, practice and what she wants other people to learn and know about it. Her books are of great help in every aspect.

Introduction

It's important to clear a few things up before we get started. Although this guide is primarily aimed at Wiccans, not all Wiccans consider themselves to be magical practitioners-some only use candles to revere the Goddess and the God in their many forms, as well as the Elements of Earth, Air, Fire, Water, and Spirit.

Furthermore, this book will still be of relevance to non-Wiccans - not all Witches consider themselves Wiccans, after all, and many practice magic without having a spiritual relationship with any deities.

Whoever you are, and whatever your beliefs, you are more than welcome here. However, it is worth pointing out that candle magic has Pagan roots—one trait found in just about any Pagan tradition is the belief in, and use of, the power of candles.

In this guide, you'll learn the basics of working with candles for magical purposes, including the reasons underlying successful magic, the best approaches to acquiring candles and preparing them for spellwork, and a selection of candle spells to try out on your own.

You'll also find ideas and resources for creating your own magic through the use of oils and herbs, as well as enhancing your work with an awareness of right timing by paying attention to the phases of the Moon and the days of the week.

However, no matter how much knowledge you acquire, it's really the practice of magic that leads to success. Be willing to try and try again, and you will ultimately find yourself with the ability to transform your life. Science is valuable, but is certainly not the end all be all of explaining and experiencing reality. This is where Wicca and other magical studies come into play. Many feel it is the duty of the magical practitioner to do this spiritual work to rebuild the relationship between humans and our friends who also inhabit this reality, even if it's interdimensional or beyond our sensory perception. This may sound complicated, but just like any skill it takes time, practice and experience.

Book 1: Intro, the Wiccan Religion

Chapter 1: What Is Wicca?

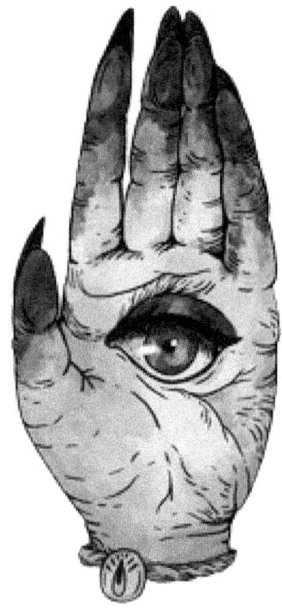

One common misconception about Wicca is that it's an ancient practice passed down through the centuries by initiates to new practitioners. While the practices within the Wiccan sphere are loosely based on ancient traditions and pagan natural magic, Wicca itself is relatively young. Many adherents of the religion claim it to be a true pagan practice passed down from prehistory, but there is little proof of this lineage within the communities. For our intents and purposes in this book we will follow the recent history of the religion.

Often referred to as the "Old Religion" or "Pagan Witchcraft", Wicca comes with its own set of tenets, practices, and beliefs that are rooted in ancient pagan traditions. As with other religions, there are numerous types and paths of Wicca which people can practice. Becoming a Wiccan can be a long process that demands concentration, focus, and studying. However, it can be a very satisfying and gratifying belief system to stick to and follow.

Wicca first gained attention in the early parts of the 20th century. Many attribute Gerald Gardner for bringing it to the public forefront. Wicca gradually started

gaining more followers over the next few decades. It exploded in popularity when followers started insisting on having their faith recognized during the late 1950's and early 1960's. From that point, Wicca began to spread throughout Europe and across the United States, where it gained popularity among the counter culture youth of the 1960's. Over the years, it has continued to gain in popularity and new forms of Wicca have increasingly popped up all over the world.

Wicca is primarily based on believing that there is a Goddess that is at the center of all creation and life. Depending on which version of Wicca you practice, some weigh gods and goddesses equally, believing there to be balance and duality in the world. While duo-theism is often seen as traditional Wicca, there are other Wiccan beliefs that range from polytheism to monism to pantheism.

In Wicca, there aren't any holy books, saints, prophets, or other forms of intermediaries. Anyone practicing Wicca is said to have direct access to the Divine or Goddess. The Divine is said to live in each and every person.

The Wiccan Creed or Rede is a central tenet followed by Wiccans that states: "If You Harm None, Do What You Will". Wicca values the harmony we should live our life by. Wiccans believe that as long as we aren't harming others, or infringing on their way of life, we should be able to proceed as we see fit. Another big belief among Wiccans is the threefold rule. This basically means whatever actions you take will end up coming back to you threefold. The threefold rule applies to both negative and positive actions.

In Wicca, a person takes responsibility for any actions they take. Wiccans believe that a person has to be responsible for their actions and words. It's completely on the individual how they react to any outside forces or issues. Wiccans believe that accepting responsibility and making amends are the best way to handle things when you've made a mistake. The concept of harmony with nature is an important aspect of the Wiccan

lifestyle. Wiccans believe that all life is sacred. People are living in a partnership with the earth and are reliant on the bounty the world provides in order to

survive. Wiccans believe that life and nature occur in one big cycle and that we as humans are a part of this cycle.

This also leads to the belief in some form of reincarnation depending on the type of Wicca you practice. It is not a central practice so not all forms believe in it. For those that do, it stems from the fact that things in nature always keep returning. For example, sea water evaporates and becomes clouds, clouds eventually give us rain. Death like life is just another part of nature's cycle.

Different Forms of Wicca

Over the years, Wicca has continued to evolve, leading to the many different forms that are being practiced today. In this next section, I'm going to discuss a few of the main forms of Wicca being practiced, some of their rituals, along with some of their beliefs. There are many other forms of Wicca being practiced. This is just a little more information for you on a few of the larger, more popular forms.

Gardnerian

This form of Wicca was founded by a man named Gerald B Gardner. He is one of the most important figures in Wicca, as he is primarily referred to as the father of modern Wicca. The reason for this is he was the first to come out in public about his beliefs.

Gardnerian Wicca requires a person be initiated. This form of Wicca works within a strict degree system. Much of the information taught in this form must be held secret under oath, therefore, cannot be shared with people outside their path. Some believe this form to be the only true form of Wicca, but that is a hotly debated argument.

In this system, the idea of Goddess over God is emphasized a great deal. Gardnerian Wicca follows a more structured religion, one that has a well-defined hierarchy within each of their groups or covens. However, different covens have little or no authority over each other. In each coven there exists a matriarchy, with a High Priestess normally considered the one in charge. This is not always the case, there are exceptions.

The Gardnerian practitioners view the Goddess as having three faces. Those faces are comprised of the maiden, the mother, and the crone. There is also a male consort that is referred to by a variety of different names.

The Gardnerian practitioners hold many ceremonies and celebrations throughout the year, either celebrating the different holidays based on the Wheel of the Year calendar or to initiate members into a higher level.

Alexandrian

This form of Wicca was originally founded by a man named Alex Sanders. This form of Wicca is very influenced by the Gardnerian form of Wicca. They both use initiations and degree systems. The main difference between the two is that Alexandrian Wicca put a heavy focus on a sense of equality between both the God and Goddess. They also focus heavily on performing ceremonial magick during Sabbats and Esbats.

Traditionalist

This is a form of Wicca that is normally used to describe the first of the Wiccan traditions, predating all other forms that are practiced today. It started with the British, and members can be initiated only by someone who is a member.

Traditionalist Wiccans must continue to maintain a high level of practices and training. They believe in structure. Each of these groups is based on the myths, literature, traditions, and folktales of their demographic and geographic region. Their beliefs are a mix between Gardnerian and Alexandrian Wicca.

Seax

This form of Wicca was founded originally by a man named Raymond Buckland. This form of Wicca is also sometimes referred to as Saxon Wicca. While this is a traditional form of Wicca, the main difference between this and some of the aforementioned forms is that Seax Wicca has public open rituals. Following this path also doesn't require any type of initiation into a lineage. Seax Wiccans are allowed to either practice in covens or on their own. They realize that not all areas will have a coven nearby to practice with, therefore, members are allowed to self-initiate and practice alone. These people are often called Solitaires. Seax

Wicca also encourages its Priests and Priestesses to modify or add practices and rituals as they deem is necessary when no regulations are already in place. In Seax Wicca, you normally deal with Germanic Runes and Deities for any type of divination.

Celtic

This form of Wicca combines Gardnerian and Druid Wicca. Celtic Wicca places a big emphasis on nature, the elements, and the Ancient Ones. Celtic Wicca believes in the magick and healing properties of stones, plants, trees, flowers, elemental spirits, faeries, and gnomes. Overall, this form of Wicca uses the same general theology, beliefs, and rituals that are employed by other paths of Wicca. The main difference is they use their own Celtic figures, deities, and seasonal holidays.

Eclectic

This form of Wicca combines many different traditions to form new traditions. Eclectic Wicca can be either practiced alone or in covens. People who follow this form of Wicca don't follow any one denomination, magickal practice, sect, or set of traditions. Instead, they are constantly learning and studying from a variety of different paths, applying what they think works best.

Blue Star Witchcraft

This form denounces the term Wicca and only refers to Witchcraft or Witches. This form of witchcraft uses many of the same beliefs and rituals as Gardnerian Wicca. They both use a degree system and initiations, however, in Blue Star Witchcraft they use a 5 level system instead of a 3 degree one.

Dianic

This form of Wicca was born out of Feminism. It focuses almost entirely on the Goddess and anything feminine. It allows for either female covens, mixed covens or individual practitioners. This form of Wicca honors Sabbats but doesn't have a ton of continuity in its rituals. Dianic Wicca also encourages females be in leadership roles and insists on having a Priestess in attendance to open a circle.

1.1 What's the Difference Between Wicca and Witchcraft?

Wiccans who don't identify as Witches don't use the term "Witchcraft" in association with their practice of Wicca—they don't use magic, and they draw a distinction between Wicca as a spiritual practice and individual relationship with the divine, and witchcraft as a practice that is not necessarily spiritual.

However, many Wiccans do blend magic into their practice to varying degrees, and may use "magic" as an interchangeable term with "Witchcraft" (often shortened to "the Craft") in association with Wicca.

In fact, some Witches who practice Witchcraft don't identify as Wiccan at all.

1.2 What's the Difference Between a Witch and a Wiccan?

Depending on who you ask, there's a big difference, or there's not much (if any) difference.

In terms of language, the words "witch" and "wicca" are related, as "wicca" was the Old English word that later became "witch." However, among Wiccans the relationship between the two words is less black-and-white—there are Witches who identify as Wiccans, Witches who don't, and Witches who don't have a preference. There are also Wiccans who don't identify as Witches. The varied uses of these words can be seen throughout contemporary writing about Wicca and Witchcraft. In addition to the name of the religion, some authors use "Wicca" as a singular word in place of "Witch," but most use "Wicca" as a plural term, meaning that several (or all) Wiccans can be collectively called "the Wicca." Finally, while the words "Wicca" and "Wiccan" tend to be capitalized—especially in reference to the religion and its members—but there seem to be no hard and fast rules regarding whether to capitalize the words "Witch" and "Witchcraft" or leave them in lower case.

Some followers of Wiccan traditions who don't adopt the name "Wicca" as a personal identifier feel no need to identify with a capital "W" for "Witch" or "Witchcraft." Others feel that capitalization of these terms is important in

distinguishing Wicca as an official religion and establishing a cultural respect for it as such. In the spirit of respect for those who feel strongly about recognizing Wicca as a religion, this guide capitalizes all four terms.

1.3 What Does Wicca Have to Do with Magic?

Once again, it depends on who you ask, and for Wiccans who don't practice magic of any kind, the answer is probably "nothing." However, many, many Wiccans **do** include magic in their practice, to the point that the two are combined in many Wiccan books and resources—including this very guide! Most Witches will refer to their practice of magic as Witchcraft but may use either term. And of course, the word "magic" is also a bit tricky, as it has its own set of meanings.

"Ceremonial magic" is older than Wicca and was an original influence for what would eventually become Wicca, but it's actually a practice in its own right—in other words, not part of the religion. This ceremonial magic has several differences from the magic practiced by Witches. Ceremonial magic was derived from occult traditions through secret societies like the Freemasons and the Hermetic Order of the Golden Dawn and is often quite elaborately ritualized. The term "high magic" is sometimes used to distinguish it from Witchcraft, which is called "folk magic" or even "low magic" by many of its practitioners. Some who practice ceremonial magic may identify as Pagans but are not Wiccans or Witches. Some simply identify as magicians.

What some call "practical magic" is a kind of ceremonial magic aimed at achieving common life improvements, such as healing physical or emotional ills, attracting love, and improving one's finances. Some Wiccans see this form of magic as non-spiritual and distinct from Wicca, but others blend the two by performing magic in alignment with their deities and for the good of all, rather than just for their own personal gain.

1.4 Wiccan Traditions

From Gardner's form of the craft (which he never called "Wicca," by the way—that came later), other traditions developed. Initiates in Gardner's lineage went

on to form Alexandrian and Seax Wicca, just to name a couple. The continuing development of this very diverse religion has gotten to the point where there are probably more Wiccan paths than can be described in one book— particularly if you include eclectic practitioners in the mix. However, those new to the Craft who are reading around on the Internet and in print are most likely to encounter one of three main "branches" on the tree of Wicca—Gardnerian, Alexandrian, or Dianic—either in their "pure form" or in forms loosely based on the original.

These three, along with a few other more commonly encountered traditions, will be discussed in further detail later in this guide.

1.4.1 What's the Difference Between One Tradition and Another?

Each Wiccan tradition has its own way of practicing the religion: the protocols for rituals, the deities to worship, the structure of worship, how a coven is organized, and any number of other details large and small may differ from one tradition to the next.

Two Wiccan traditions may have some of the same things in common, such as a similar way to begin a sabbat ritual, but differ widely in other ways, such as the pantheon their patron deities are selected from.

While there are set rules in each tradition, it's generally understood that covens and solitary practitioners alike may add to the tradition's teachings and adapt the rules as necessary, so long as the tradition's main teachings remain intact. This will depend on how "orthodox" the coven or solitary prefers to be.

Of course, once too many changes are made, the tradition is no longer being followed, which means it's likely that a new tradition is being formed.

1.4.2 Do I Have to Follow a Specific Tradition?

In essence, all Wiccans use the work and beliefs of one tradition or another, at least to some extent.

Unless you're literally making up every single aspect of your practice (in which case, you're not actually practicing Wicca), then you're following in the footsteps of those who came before you.

That being said, there's a lot of variety in terms of how strictly any given Wiccan adheres to the "way it's always been" along a particular path.

Covens typically follow specific Wiccan traditions that dictate their structure, rituals, and spell-work. While covens tend to adhere pretty strictly to their tradition, they may from time to time make exceptions, but this will depend on a unique set of circumstances that prevail in the group.

Solitary practitioners also follow traditions. Some follow a specific tradition as closely as they can, while other prefer to put their own twist on older versions of practice.

Some people follow many different aspects of several traditions, preferring to mix and match. This is called Eclectic Wicca, something that we'll look deeper at a little later. Finding and following a tradition in Wicca is a wonderful thing because it's a way to learn and grow into your shoes, so to speak. It can be a great feeling to know that you found the right religion for you, and this is what following a tradition can provide.

Sometimes there can be some trial and error involved, though. If you're checking out a coven in your area and find that the tradition the coven is following isn't exactly what you had envisioned for yourself, simply search for other options and learn as much as you can along the way until you find the perfect fit.

That is, of course, one of the most appealing parts of being Wiccan: the ability to adapt and grow into the right path. You may even find yours by starting with an established tradition, and then moving on to your own eclectic practice. This approach is great for the independently-minded newbie.

Just keep in mind that wherever your ultimate path leads you, knowledge is crucial, so you should always be willing to learn— whether it be from books like this one, or from a coven or circle in your area. We'll take a closer look at these "in-person" options in the next few sections of this guide.

1.5 Wiccan Beliefs

We have seen Wicca's Journey through the past century as it adopts ancient traditions and newer ones. With all the different branches and traditions, almost

anyone can find a finely tuned Wicca group that adheres to their political or spiritual ideals. But at the core of any tradition there are fundamental and universal beliefs based on Gardner's publicized teachings. These beliefs may be derived from other religions and practices, but overall are seen today as Wiccan. Many different people identify as Wiccan, not every person within the Wiccan sphere believes the same thing, so keep an open mind as we explore some of the popular beliefs in Wicca today. One main source of differing opinion is whether or not the gods and goddesses in Wicca are actual beings or simply symbolic representations similar to Carl Jung's archetypes. You can make your own choice on this big question, and with experience your choice may be validated or disproven.

We will go over some of the core values of Wicca followed by an easy reference guide. Some features covered will include: duotheism, polytheism, monotheism, atheism, magic, witchcraft, elements and death. All of these philosophies are filtered through a moral lens that is upheld regardless of belief. These descriptions will be brief, but we will discuss them in detail in subsequent chapters.

1.5.1 Belief in God

Wicca is generally believed to be a dualistic religion with a feminine goddess and masculine god who work together as the governors of Earth and all existence. While this is the common theme, most Wiccans believe in an eternal 'source' that is infinite and not able to be known with the human senses. Many Wiccan traditions also adhere to the idea there are various other aspects of the god and goddess that manifest in various forms. These forms can be thought of as gods or goddesses, but also as spirits, entities or forces. All in all, it is safe to say the eternal source is all-encompassing and permeates all existence. The god and goddess are male and female divisions of the source, and any other life forms are comprised of masculine and feminine energies that can be symbolic of the god and goddess as they create Earth and its inhabitants through their infinite dance of death and rebirth.

1.5.2 Magic

Magic tends to avoid a distinct definition; it encompasses a wide range of practices; conjuration, astrology, tarot, prayer, meditation, spells, sigils, and many other techniques can be considered magical.

Overall, magic aims to improve your life through communion with nature or manipulating unseen forces for your personal benefit. Some consider selfish or evil magic to be black magic, while good or selfless magic is called white magic.

1.5.3 Witchcraft

Witchcraft is considered a form of magic that focuses on natural magic and herbal magic. These techniques are powered by the archetype of the witch in all her forms. The goddess in Wicca can be seen as these forms. Herbalism, elemental magic, full moon sabbats, and many sublunary practices are in league with witchcraft. This current of power is often very feminine and aims to break taboos. The underprivileged and oppressed masses are the populace of witchcraft, which aims to rewild the Earth and rebuild humanity's relationship with nature.

1.5.4 The Five Elements

The five elements are found in many cultures. Air, earth, fire, water and aether are the primary five in Wicca. These elements are thought to be what all things are made of. Modern science has disproven this concept as a literal philosophy, but symbolically these elements are still very powerful.

1.5.5 Death

In Wicca death is not feared as a negative thing. It is viewed as a transit to another plane of existence. Many Wiccans welcome death and view it as a positive thing. Death is not the end of life for Wiccans.

Wiccans also make it a point to honor their ancestors who have passed. Ancestral altars and offerings are commonplace in Wicca. These practices help prepare and accept death as inevitable, while also building relationships with the dead. It always helps to have friends on the other side!

1.5.6 Initiation

As per Gardner's original structure, one must enter through rites of passage to be properly initiated into a Wiccan coven. Gardner taught that these rites must be performed to initiate one into the religion. These initiation rituals have been practiced since Gardner's time and keep a lineage with his original rites. As we've mentioned Gardner claims to have been taught these rites from a coven he joined that claimed to be a lineage of pre-Christian pagan systems of initiation. Many Wiccans today do not adhere to this idea, instead just keeping the lineage history as starting with Gardner's first rites. Gardner taught it takes a year and one day from the time someone starts practicing the craft to the instance of initiation, but many sources claim he broke this rule often. For a general overview of these rites there are three degrees; first is starting your practice, second being familiarization with ritual tools and rites, then third being the participation in the Great Rite, this rite being a sexual initiation performed physically or symbolically with magical tools, more on the details on these practices in later chapters. Gardner claimed these rites must be performed in the nude, but many covens today disregard this idea, opting for robes or even casual clothing.

Self-initiation is also popular among lone practitioners or couples who do not wish to join a group. Paul Huson's wonderful book *Mastering Witchcraft* was one of the first to offer effective insight into self-initiation, and still stands strong today as an effective book. Self-initiation is sometimes ridiculed by pagan groups, but it can be effective. Remember, there is not only one way to become a Wiccan that works for everyone.

Chapter 2: History of Wicca

The history of witchcraft dates back to the Paleolithic about 40,000 years ago. Archaeologists have discovered cave paintings of this period depicting witchcraft in its basic form. Our ancient ancestors would not have considered themselves witches, but they used practices associated with witchcraft today.

Witchcraft evolved from that time on and was much more commonly referred to as such from before the Middle Ages. The practice of witchcraft was fundamental to many cultures of this period and was widely practiced in Europe where it is most often referenced. The emergence of Christianity as the main religion of the time would bring unspeakable misery to those who practice witchcraft.

Many of the so-called Witches of that time, who for the most part were healers who used basic herbs to treat their villages, were persecuted as a result of the edicts of Pope John XXII in 1320. The history of witchcraft was mainly peaceful until that time, since witches were not directly sought by the Inquisition, but this edict authorized the Inquisition to pursue Wizards as well. Modern practices are widely called neopaganism, although this term does not accurately represent the many varieties followed in modern times. Traditional witchcraft as a way of life with a very limited direct structure is probably the most common, but there are more irregular religious forms of witchcraft. Wicca is perhaps the best known of them and is very much a religion involving witchcraft. During the history of witchcraft, there were established general principles governing all congregations or witches, which led to each Coven practicing the Arts in their own way, as directed by their individual direction. Solo practice is also wide and unique, always following the same beliefs.

Wiccan beliefs many people practice today can trace their ancestors to our ancient stone age past. Evidence of the beginning of Wicca's long history can be seen for the first time in the cave paintings of the Pyrenean regions of France and Spain dating back about 17,000 years. Concerned about the success of the hunt,

 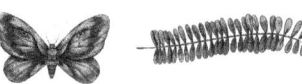 

these paintings are usually very far underground and are clearly destined to invoke the help of the Goddess Mother Earth.

A major change in the history of Wicca came with the spread of Agriculture in Europe about 10,000 years ago. Peoples' relationship with the Earth has changed and their need for a wider range of deities to help and protect them has expanded. As communities grew, it became necessary for a specialized priesthood to evolve. In the history of Wicca, Celtic Druids are often established as direct ancestors of today's Wiccan. Druids trained in their craft for twenty years before becoming very important and influential members of their communities. Often considered the culmination of the history of Wicca were able to move freely between tribes and kingdoms. The power of the Druids was so great that many historians now believe that the Romans brought Britain into the Empire to put an end to their influence in Gaul. With the fall of the Druids, religious beliefs returned to a more personal and disorganized level. This was the situation until the suppression of these beliefs from the middle of the first millennium by the new Christian religion. From this moment to the present day, the history of Wicca has changed from being an openly practiced religion and by necessity has become "underground". The Latin word "pagan" simply means an inhabitant of the countryside or the rustic, the ancient ways were kept alive in rural areas by "wise women" who would have used their knowledge of magic and plant lore, to help their neighbors, and it was at this time in the history of the god and goddess That the ancient ways were kept alive in the areas

Fortunately, in the mid-twentieth century there has been a revival of interest in the old-fashioned way, with the publication in 1954 of Gerald Gardner's book "Witchcraft Today" is generally considered to be a renaissance time in the history of Wicca, to the point that today it is the 5th largest religion in the United States, with nearly 1 million active participants.

Scholars suggest Wicca was developed in England sometime between 1920 and 1930. Gerald Gardner is viewed as the inventor of this version of Wicca, although there were forms of it that predated Gardner's Wicca. Gardner was influenced greatly by the writings of notable magician Aleister Crowley and other Victorianera ceremonial magicians. Crowley developed a religion himself known as Thelema. Other notable societies during this era include freemasons, Golden Dawn and Theosophist movements. Wicca draws from these groups both in structure and practice, while also mixing the folk magic of European tradition.

There is no set leader in Wicca, but the general structures and philosophies were presented publicly by Gardner with assistance from Doreen Valiente in books openly published and available to the wider population in the 1950s. These books held the general ideas of Wicca, while many deeper teachings were reserved for oral teachings within the religion's meetings and rituals. As with any religion these core teachings have been separated into various sects and lineages with slight variations on beliefs and practices. These traditions have their own respected leaders and philosophies; this leads to much debate on what actually defines Wicca.

We see that Wicca takes many of its ideas and practices from many other religions. These basic ideas are formed as a part of a notion that there existed a pre-Christian cult of witchcraft in Europe that still exists today. Many Wiccans believe they are continuing this lineage with practices similar to these witches who were not in league with Satan as the persecutions alleged but were communing with nature and the spirits therein. This lineage is up for debate, many believing its true nature is held secret, while others believe the practices openly performed within Wicca are the actual lineage being upheld. Regardless of the truth of the lineage,

It's hard to say if the first Wiccans were actually the surviving members of an older lineage, whether blood or spirit, but nonetheless Wicca provides a powerful current to tap into. Garner whole-heartedly promoted the idea of Wicca being a true lineage of with cults that survive in Europe, his books *Witchcraft Today* and *The Meaning of Witchcraft* both contain his passion and fervor for this idea. Many scholars today see the parallels of masonry and Golden Dawn practices rather than witch trial era practices and especially not ancient paganism, which has shown to be more extreme in practice and lifestyle.

Gardner further claims he was initiated into a coven in Hampshire in the 1930s, but this claim is unfounded. Gardner eventually founded his own coven in the 1940s based on the alleged teaching he had learned in the Hampshire coven.

Once the 1950s arrived Wicca was seeing its first resurgence as a popular religion. This is around the time many laws against witchcraft were being lifted, science did the craft a favor during these times as many powerful leaders dismissed witchcraft as unreal and superstition. Now Gardner could publicize his teachings without the fear of social ridicule or lawful persecution.

During his life Gardner never actually named his religion Wicca. The term came from him referring to practitioners of the craft 'the Wicca.' He typically named the practices witchcraft or old religion. After his death in 1964, Wicca became the normalized term for a general name of the practice while adherents to Gardner's specific structure was termed Gardneriansim.

During the 1960s and around the time of Gardner's passing, the practice continued to grow rapidly. The 60s were a time of extreme social change for the western world; soon these ideas found their way to the youth of the decade, who were more openminded than their parents, openly seeking any new ideas they could find to fit into their radical mindset and hippie aesthetic. Gardner's Wicca soon sees its structure being altered and rebranded, notably Alexandrian Wicca, which is identical to Gardner's teachings, but with greater focus on Ceremonial Magical practices that were so popular in the Victorian era. As Wicca branched off into different traditions it made its way overseas to America and Australia.

As the 1970s began, Wicca became a more favorable term compared to witchcraft, it seemed friendlier and more welcoming than the pop culture idea of witches and 'dark magic.' Along with the new decade, Wicca is seen to merge with more political ideas like environmentalism and practices from India like yoga and meditation, although these Indian philosophies are found in Theosophy and Crowley's writings respectively.

We see dozens of different branches of Wicca being formed for any slight change in practice and social-political ideals; the 70s found many groups wishing to take advantage of Gardner's base structure and make it their own, for better or worse. These different branches have come and gone, but all focus mainly on the core idea of natural magic mashed with whatever the leader of a certain group wished to propagate.

With this wider acceptance of witchcraft, we see books and material being offered to the public containing effective methods for an individual to practice witchcraft without the help of a secret society or coven. Many denounced these books claiming one can only be initiated through a lineage or coven, this is quite untrue, but a popular take from leaders of various groups hoping to gather more followers. It is safe to say anyone can self-initiate by themselves, but keep in mind this can be dangerous, but so can following a false guru. Choose what works best for you; there is no one true path.

Chapter 3: A Quick Intro to Wiccan Altar

As the physical focal point of just about any Wiccan ritual, the altar is crucial to spell-casting and general practice, and it also serves as a central force in any number of celebrations throughout the year: celebrating Sabbats and Esbats (full moons), practicing meditation, saying prayers, or creating spells are all activities during which the altar can be a focal point. If you don't wish to create a permanent altar in your home, you can certainly set one up outside in a private, secluded space or you can construct a small, moveable altar that can be put away after a ritual or ceremony is over. Practicing Wicca outdoors is a preference for many, as it allows you to communicate more closely with nature and the spiritual.

There are no particular requirements when it comes to what the altar looks like, though it does need to have an accommodating flat surface upon which to place tools, ornaments, and other ritual items. Many Wiccans prefer a round shape, both because of its feminine and egalitarian associations and for its practical use in creating the sacred circle. Additionally, as with other Wiccan tools, the ideal altar is made of natural materials—wood or stone, not plastic or other human-made material. Other than these basic requirements, the altar can be made of whatever you have on hand, an underused desk or a coffee or end table. It is not necessary to purchase something new, though if you intend to use your altar with any frequency, it might be a good idea to find one that you can use continuously, rather than having to clear it up and put it away frequently.

Once you have the surface of your altar, be sure to adorn it with whatever colors and decorations you feel give it a magical aura - this is the goal, of course, to transform an ordinary surface into an extraordinary place in which your intentions are heard and your rituals are successful. You can change this according to the seasons, of course, using browns and golds during autumn and greens and yellows during spring; always be in tune with natural cycles when you can. The altar is also a place to keep energy channelling crystals or stones, images of deities or other symbolic representations, and candles. However, the main function of the altar during ritual is to hold your tools in some kind of

thoughtful arrangement. As with all things Wiccan, this arrangement is mostly up to the individual practitioner, but there are a couple of standard arrangements that you can follow: first, a simple way to arrange your altar is to arrange all tools associated with the Mother Goddess (water and earth elements) to the left of center, while all tools associated with the Horned God or male deity (air and fire elements) to the right of center.

Again, many Wiccans will simply arrange their altar according to their own intuitive feeling, and you should feel free to do such, especially after you've had some time to practice and start to understand how energy works best for you.

The most important issue to remember when setting up your altar is that no one way is right or wrong, that no matter how large or small your area is, it is still meaningful. Indeed, you are the one to endow the space and the tools with energy and intention, so it should feel right for you. It should be a space of power, of energy, of serenity—and of practical use. If it's too crowded or if you cannot find what you need, then you know that it's not working as well as it could. In addition, each ritual need not be practiced on the same altar; a tree stump behind your home might serve particularly well for a harvest Sabbat, while your small home altar serves you better for daily meditation. The above are just some ideas to get you started.

Chapter 4: Goddess in Wicca

4.1 Origins of the Goddess and the God

Many thousands of years ago, long before any of the religions in existence today were developed, human beings experienced divinity very directly. There was no need for churches or temples, or written texts explaining the existence and desires of an invisible, far-away, supernatural "overseer." Instead, early humans encountered the divine in their immediate surroundings. Plants, animals, rocks, mountains and streams were infused with spirit energy, as were words, songs, and stories. Nothing was "supernatural," since there was no separation between the perceived physical world and the invisible spirit world.

In some cultures, individual objects had their own distinct spirits, or "souls," while in other cultures, everything was part of the same divine source. In describing the origins of religion in human society, historians and anthropologists call the first concept "animism" and the second one "pantheism," though in practice the two worldviews would have had some overlap, as they still do today.

No one knows exactly when or how the phenomenon of individual deities first came about. We only know that as human culture evolved, so did our way of perceiving and describing this primordial spiritual energy.

The earliest deities we have records of tended to be associated with the essential components of the physical Universe - the sky, the Sun, bodies of water - and the most basic of life's needs and functions - safety, shelter, success on a hunt. The Sumerian sky god Anu is one of the earliest known examples, though there are doubtless older ones which are lost to history. Over time, as the development of agriculture led to permanent settlements and life became more complex, the mythology of these ancient societies began to include deities who were associated with more sophisticated pursuits such as poetry, schools, and crafts - like the Roman goddess Minerva, who governed all three.

Not all deities were of equal importance or power. Some "lesser" deities guarded or inhabited specific natural places, such as a spring or a grove of trees, while other "greater" deities had the command of weather, battles, the annual harvest, and other crucial facets of life.

For the most part, deities were local-meaning they were only known to the people living in a given area. But as some societies began expanding beyond their original territories and settling in new regions - like the Romans, the Celts, and the Germanic tribes—they brought their deities with them, spreading their influence far and wide across continents. The Celtic Sun god Belenus, for instance, is one of the oldest and most widely known deities in Europe. An even older goddess, Innana spread through space and time across Mesopotamia and into Greek civilization, where she became Aphrodite.

By the time Christianity was developing and gaining influence, there were probably tens of thousands of individual deities throughout the world, if not more. In many places, such as India, Japan, and parts of Africa and Native America, some of these deities continue to be honored today.

In most of the Western world, however, this is not the case. The rise and spread of the Judeo-Christian "God" eventually all but stamped out the ancient, "pagan" religions, particularly throughout Europe. And since the people in these regions were largely illiterate, relying on the oral tradition to pass down their beliefs and customs from one generation to the next, there's not much specific information to be found about what is now often referred to as "the Old Religion."

Nonetheless, the deities themselves never truly "died out," as the myths, epics, and other legends that kept them immortal were never completely forgotten. And small pockets of pagan worship, along with other practices that would later come to be called "Witchcraft," remained active in Europe - even through the worst of the centuries of persecution.

Furthermore, there were always at least a few curious people in each generation who studied the lore of the ancient past, keeping the flame of occult knowledge alive, and developing new ways to explore and practice what our pagan ancestors had always understood. Gerald Gardner, widely considered to be the founder of modern Wicca, was one of these people.

In the early decades of the 20th century, Gardner explored many avenues of religious mysticism and occult teachings, befriending a wide variety of influential thinkers along the way. He wound up meeting with a group of Witches practicing what Gardner believed to be an ancient religion, which had been secretly kept alive throughout the centuries since pre-Christian times. This group, known as the New Forest Coven, initiated Gardner and presented him with some of the spiritual teachings that he later brought to his own coven, Bricket Wood. Other occult influences, such as Freemasonry and ceremonial magic, along with Gardner's own intuitive innovations, made up the rest of the beliefs and practices that he and his initiates began to follow.

The core element of this new version of "the Old Religion" was the worship of a pagan god, usually referred to as the Horned God, and a pagan goddess, often referred to as the Great Mother.

These were believed to be ancient deities of the British Isles, who had been buried in obscurity by Christianity, but were now being pulled back into modern awareness through a duotheistic religion that later came to be called Wicca, which was rooted in gender polarity—the male and female being both opposite and equal, and present in all of nature. (Gardner's cosmology also involved a supreme higher power, which he called the "Prime Mover," but this power was beyond the ability of humans to know or understand, and therefore not of much practical concern.) The God and Goddess, as they are referred to in their most general form, are more often described as archetypes—the masculine and feminine energies arising from the collective unconscious—than as historically known deities from a specific culture or location.

However, they can also be thought of as encompassing several individual "aspects," or "lesser" deities. Some of these aspects are also archetypes, but many are actual known deities from a variety of ancient cultures, including the Egyptians, Greeks, Romans, Celts, Norse, and Saxons. For example, the "Horned God" could have been based on a number of ancient deities, such as the Greek god Pan or the Celtic god Cernunnos (or his later English counterpart, Herne).

Likewise, the "Great Mother" could be said to contain various goddesses, such as the Greek Gaia or the Egyptian Isis.

This syncretism—the combining of different deities into one— seems quite logical in Wicca, since it was also a feature of the ancient religions that Wicca draws inspiration from. Over the millennia, many thousands of deities were "absorbed" into others, including many in the ancient civilizations of Egypt and Greece, as we will see later on.

This multifaceted nature of the deities is no doubt a big factor in the rise and spread of Wicca, as it allowed for various interpretations of their identities. In fact, others in the British occult circles of the time added their own concepts to this newly emerging religious movement. Robert Cochrane, who formed his own coven a few years after Gardner, emphasized the three-fold element of the Goddess—the Maiden, Mother, and Crone—rather than focusing mainly on the Mother aspect. And although Cochrane's form of the Craft ultimately branched away from Gardner's, the Triple Goddess is now a mainstay in most forms of Wicca.

Later, Janet and Stewart Farrar, who had been part of the Alexandrian Tradition of Wicca, incorporated the old English mythology of the Oak King and the Holly King into their practice.

These were not replacements for the Goddess and God, but rather additional forms of the masculine deity - brothers whose cyclical battles represent the dark and the light times of the year.

As Wicca spread from Europe to the Americas and beyond, more and more variations on Gardner's initial vision and concepts began to crop up. For example, some traditions might worship a Sun God rather than a Horned God, or even the Green Man, another archetype that comprises various Earth gods.

There are many different such archetypes, or "titles," found in Wicca, including the Earth Goddess, the Moon Goddess, and the Father God. These variations can be confusing to people who are new to Wicca, especially because you're likely to find at least slightly different information in every book you read, depending on the author's particular tradition (or lack thereof) and experience.

But it's important to understand that all of the different archetypes and individual deities can be thought of as being part of—or aspects of— the overall Goddess and God. There's no exclusivity or competition as there has so often been with monotheistic religions. Wiccans simply worship their deities in the forms that they connect with most on a personal level.

Those who belong to covens follow their coven's tradition regarding deities, so if the coven worships the Goddess as Selene and the God as Apollo, then these are the aspects who are honored in coven ritual. In keeping with the tradition of the earliest Wiccans, coven's names for the deities are almost always kept secret, known only to initiated members.

There is truly an incredible variety of names, titles, and visual renderings of the God and Goddess among the various traditions, covens, and individual practitioners of Wicca. No one way of approaching the worship of these deities is more correct than another—although many orthodox members of lineage-based traditions such as Gardnerian and Alexandrian Wicca might argue with that assertion.

But since Wicca, as a religion, has no official leaders or authoritative texts, there really isn't anyone who can say that another person's understanding of the Goddess and God is somehow wrong or inauthentic. If this wasn't the case, then Wicca wouldn't be the widespread and ever-growing spiritual practice that it has become.

For all the diversity within the Wiccan concept of deity, however, there are certainly some core characteristics of belief, myth and legend, and practices regarding the God and Goddess that are commonly found throughout various forms of Wicca. Let's turn now to a closer look at these multifaceted deities and their roles within the Wiccan concept of life, death, rebirth, and the perpetual cycle of Nature.

4.2 Goddess

As the feminine half of the Wiccan duo, the Goddess is associated both with the Earth and with the Moon. If the God is viewed as the source of life, it is the Goddess who brings life forth and sustains it. As the Earth Mother, she tends the land - the forests, fields and crops - as well as livestock and other domesticated animals.

Through her cycles of flourishing and then dying back in order to ultimately yield new life, she responds to the change of seasons in her timeless co-creation with the God.

Aspects often representing the Goddess in Wiccan traditions include the Egyptian goddess Isis, the Greek goddess Diana, and the Celtic goddess Brigid, among others.

4.3 The Triple Goddess

The revering of the Triple Goddess in many, if not most forms of Wicca, is often attributed to the influence of Robert Cochrane. Cochrane was inspired by British poet and scholar Robert Graves, who wrote *The White Goddess: A Historical Grammar of Poetic Myth,* in which he proposed that a White Goddess of Birth, Love, and Death had been worshipped under many names, throughout pre-Christian Europe and the ancient Middle East.

Although historical evidence of these goddesses is not as prevalent as Graves suggested, there are a couple of known examples, such as the Celtic Brigid, who is considered a triple goddess because of her three domains: healing, poetry, and smithcraft, and the goddess Hera, who appears in Greek mythology in the guises of Girl, Woman, and Widow.

The three aspects of the Wiccan Triple Goddess, the Maiden, Mother, and Crone, represent the three phases of a woman's life in terms of physical reproduction - before, during, and after the body's ability to have a child. These names are also given to the Moon in her own cycle of waxing to Full and then waning to dark.

Some traditions emphasize the Moon connection over the life cycle by worshipping a Triple Moon Goddess, while others keep the relationship with the Earth more evenly represented by simply calling her the Triple Goddess.

But whatever she is called, each aspect—or archetype—contained within this multifaceted deity has her own particular associations, characteristics, and representative deities from pantheons around the globe.

4.3.1 The Mother

At the Full Moon, the Goddess transforms from Maiden to Mother. This is the Summer season on Earth, when the forests become lush with life, the crops flourish, and the newborn animals grow into maturity.

The Mother is associated with midday and manifestation, as well as adulthood, responsibility, nurturing, and life in all its fullness, as she cares for all of creation.

In many Wiccan traditions, this is considered to be the most powerful of the three forms of the Goddess, as evidenced by the use of the name "Mother Goddess" in Gardner's original coven. She is often represented by the Celtic goddesses Badb and Danu, as well as the Greek goddesses Demeter and Selene, the Roman Ceres, among others.

4.3.2 The Crone

As the Moon wanes and the Earth's bounty begins to die off in preparation for the Winter season, the Goddess is finished with her duties of motherhood, and so the Crone comes into her power. The Crone is often represented by ancient goddesses of the underworld, such as the Russian Baba Yaga, the Celtic Morrigan and Cailleach Bear, and the Greek Hecate.

Chapter 5: Other Beliefs

Borrowing as it does from many older spiritual traditions, Wicca is inherently a "patch-worked" system of beliefs. In addition to relationship with deity and the participation in the natural cycles of life, other beliefs and practices contribute to the Wiccan religion. These beliefs are as personal and idiosyncratic as the choice of deities one resonates with, and include reincarnation, animism, the existence of unseen dimensions, sometimes called "the Otherworld," and the existence of fairies and/or other unseen spirits.

5.1 Reincarnation

A major tenet among Wiccans, the idea that we live many times over in different times and places on Earth is found in several religions, including Jainism, Hinduism, and Buddhism, as well as in other ancient and modern cultures.

Wicca has adopted this belief in many ways, which differ from coven to coven and individual to individual. While some Witches believe that we can and sometimes do choose to reincarnate in non-human forms—i.e. as animals or plants—many others believe that we only come back as humans.

Either way, reincarnation is seen as a logical extension of the life/death/life cycle observed in nature and celebrated throughout the Wheel of the Year. It is also used as a lens through which to look at life struggles and lessons, as the belief that we've chosen our life circumstances before being born into our new bodies is common. While it's never possible to scientifically verify the existence of past lives, many Wiccans and other spiritual seekers feel to be aware of at least some details of a past before this life, while others may have a sense of having "been here" before. This feeling may occur in or near a particular place where a past life was lived, or manifest in an affinity for a particular time period in history or a country or continent that has never been visited in this lifetime. A common "past life history" among Witches involves at least one prior life as a Witch, often one that ended in some form of persecution. Many of these Witches feel they have chosen to come back at a time when their form of religion is accepted—at least enough not to put them in real danger.

Wiccans and spiritual healers of many traditions today employ meditation, past-life regression, and dream analysis techniques to help people recall their past lives as a way of understanding their current problems. It is thought that whatever spiritual lessons were not learned in the past can be actively worked on in this life, which sets up the soul to learn new lessons, both in this and future lives.

5.2 The Afterlife

Wiccans generally believe in an afterlife of some form or another. However, this is not an "absolute" place where we remain for eternity—for example the Christian Heaven and Hell-but rather the place where our souls spend time between incarnations. Names and descriptions for this realm vary widely and may be based on older belief traditions or be more idiosyncratic, with each individual's experience and perception informing her or his notion of what's beyond that which we can physically perceive as this life. The spiritual realm is known as the Otherworld, the Afterworld, Summerland, and the Shining Land, among other names. Some describe it as a naturally abundant and beautiful place, while others see it more as an entity that doesn't resemble any physical reality on Earth.

It is nevertheless interconnected with all things in the Universe and many who practice divination believe it to be the source of the answers to their questions. It is thought by some Wiccans that the afterlife is a place to make choices about our next incarnations based on what we've learned, or haven't yet learned, so far in our soul's journey.

5.3 Animism

In its most basic form, animism is the belief that everything in the material world has a "soul" or a "spirit." This applies to all nonhuman animals as well as the geographical and ecological phenomena of rocks, trees, and anything else found on Earth. Many indigenous cultures operate from an animistic perspective, including several Native American belief systems and the traditional Japanese Shinto religion.

Animism provides a way of seeing into the divine relationship between humans and the natural world, as particular stones, trees, and streams may be imbued with a special sense of energy and held as sacred sites of worship. The Celtic belief in fairies (also spelled "faeries") can be seen as a form of animism, as they are themselves generally invisible but thought to live in hills, mounds, woodlands, and other natural phenomena. For some, animism also powers the workings of magic, as objects used in ritual may be thought to possess their own spirit energies, which are joined with those of the Witch to effect the positive change being sought.

Book 2: Wicca Wheel of the Year

Chapter 1: What Is Wicca Wheel of the Year

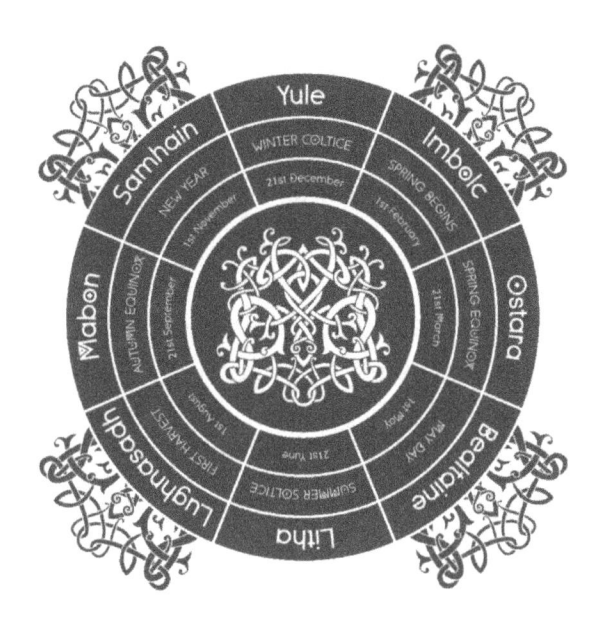

In accordance with Wiccan belief, the Wiccan calendar celebrates nature in its reverence for seasons, phases of the moon, and other natural phenomena. While Wicca believers may not always be practicing the religion within a group or a coven, they are always in solidarity with other practitioners when they celebrate the various Sabbats—special holidays—that fall on the Wiccan calendar. The calendar is one of the specific tools that bring the wide-ranging and diverse elements of Wiccan belief together.

Of these eight holidays, four are considered "solar holidays," centering on the solstices and equinoxes, while the other four are considered "earth holidays," centering on the earth's revolutions around the sun and at quarter points between solstices and equinoxes. The solar Sabbats are often called the "lesser Sabats," while the earth holidays are called the "greater Sabbats." This isn't a distinction of importance, however, but one of acknowledging that the earth

Sabbats appear to possess greater natural energy—which makes sense as they are more rooted in the earth, in the natural world that is closest to us.

These holidays, listed in greater depth below, are not necessarily unique to the Wiccan calendar, as many of them, particularly the earth Sabbats, are connected back to pre-Christian pagan celebrations. As with some of its beliefs, Wicca does work to reconnect with this pagan past, and this shows also in its festival times. Many of these Sabbats are also celebrated by other neopagan groups, as well, but what makes their presence in Wicca unique is in the emphasis on the combined divine energy of the god spirit and the Mother goddess in equal quantities. Responsible for all creation, these energies must interact in many ways throughout the year to continue to nurture current life and to bring forth new life. The sun energy is represented by the god spirit (in many branches of Wiccan, this is called the Horned God), while the Mother Goddess is the symbolic figure of the earth (Mother Earth). They are alternately seen as Mother and Child or as lovers who procreate the world into existence, both symbiotic relationships.

This symbology suggests the passing of the seasons: the god figure, who represents the sun, is born (Spring) and reaches the full height of his power (Summer), only to weaken (Fall) and symbolically die (Winter), only to be reborn. The Mother Goddess, in contrast, is the constant: she is always with us, no matter the strength of the sun or the power of the light. But she is also the constant companion to the sun, responding to his rays by replenishing the earth in the seasons of spring and summer, growing colder in his absence during fall and winter. This kind of spiritual reverence of the cycle of seasons is not new to Wicca, of course; it can be seen in nearly all ancient cultures, wherein the very life and survival of a people were wholly dependent on agricultural cycles. Wicca belief promises a return to channeling that kind of spiritual gratitude and harmony with the earth and nature that modern industrial life has largely been divorced from. Even farmers who still yet depend on seasonal cycles and the vagaries of weather are now so industrialized, in most cases, that this kind of connection to the earth and this kind of understanding of the symbiosis between the dual powers that deliver our life energy is often lost. This has been part of the appeal of Wicca, to reconnect people to a larger sense of connection between self and nature, between male essence and female essence, between the earthly and the spiritual.

Chapter 2: Various Seasons

2.1 Samhain

Samhain marks the end of the harvest season and the beginning of the darker half of the year, when the sun's energy wanes. Samhain, the halfway point to Yule or the Winter Solstice, is also a night when the veil between the physical and spiritual worlds is at its thinnest. The rituals in this section focus on honoring your ancestors and holding a *"dumb supper"*- a silent dinner to honor the deceased.

2.1.1 Samhain Ancestor Ritual

Samhain is a time to honor and pay tribute to your ancestors or deceased loved ones. This simple ritual will help you show your appreciation and share memories. It uses a purple candle for spirit communication and heirlooms to connect you to your departed loved ones or ancestors.

Ritual Setting

Altar

Tools and Supplies

Festive decorations for Samhain—flowers, crystals, or mementos

- Wand or athame
- Elemental representation
- Deity representation
- 1 pillar candle—purple
- 1 cone or stick incense—cinnamon, clove, patchouli, rosemary, or sage
- Fire-safe plates or candle holder and incense holder
- Photograph or heirloom for each person you want to connect with

- Lighter or matches
- Bell
- Offering of choice—food, craft, or something important

Prior to the ritual

1. Shower or bathe, visualizing all old or unwanted energies leaving your being.
2. Cleanse the altar.

Preparing the altar

Place the festive decorations and tools on the altar. Place the elemental representations in a pentacle configuration. Place the deity representation at the top of the altar. Place the candle and incense (on the fire-safe plates) and any symbols, photographs, or heirlooms of your deceased loved ones or ancestors around the altar, in positions you feel are best.

The ritual

1. Cast a circle of protection. Hold the wand or athame as an extension of your hand to gather and direct energy as you call upon the elements. Starting from the east and ending north, call upon the element of air for mental clarity, the element of fire for power, the element of water for fluidity, and the element of earth for stability.
2. Invoke your chosen deity or deities by saying something like: *"Lord and Lady, I invite you to join this sacred circle."*
3. Light the candle and incense and say the name(s) of your loved one(s).
4. Ring the bell to raise energy and then say to your loved one(s): *"I call out to you to welcome, honor, and thank you. You are gone but never forgotten, for I remember. I hold close our memories together, and you will continue to live on within me."*
5. Spend time sharing memories and thanking your loved one(s) for being part of your life, silently or out loud.
6. Place the offering on the altar. Thank your loved one(s) for their presence and say your goodbyes.

7. Thank the deities for their assistance by saying: *"Lord and Lady, I humbly thank you for your presence here. Go if you desire or stay if you'd like."*
8. Release the elements in reverse order by beginning facing the north and ending east, thanking each element for their assistance and bidding them farewell. Then open the circle by saying: *"I open this circle and release the energy back into the earth."*
9. Extinguish the candle and incense. Leave the offering on the altar.

2.1.2 Dumb Supper

A "dumb supper" refers to a silent dinner or "feast to the dead" at which a seat must be provided for the deceased. This ritual involves eating a meal, writing letters to the deceased, and burning the letters in a fireplace or fire-safe cauldron. The ritual should be conducted in complete silence.

Ritual Setting

Dining room table or area where food can be served

Tools and Supplies

- Festive decorations for Samhain—black décor is traditional but not required
- Photographs or heirlooms of the deceased
- Festive food, drink, and place settings for each guest
- Wand or athame
- Elemental representations
- Deity representation
- Taper or votive candles for each place setting—white, purple, or black
- Fire-safe plates or candle holders
- Pens and paper, for guests to write letters
- Lighter or matches
- Bell
- Fireplace or fire-safe cauldron

Prior to ritual

1. Shower or bathe, visualizing all old or unwanted energies leaving your being. Wear black or festive clothing for this event.

2. Cleanse the altar.

Preparing the altar

Decorate the room and place the decorations and photographs or mementos of the deceased on your dining table. Set a place setting for each guest, including one for the deceased. Prepare the food and drink. Position the elemental and deity representations around the room. Place the candles on fire-safe plates on the table, one for each person, including the deceased guests. If you will be calling multiple spirits, place the equivalent number of candles at the empty place setting. Once the guests arrive, have each guest write a letter to the spirit they wish to commune with and bring their letter to their place setting.

The ritual

1. Silently cast a circle of protection to call upon the elements. Hold the wand or athame as an extension of your hand to gather and direct energy.

2. Invoke the deity silently by closing your eyes and willing the assistance of the God and Goddess.

3. Serve the food and drink, light the candles, and ring the bell to shift the energy in the room, commencing the celebration.

4. Eat in silence, spending the time thinking about your departed loved ones and the messages you wrote.

5. At the end of the feast, help the guests burn their letters in a fire-safe cauldron or fireplace. Burn your own letter as well.

6. After all the letters have been burned, ring the bell again to end the supper.

7. Silently thank the God and Goddess for watching over the feast.

8. Silently release the elements, open the circle, and extinguish the candles and any embers in the fireplace or cauldron.

9. The room should remain silent. If you wish to speak, you may leave the room and converse elsewhere or dismiss your guests and end the supper.

2.2 Yule

Celebrated on the date of the Winter Solstice, Yule is the point on the Wheel of the Year when we acknowledge the beginning of the return of the light. The nights have reached their longest point, creating a sense of darkness that is almost overbearing. The air is cold, the deciduous trees are completely bare, and for those in northern climates, the season of snow is in full swing.

Yet as far as the Sun is concerned, this is a turning point toward increased daylight, and the promise that warmth of the growing season will eventually return. The longest night will now be behind us, and the Sun will stay with us later each day, rising ever higher in the sky until the Summer Solstice, the turning point on the opposite side of the Wheel.

However, it will be a few weeks before this is noticeable, as the increase in daylight is only gradual at first. The Sun actually appears to not alter its path across the sky at all during the days around the Winter Solstice. In fact, the word "solstice" comes from a Latin phrase meaning "sun stands still." Likewise, much of Nature seems to be still at this point. Birds have migrated south, many animals hibernate, and the snow covering the ground seems to have a quieting effect on the landscape. This is a time of turning inward, hunkering down, and tuning in to our deepest selves.

Many people see these short days and long nights as a time of self-reflection, spiritual study, and intention-setting for the coming year. But before the deep winter sets in, we gather with friends and family to celebrate the renewal of the Sun and the hope that comes with emerging from the darkness. This has always been a traditional time for both spiritual observance and merriment, and still is today, as we can see in the many different holidays and festivities associated with the start of the winter season.

In many Wiccan traditions, Yule is the start of the new year. The seasons of the Wheel, and the annual story of the God and the Goddess have completed the circle and now begin again.

The Goddess gives birth to the God, fulfilling the intention the divine pair set when they coupled at Beltane. As the Sun God, his symbolic death and return to the underworld at Samhain led to the darkness of the past six weeks, and now his rebirth brings back the light. The Goddess has transformed once again from her Crone aspect back to the Mother, who will now rest awhile from her labor and emerge rejuvenated in the spring.

This segment of the mythological cycle is at the heart of the

Wiccan understanding of reincarnation—after death comes rebirth into new life. The Sun illustrates this truth through its cyclical disappearance and reappearance. The Earth, which never disappears, represents the never-ending presence of the divine Universe.

Winter Magic and Merriment Of all the solar Sabbats, Yule is probably the one most clearly rooted in an ancient pagan holiday, as it takes its name from a festival held in Germanic and Scandinavian cultures around the time of the Solstice (though the original Yule likely lasted for several days). Of course, many other peoples of the ancient world also observed the Winter Solstice, as we can see by the number of Neolithic monuments—like

Newgrange in Ireland—built to align with the sunrise on this day. The Romans celebrated Saturnalia around this time, which involved feasting and exchanging gifts as well as ritual sacrifice. In Persia, this was when worshippers of the god Mithra celebrated his birth. And the Druids of the Celtic Isles are said to have gathered sacred mistletoe and sacrificed cattle on the solstice.

But while some forms of Wicca may base their Yule celebrations on some of these other regional traditions, in general the Norse and Anglo-Saxon customs that give the Sabbat its name are what the day is best known for. In the lands of Northern Europe, the Solstice festivities were the last opportunity for most people to socialize before the deep winter snows kept them from being able to travel. Great gatherings were held by the Germanic tribes where feasting, drinking, and ritual sacrifice of livestock took place. Bonfires were lit and toasts were drunk to the Norse gods such as Odin and Thor. These activities helped ensure a prosperous growing season in the coming new year, which was dawning now with the Sun's reemergence from the dark shadows. Some of the traditions observed during these ancient festivals— such as the Yule log, decorating with evergreen boughs and branches, warm alcoholic beverages known as wassail, and group singing—continued on through the centuries and are still part of many Christmas celebrations today.

The Yule log in particular was widespread in Europe, with many different regional customs attached to it. Traditionally made from a large log of oak, it was decorated with pine boughs, holly, or other evergreen branches and doused with cider or ale before being lit at the start of the festivities. In many places, this fire was lit with a piece of wood saved from the previous year's Yule log.

The log was supposed to be harvested from the land of the household, or else given as a gift—to purchase it was deemed unlucky. The Yule fire was tended so that it didn't burn out on its own, in part so that a piece of the log could be saved to start the following year's fire. The length of time for the fire to burn varied but was usually between 12 hours and 12 days.

The Yule festivities—caroling, games, the exchanging of gifts— took place around the warmth of the fire. In some places, the ashes from the Yule fire were used to make magical charms, sprinkled over the fields to encourage the crops, or tossed into wells to purify the water. As with so many other pagan festivals, we can see that the magical power of fire was alive and well at Yule! The most obviously pagan remnant surviving in today's holiday traditions is probably the use of mistletoe. This parasitic plant (called so because it grows attached to a host plant, usually oak or apple trees) was significant to both the Norse and Celtic cultures, as well as the ancient Greeks and Romans. It's not clear why "kissing under the mistletoe" became a tradition, but it's thought to come from an ancient Norse myth involving the goddess Frigga and the death and restoration of her son Baldur. The significance of mistletoe at the Winter Solstice likely comes from the Druids, who viewed the plant's ability to stay green while the oak it grew on was without leaves as a sign of its sacred powers. The mistletoe was ritually harvested at this time with a golden sickle and fed to the animals to ensure fertility. It was also valued for its protective properties, particularly against fire and lightning, and was used in medieval times for healing. Interestingly, once the Christian Church had coopted Yule and other Solstice festivals in its quest for domination, mistletoe was prohibited as a decoration, most likely due to its association with magic.

2.2.1 Celebrating Yule

Many covens meet just before dawn on the day of the Solstice to hold their Yule rituals, and then watch the rebirth of the God enacted as the Sun rises. In some traditions, the fires and/or candles are lit in encouragement of the Sun God's emergence, welcoming his returning light. Themes of ritual may include regeneration, light in the darkness, and setting intentions for the new year. In some Wiccan traditions, this is the time to ritually reenact the battle between the Oak King and the Holly King.

These twin brothers represent the opposing poles of the Sun's annual journey through the seasons. The Holly King, representing the dark half of the year, reigns until the Winter Solstice, when he is cut down by the Oak King, who heralds in the beginning of the waxing daylight. This cyclical story serves as a reminder that light and dark are both essential parts of existence in Nature—neither can exist without the other.

For solitary Wiccans who live "double lives" as far as mainstream society is concerned, Yule can be a challenging Sabbat to make time for, swamped as so many are with the obligations of the Christmas season. However, since plenty of the traditions associated with both holidays overlap, it's easy enough to infuse more conventional practices with a little Yule magic.

For example, hang a sprig of holly above your door to ensure protection and good fortune for your family and your guests. Magically charge your Christmas tree ornaments before placing them on the branches. Whisper an incantation to the Goddess over any cookies, spiced cider, or any other holiday goods you make for your friends, family or coworkers. You can spread the blessings of your own personal holiday throughout your community without anyone even knowing it!

For those without indoor hearths, a Yule log can be fashioned from a small tree branch—flatten it on one side so it will sit evenly on the altar and drill small holes to place candles into. Go outside and gather boughs of fir, juniper or cedar, as well as pinecones, holly berries, and any other "natural decor" to bring the energies of protection, prosperity, and renewal into your home.

Use mistletoe to bring peace and healing to your life by placing leaves in a sachet or hanging it over your door. Honor the rebirth of the Sun by inscribing discs, pinwheels, or other solar symbols into a large red, orange or yellow pillar candle. Light it at dawn on the day of the Winter Solstice to welcome the Sun and the new beginning of the Wheel of the Year.

2.2.2 Yule Correspondences

Colors: red, green, gold, silver, white, orange

Stones: bloodstone, garnet, emerald, diamond, ruby, clear quartz

Herbs: bayberry, blessed thistle, frankincense, chamomile, mistletoe, ivy, rosemary, all evergreens, oak and holly trees

Flowers: sunflowers, dried flowers from summer

Incense: frankincense, cedar, juniper, pine, cinnamon, myrrh, bayberry

Altar decorations/symbols: candles, evergreen wreaths and boughs, holly, mistletoe, pinecones, Yule log, snowflakes, pinwheels, yellow discs, other solar symbols and imagery

Foods: fruits, nuts, baked goods, cider, spiced cider, eggnog, ginger tea, wassail

2.2.3 Inner Light Meditation

No matter which holiday(s) you observe in December, it's hard to avoid the noise and bustle of the general holiday season. The commercialism of mainstream society is at its height, there are many social gatherings to go to, and everything seems to feel busier. It can be a struggle to stay balanced and grounded at this time, especially for people who are strongly affected by the lack of sunlight at this point in the year. This simple visualization can help you connect with your inner light, your center, where your connection to the divine resides.

Meditation is very helpful for people from all walks of life. For Witches, it's a key tool for cultivating a magical state of mind. Here, the candle is a physical symbol for what you're connecting to on the ethereal plane: your inner flame. Adding a little greenery to the scene, even if it's just a few pine needles, brings in the Earth element as well, but it's not strictly necessary for the meditation.

You will need:

- 1 white votive candle
- Small evergreen (pine, cedar, etc.) branch or bough
- (optional)

Instructions:

Arrange the evergreen on your altar in a visually pleasing manner. Light the candle and sit quietly, gazing at the flame for a few moments. Then gently close your eyes. See the flame as a white light spreading from the center of your heart throughout the rest of your body. Hold this visualization and breathe deeply and slowly. When you find you've wandered off in your mind, gently return your focus to the white light suffusing your entire being. After 5 to 10 minutes, allow the light to relax back into the form of a candle flame sitting in the center of your heart. When you feel ready, open your eyes. All is well.

2.2.4 Magical Yule Brew

This delicious tea is a nice non-alcoholic alternative to the traditional wassail, though you can turn it into a hot toddy if you like by adding whiskey, brandy or vodka. Wassail (mulled cider or wine) was originally part of fertility magic among the ancient Norse. It was poured onto the ground at Midwinter to encourage abundant crops in the coming year. To turn this tea into a magical brew, be sure to charge all ingredients before making it, and say a blessing as you pour the water over the tea and herb mixture. Then drink it in advance of (or during) ritual and/or spellwork. This recipe is for one cup, but you can adapt it to serve more. Just add one teabag, one lemon slice and one cinnamon stick for each additional person and increase the rest of the ingredients as you see fit.

If you don't have muslin bag or cheesecloth to keep the herbs and spices in while steeping, you can let them float loose in the pot and use a strainer when pouring the tea into mugs. If you don't have a teapot, use a large mug or bowl and cover it with a plate while the tea is steeping.

You will need:

- 1 cup hot (boiled) water
- 1 teabag of black tea
- 1 lemon slice
- 5 whole cloves
- ½ teaspoon dried chamomile
- ¼ teaspoon allspice berries
- Pinch grated ginger
- 1/8 teaspoon orange zest
- 1 cinnamon stick
- Honey to taste
- Muslin bag or square piece of cheesecloth and kitchen twine (optional)
- Teapot
- Mug(s)

Instructions:

Place the herbs and spices except for the lemon, cloves, and cinnamon stick into a muslin bag or cheesecloth sachet.

- Place this into the teapot along with the teabag.
- Pour the hot water over the tea and herbs and cover, letting steep for 3-5 minutes.
- Stud the lemon slice with the cloves.
- Pour the steeped tea into the mug and add the lemon slice.
- Sweeten with honey and stir with the cinnamon stick. Enjoy!

2.3 Imbolc

Imbolc is the first of the three spring festivals and takes place directly between the Winter Solstice and the Spring Equinox. The rituals in this section support love and creativity.

2.3.1 Imbolc Ritual for Love

This ritual for love can be used to attract love into your life or to manifest self-love. Perform this ritual on Imbolc or during the month of February, when love is in the air thanks to Valentine's Day. This simple ritual uses fire, your desires, and rose petals.

Ritual Setting

Altar or outdoors

Tools and supplies

Festive decorations for imbolc—hearts, red cloth, rose quartz stones, or fresh flowers

- Wand or athame
- Elemental representations
- Deity representation
- Pen and paper
- Fire-safe cauldron, if indoors, or firepit, if outdoors
- Lighter or matches
- 4 or 5 dried rose petals

Prior to ritual

1. shower or bathe, visualizing all old or unwanted energies leaving your being.
2. cleanse the altar.

Preparing the altar

Place the festive decorations and tools on the altar. Place the elemental representations in a pentacle configuration or facing their respective cardinal directions around your fire area. Place the deity representation at the top of the altar.

The ritual

1. Cast a circle of protection. Hold the wand or athame as an extension of your hand to gather and direct energy as you call upon the elements. Starting from the east and ending north, call upon the element of air for mental clarity, the element of fire for power, the element of water for fluidity, and the element of earth for stability.
2. Invoke the lord and lady or love deity by saying: "lord and lady (or name of love deity), i invite you to join this circle tonight. Lend me your strength and grant your blessings."
3. Using the pen and paper, write down the things that you want to attract and manifest in your life. Be as specific as you can.
4. Fold the paper and put it in the fire-safe cauldron or firepit.
5. If not using a lighter, ignite a match and toss it on top of the paper.
6. Sprinkle the rose petals over the flames and say: "burning blaze, hear my desire, accept these petals and my request to manifest love from this fire."
7. When you are ready, thank your chosen deity: "lord and lady (or name of love deity), i thank you for the strength you share and the blessings you give."
8. Release the elements in reverse order by beginning facing the north and ending east, thanking each element for their assistance and bidding them farewell. Then open the circle by saying: *"I open this circle and release the energy back into the earth."*
9. Sprinkle any leftover ash into the wind as an offering.

2.3.2 Brigid Creativity Ritual

Imbolc has associations with fire, creativity, and the goddess brigid, who is associated with crafts of any kind, so connecting with her is ideal for sparking creativity. This ritual uses a connection to a specific celtic goddess, an orange candle to represent creativity, and an oil.

Ritual setting

Altar

Tools and supplies

Festive decorations for imbolc—orange cloth, fresh flowers, brigid's cross, or imbolc items

- Wand or athame
- Elemental representations
- Deity representation for brigid
- 1 pillar or taper candle—orange
- Fire-safe plate or candle holder
- Oil, for anointing—olive, sweet almond, or apricot kernel
- Lighter or matches
- Cake and ale—homemade treats and a drink of your choice Prior to the ritual

1. shower or bathe, visualizing all old or unwanted energies leaving your being.
2. prepare the cake and ale.
3. cleanse the altar.

Preparing the altar

Place the festive decorations and tools on the altar. Place the candle on the fire-safe plate. Place the elemental representations in a pentacle configuration around the candle or facing their respective cardinal directions. Place the deity representation at the top of the altar.

The ritual

1. Cast a circle of protection. Hold the wand or athame as an extension of your hand to gather and direct energy as you call upon the elements. Starting from the east and ending north, call upon the element of air for mental clarity, the element of fire for power, the element of water for fluidity, and the element of earth for stability.
2. Invoke the goddess Brigid by saying: "Brigid, goddess of fire and the forge, i call and invite you here today."

3. Anoint the candle with the oil to increase the potency of its energy. To anoint the candle, pour oil near the top of the candle and use your hands to rub the oil down the candle. Be careful not to get oil on the wick.
4. Light the candle and say: "Great goddess, bestow upon me your power and guidance and lend me your power of creativity."
5. Spend 10 to 20 minutes in meditation, focusing on your intentions and on brigid. Feel her fiery energy wrap around you and let yourself fall into a centered state.
6. When you feel ready, thank Brigid by saying: "Brigid, goddess of fire and the forge, i thank you for your presence here today. Accept my offering for lending me your strength and wisdom."
7. Set out a portion of the cake and ale offering for Brigid. Then take a bite and have a sip of your own.
8. Release the elements in reverse order by beginning facing the north and ending east, thanking each element for their assistance and bidding them farewell. Then open the circle by saying: *"I open this circle and release the energy back into the earth."*
9. Extinguish the candle. Cover the cake and ale offering and leave it on the altar overnight. The next day, dispose of it by returning it to the earth.

2.4 Ostara

As the first solar Sabbat of the calendar year, Ostara marks the Spring Equinox, one of two points in the Sun's journey at which day and night are of equal length.

The Sun has crossed the "celestial equator," and will shine on

Earth for longer each day until it reaches its zenith at the Summer

Solstice. For Earth's inhabitants, this is a fortuitous moment, as the scarcity of winter comes to an end and the growing season begins in earnest. On the modern calendar, this is the first day of spring.

Depending on where you live, there may still be snow on the ground, but the Earth is beginning to thaw and rivers rise and overflow their banks. Green grass and spring flowers emerge, lambs, rabbits and chicks are born, and the promise of further new life is felt on the breeze, which is milder than it was just a few weeks ago.

The waxing light is truly felt now, as the Sun's power seems to quicken. The lengthening of the days, first perceived at Imbolc, seem to be growing at an even faster rate as the Sun sets later and further north with each passing day. But just at this moment, the light and the dark exist in equal measure, and this gives Ostara its primary theme of balance.

This balance is observed not only between night and day, but also generally in weather patterns—the harsh, bitter cold of winter is behind us and the relentless heat of summer has yet to arrive. In colder climates, it's not unusual for spring and winter to take turns during these days, with one day feeling more like February and the next more like May. Nonetheless, the fertility of the Earth becomes more and more undeniable as the slow energies of winter give way to the fresh new vibrancy of spring.

This is a time to reunite with the Earth in a tactile way after many months spent largely indoors. Gardening begins in earnest now, as soil is prepared and seed trays are set out in the sunlight to sprout. Those who practice green Witchcraft may perform seedblessing rituals if they did not already do so at Imbolc.

Magical gardens are plotted out in order to grow the herbs, flowers and vegetables that will later be harvested for feasting, ritual and spellwork. As the first green shoots poke up through the soil, we truly begin the active half of the Wheel of the Year, turning our focus to outward action until the inward, passive half begins again at the Autumn Equinox. Ostara is also a time to reflect on the balance between the male and female energies of the Universe, each of which requires the other to exist. This gender polarity is at the heart of traditional Wicca, with the Goddess and the God in constant co-creation throughout the changing of the seasons. At this point on the Wheel, the Goddess of the Earth is in her fertile Maiden aspect, while the Sun God grows into his maturity. There is a youthful joy between the two as they make their forays into romance and desire. In some Wiccan traditions, this is considered the time when the divine pair comes together to conceive the next incarnation of the God, who will be born nine months later at Yule. In many others, the coupling of the divine pair happens at Beltane, when the new energies of growth and light have progressed further into wild abundance. Nonetheless, in Nature we see the mating of animals and insects is well underway as "spring fever" takes hold.

2.4.1 Fertility and the Goddess of the Dawn

As midpoints of the solar year, the equinoxes were not typically as widely celebrated as the solstices in pagan Europe. However, there are megalithic sites in Great Britain that align with the Sun on this day, as there are in many other parts of the world. Many ancient cultures in the Mediterranean region did hold festivals during this time, such as Sham el-Nessim, an Egyptian holiday which celebrates the beginning of spring and can be traced back almost 5,000 years. In Persia, the festival of Nowruz, (meaning "new day") marked the Spring Equinox, and the Jewish calendar sets the dates for Passover based on where the New Moon falls in relation to this day.

In northern Europe, the Latvian festival of Lieldienas was a pre-Christian equinox holiday before it was absorbed into the Christian Easter. And the Norse pagans are said to have honored their female deities with a festival called Dísablót, though some sources place this holiday at the Autumn Equinox or closer to Imbolc.

The Scandinavian tribes and the Anglo-Saxons are where most of our modern Ostara traditions come from, most particularly in the name of this Sabbat. A Saxon goddess named Eostre (also spelled Eostra) is described by an 8th-century scholar who mentions a feast held in her honor at springtime. Little is known about her, and even less is known about her Germanic equivalent, Ostara, for whom the month of April was named in ancient Germanic languages.

However, many place names in some Scandinavian countries suggest that this goddess was fairly widely worshipped before the Christianization of Europe. The name "Eostre" has been translated as "east," "dawn," and "morning light," and so she has seemed a fitting deity to honor at the beginning of the growing season, even if much of the symbolism and lore about her in modern Wicca and other forms of Paganism has essentially been borrowed from other, better-known goddesses like the Norse Freya.

Symbols and customs of Ostara are recognizable to many as being part of the "Easter" season, such as the rabbit or hare and the egg—both symbols of fertility. The hare—a larger, more rural relative of the rabbit—is believed to be an ancient symbol of the Earth goddess archetype. Hares were also associated with the Moon, and in some places with witches, who were thought to be able to transform themselves into these quick-moving animals.

The fertility association is fairly obvious, as rabbits are known for their fast and prolific reproductive abilities. But there is also an element of honoring the Sun through hare symbolism, as these animals are usually nocturnal, but come out into the daylight during Spring to find their mates. Rabbits and eggs have traditionally gone together, both in ancient days and in modern Easter customs. This stems from our pagan ancestors' observations that plover eggs could sometimes be found in abandoned hares' "nests" in the wild. The egg itself was a potent symbol of new beginnings and the promise of coming manifestations in many cultures. Painted eggs were part of the ancient Persian Nowruz celebrations, and egg hunts have been traced back at least 2,000 years to Indian and Asian spring customs.

In Anglo-Saxon England, eggs were buried in gardens and under barns as a form of fertility and abundance magic. Offerings of eggs were made to female deities in ancient Scandinavia and in Germany. Interestingly, the egg also speaks to the theme of balance at Ostara, through the tradition of standing an egg on its end in the moments right around the exact time of the Equinox.

Of all the Sabbats, Ostara is the clearest example of how the Christian Church went about converting the pagan populations of northern Europe. By choosing the spring for its own celebration of renewal (in the form of the resurrection of Jesus) and adopting the name of this older festival, it effectively absorbed and dissolved this and other Spring Equinox holidays. However, as with Yule and Samhain, the old pagan customs and traditions have stubbornly stuck around, and are even widely practiced in mainstream society.

2.4.2 Celebrating Ostara

As the weather grows warmer, Ostara is a particularly wonderful time to get outdoors and take in the seasonal changes taking place all around you. If you haven't been in the habit of truly noticing spring's unfolding before, choose a place to visit regularly and study the transformation of the trees and other plant life. Greet the bees and other insects with joy as they begin to appear, and thank them for their role in sustaining life. Take every opportunity you can to watch the Sun set just a little later each evening. And if you don't already have a garden to prepare, consider starting one—even if you only have a windowsill to grow a magical herb or two.

Coven rituals often focus on the goddess Ostara or another goddess of spring. Witches may meet just before dawn to watch the Sun rise on this perfectly balanced day. Dyeing eggs is a fun activity to do with fellow Wiccans, perhaps using color correspondences to create magical eggs for later spellwork.

Natural objects are always a welcome part of rituals at any time of the year, but especially at the Spring Equinox, the first Sabbat after winter when flowers, buds and blossoms are truly available to be gathered. Sprinkle petals around your altar, float them on water in your cauldron, and wear them in your hair if you like, but be careful to harvest spring wildflowers responsibly, as they serve as much-needed food sources for our much-needed pollinators!

2.4.3 Bark and Flower Balancing Spell

Both the Spring and the Fall Equinoxes provide excellent opportunities to work for balance in our lives. This can mean achieving better physical health, learning how to deal more skillfully with an emotional challenge, or balancing the monthly budget. Anything you're dealing with that's hindering your ability to make progress in the outer world is a good area to focus on releasing, so that the energies of positive manifestation have more room to come into your life. For best results, identify a goal that aligns with the physical, mental or emotional realm in order to take full advantage of the magical correspondences of your chosen spring flower.

As for the bark, this should be gleaned (i.e. gathered from the ground) and **not** cut from a living tree. Many trees actively shed their bark at the onset of spring in order to make room for their own new growth.

Trees associated with establishing balance include ash, birch, cedarwood, poplar, willow and white oak. If none of these grows where you live, look up the magical correspondences of the trees that do grow in your area, or ask the God and Goddess to guide you in finding the right bark for this spell.

Flowers used in balancing magic include:

- Mental: daffodil, iris, lilac, violet (yellow candle)
- Emotional: crocus, daffodil, iris, violet, tulip (pink or light blue candle)
- Physical: alpine aster, iris, honeysuckle, lilac (green/light green candle)

You will need:

- Piece of gleaned tree bark
- Handful of flower petals
- Spell candle in a color corresponding to your goal
- Pencil (or ink and quill)

Instructions:

Start by meditating on your goal.

What does **balance** in this situation or area of your life look and feel like to you? Identify a word or short phrase that encapsulates the achievement of your goal, such as "optimal health," "harmony in the home" or "all bills paid."

Write this on the bark. Don't worry if the pencil lead doesn't show up, as the letters are still being traced into the essence of the bark's energy.

Light the candle and lay the bark on your altar or work space. Sprinkle the daffodils around the bark in a circle three times, moving clockwise.

With each rotation, say the following (or similar) words:

"As the day is balanced with the night, and the darkness balanced with the light, I find balance in my life."

Allow the candle to burn out on its own.

Within 24 hours, return the bark to the Earth, either where you found it or another place in Nature.

2.4.4 Ostara Egg Garden Fertility Spell

Many cultures around the world have long traditions of using eggs in magic, for healing, divination, protection and other purposes. Here, the properties of fertility and promise inherent to the egg is combined with the same energies that are so magnified at the height of Spring. For those already preparing their gardens, this is a highly opportune time to work this spell, as you're already out digging in the soil! But if you don't have a garden, shift the focus to creating an abundant and thriving home, and bury the egg in your yard.

You will need:

- 1 hard-boiled egg
- Green marker or green paint and brush

Instructions:

Boil the egg with the specific intention for this spell. You might even say a blessing over the water before you start. When the egg is dry and cool enough, draw a symbol of abundance appropriate to your goal—a flower or other plant, a house, a dollar sign or even the Sun.

Once the symbol is dry, hold the egg in your hands and raise it toward the sky. Say the following (or similar) words:

"As the light and warmth increase, so does the bounty of my life. So let it be."

Bury the egg in your garden or somewhere near the front door, visualizing golden light radiating from the egg throughout the soil, nourishing the roots of your growing plants or the foundation of your home.

2.5 Beltane

Beltane, the third spring festival, is a time when the sun begins to overtake the night as the Summer Solstice approaches. During Beltane, the land is fertile and life is abundant, so it's the perfect time to celebrate growth and new beginnings.

2.5.1 Meditation Growth Ritual

The growth we observe during the time surrounding Beltane makes the festival an ideal time to celebrate your own growth in life. This ritual will allow you to pause and focus on yourself. You'll make use of foraging, meditation, and the outdoors to ground and connect yourself with nature.

Ritual Setting

Outdoors

Tools and Supplies

- 1 piece foraged wood, to use as a wand
- 7 foraged stones—5 to represent the elements and 2 to represent deities

Prior to the ritual

1. Shower or bathe, visualizing all old or unwanted energies leaving your being.
2. Go outdoors and forage for stones and wood. Notice which colors, shapes, sizes, markings, or other attributes of each item call out to you.
3. Find an area outside where you will be comfortable sitting. A shady spot under a tree would be wonderful.
4. Mentally cleanse and set your intentions for each foraged item.

Preparing the worship area

Mentally cleanse the area by pushing your own energy into the space. Use the elemental and deity stones to create a circle around you.

The ritual

1. Sit in the middle of the circle.

2. Cast a circle of protection. Hold the piece of foraged wood as an extension of your hand to gather and direct energy as you call upon the elements. Starting from the east and ending north, call upon the element of air for mental clarity, the element of fire for power, the element of water for fluidity, and the element of earth for stability.
3. Invoke the God, Goddess, or other deity of your choice by saying: *"Deity, I invite you to join this sacred circle."*
4. Close your eyes and sit in a comfortable position. Allow yourself to feel and listen to the world around you. Feel the earth beneath you. Listen to the breeze winding through the trees. If you're under the sun, can you feel its warming rays?
5. Focus on your intentions for growth and allow any messages or thoughts to flow freely. Once you feel in sync with the earth, meditate for 20 minutes.
6. When you have finished meditating, thank your chosen deity by saying: *"Deity, I thank you for the wisdom you share and the blessings you give."*
7. Release the elements in reverse order by beginning facing the north and ending east, thanking each element for their assistance and bidding them farewell. Then open the circle by saying: *"I open this circle and release the energy back into the earth."*
8. Use your foraged items to create a geometric shape or pattern as an offering to deity. Allow yourself to feel lighter as you return to your normal daily routine, leaving hindrances behind and letting yourself grow.

2.5.2 Beltane Flower Ritual

This ritual invokes the May Queen and King, two deities that represent flowers, the forest, nature, life, and other elements of spring. Here, the May Queen and King will lend their energy as you create a floral crown to embody the season when many flowers are in bloom. Beltane is the perfect time to honor nature's abundant life. Wear this crown when dancing or at an event, or save it as a decoration.

Ritual Setting

Altar

Tools and Supplies

For the ritual

- Wand or athame
- Elemental representations
- Deity representation—statues of May Queen and King, or candles
- Lighter or matches
- 1 cone or stick incense—patchouli, mugwort, orange, rose, or frankincense
- Fire-safe incense plate
- For the crown
- Floral wire
- Wire cutters
- Floral tape
- Fresh flowers and greenery—foraged, picked, or purchased
- Spool of twine or ribbon
- Boline or scissors

Prior to ritual

1. Shower or bathe, visualizing all old or unwanted energies leaving your being.
2. Cleanse the altar.

Preparing the altar

Place the tools and crown-making supplies on the altar. Place the elemental representations in a pentacle configuration. Place the representations of the May Queen and King deity at the top of the altar.

The ritual

1. Cast a circle of protection. Hold the wand or athame as an extension of your hand to gather and direct energy as you call upon the elements.

Starting from the east and ending north, call upon the element of air for mental clarity, the element of fire for power, the element of water for fluidity, and the element of earth for stability.

2. Light the incense on the fire-safe plate and invoke the May Queen and King: *"May Queen, Goddess of the Flowers and Spring's Breeze, May King, God of the Forest and Gusting Winds, join me today to honor nature and its abundant life."*
3. Trim and shape the floral wire to the desired size and fit so that it will sit loosely on your head. Twist the ends to create a circle and cover them with floral tape.
4. Add a layer of greenery around the wire, securing the pieces with floral tape.
5. Add a second layer of flowers over the greenery, securing the pieces with floral tape.
6. Once your crown is finished, create a bundle of leftover flowers and greenery to leave as an offering to the May Queen and King. When you are finished, say: *"By the powers of nature, I combine these flowers and honor Beltane. I thank the May Queen and King for your presence here today; you may go if you desire. Your presence will be forever felt through this crown of flowers."*
7. Release the elements in reverse order by beginning facing the north and ending east, thanking each element for their assistance and bidding them farewell. Then open the circle by saying: *"I open this circle and release the energy back into the earth."*
8. Extinguish the incense or allow it to burn out. Leave the flower crown on the altar as an offering.

2.5.3 Litha

(Minor Sabbat) June 20–22

Litha is the longest day of the year and is a celebration of the Goddess and God at the height of their power. Together they rule over the lush, growing Earth, their mature married love ensuring the success of the ripening crops. The Goddess is heavy with pregnancy, mirroring the laden fields, and the mature Sun

God nurtures and protects her. Litha is tinged with sadness because after this date, the sun begins to weaken, and the days grow shorter. Many modern Wiccans light bonfires in tribute to the sun, observe the sun rise and set, gather herbs, and charge crystals with sun energy. Litha is a good time to work magick for protection, healing, renewal, and inspiration.

2.5.4 Lughnasad
(Major Sabbat) August 1

Lughnasad also known as Lammas is the Wiccan celebration of the first harvest and is a celebration of grain. It is the beginning of fall, when the days will grow visibly shorter. It is a time for giving thanks for Earth's bounty and for ritually blessing grain and loaves of bread as the embodiment of the combined powers of the Goddess and the God. Bread is extremely important in Lammas because it combines the Elements of Earth, Air, Fire, and Water to become a food that has sustained people since the discovery of grain. Modern Wiccans may celebrate by baking bread, making corn dollies to honor the harvest, decorating sheaves of grain with flowers or ribbons, and giving thanks to the Goddess and God by offering them bread and wine. Lammas is a good time to gather herbs and plants for magickal workings and to cast spells for courage and protection.

2.6 Mabon
On Mabon, or the Autumn Equinox, the Earth experiences equal nighttime and daytime (like the Spring Equinox). It's the second of the three harvest festivals. During this time, you'll often notice a wave of fruit and vegetables being harvested and showing up in supermarkets (or even in your own garden). Mabon is an ideal time to reflect and focus on goals.

2.6.1 Mabon Accumulation Ritual
During Mabon, the second harvest, we honor what we've reaped from the earth. It is a time to celebrate nature and all it provides. This ritual is an opportunity to write down our thanks for what the earth gives us, creating a time capsule for the Wheel of the Year.

Ritual Setting

Altar

Tools and Supplies

For the ritual

- Festive decorations for Mabon—root vegetables, apples, grapes, harvest decorations
- Wand or athame
- Elemental representations
- Deity representation
- For the capsule
- Pen and paper
- Mason jar or empty coffee can with lid
- 1 (4- or 5-piece) bouquet of greenery and flowers
- 1 clear quartz or yellow crystal—yellow agate, citrine, yellow topaz, or tiger's eye
- 1 ounce dried sage

Prior to the ritual

1. Shower or bathe, visualizing all old or unwanted energies leaving your being.
2.
3.
4. Cleanse the altar.

Preparing the altar

Place the decorations, tools, and supplies on the altar. Place the elemental representations in a pentacle configuration. Place the deity representation at the top of the altar.

The ritual

1. Cast a circle of protection. Hold the wand or athame as an extension of your hand to gather and direct energy as you call upon the elements.

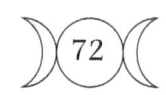

Starting from the east and ending north, call upon the element of air for mental clarity, the element of fire for power, the element of water for fluidity, and the element of earth for stability.

2. Invoke the God and Goddess by saying something like: *"God and Goddess of the Mabon Harvest, I invite you to join my sacred circle."*
3. Using the pen and paper, write a letter about all that you're thankful for. Think about everything you've accumulated thus far in your life and all the earth has given you.
4. Place the letter in the jar along with the bouquet.
5. Place the crystal in the jar and sprinkle the sage on top, saying: *"I am thankful for all that I have and blessed for all my experiences. It's time to look within and celebrate all that I've accumulated."*
6. Cover the jar with its lid and thank the God and Goddess: *"God and Goddess of the Mabon Harvest, I humbly thank you for your presence here. Go if you desire or stay if you'd like."*
7. Release the elements in reverse order by beginning facing the north and ending east, thanking each element for their assistance and bidding them farewell. Then open the circle by saying: *"I open this circle and release the energy back into the earth."*
8. Bury the capsule outside. If you'd like, you can retrieve it and repeat the ritual the following year.

2.6.2 Mabon Release Ritual

Mabon is a time to take stock of all that you have, both physically and spiritually, and to release what no longer serves you. This ritual will help you think about what it's time to let go of, as well as what might be holding you back. You'll use divination to help you get to the root of what you need to release.

Ritual Setting

Altar

Tools and Supplies

- Festive decorations for Mabon
- Wand or athame

- Elemental representations
- Deity representation
- 1 crystal—smoky or clear quartz
- Tarot deck, Oracle deck, or other divination system
- Journal and pen
- Offering of choice

Prior to the ritual

1. Shower or bathe, visualizing all old or unwanted energies leaving your being.
2. Cleanse the altar.

Preparing the altar

Place the festive decorations and tools on the altar. Place the elemental representations in a pentacle configuration. Place the deity representation at the top of the altar. Place the crystal and divination deck in the middle of the pentacle.

The ritual

1. Cast a circle of protection. Hold the wand or athame as an extension of your hand to gather and direct energy as you call upon the elements. Starting from the east and ending north, call upon the element of air for mental clarity, the element of fire for power, the element of water for fluidity, and the element of earth for stability.
2. Invoke deities by saying something like: *"Deities of Mabon, I welcome you to my sacred circle."*
3. Close your eyes and meditate for 5 to 10 minutes on your year thus far until you have a sense of what needs to be released.
4. Begin to shuffle your divination deck until you feel compelled to stop.
5. Fan out the cards on the altar. Pull three cards and ask three questions: Which area in my life is out of balance? What no longer serves me currently? How might I bring balance back to my life?

6. Spend 5 to 10 minutes reflecting on the three cards, using them to help you interpret what you need to release. Use the journal to take notes.
7. Thank the deities and leave your offering: *"Deities of Mabon, I humbly thank you for your presence here. Go if you desire or stay if you'd like."*
8. Release the elements in reverse order by beginning facing the north and ending east, thanking each element for their assistance and bidding them farewell. Then open the circle by saying: *"I open this circle and release the energy back into the earth."*
9. Leave the offering on the altar.

Book 3:
Wicca for Beginners
- Starter Kit

Chapter 1: Basic Wiccan Principles and Ethics

The Four Elements Are Part of All Magic

In Wicca, there are five elements that govern all of life. Four of them are physical and the fifth is Spirit, intangible but always present. The Pentacle, or the five pointed star that is synonymous with Wicca, is based on the five elements. The points on the star correspond to elements.

The four physical elements are Earth, Air, Fire and Water. Each of these elements has different properties and traits. Whenever you perform a spell you will call upon each element in order to gain power for the spell. Your altar should contain at least one item representing each element.

Earth is represented by the color brown, stones and rocks, or actual earth.

Air is represented by the color yellow, feathers, and incense.

Water is represented by the color blue, seashells or seaglass, and fish.

Fire is represented by the color red, wood or ash, and flames.

Each element has a wide range of emotions, intentions, and properties associated with it. Learning to use and call upon the elements is an important part of learning how to be a practicing witch.

The Law of Intention

The Law of Intention states that your spell will be more influenced by the intention in your heart than the words that you say. So, whenever you cast a spell, you should be prepared to deal with whatever happens as a result of your intention. Many witches will meditate on a particular spell before performing it to make sure that their intention is positive before doing the spell.

Sometimes spells can have unintended consequences, and if you perform a spell with less than honorable intentions you may still have to deal with negative Karma and a solid hit of negative energy from the Law of Threefold Return. Once you perform a spell you can't take it back, so it is a good idea to know your intention before doing a spell.

That means that you have to have a little self-awareness, which you can develop through meditation. You should always be calm and clear headed when you cast a spell. Never cast a spell when you are angry or irritated because that could bleed through into the spell and totally change the intention that you are directing outward. A good way to prepare for spellcasting is to meditate, take a ritual bath, and be well rested before you begin.

Take Responsibility for Your Own Spells

Whether you are writing your own spells or performing spells that were written by someone else you have to be responsible for your own spells. The intent of the spell and the action that results from it are your responsibility. Spells are nothing to play with. That's why it's important not to perform spells that will hurt or manipulate another person.

Spells rarely work in the way that you think they will. When you perform a spell what you think will happen is often not what happens. That's because once you put your energy and intention into the world the Universe will pick it up and run with it. But you are still responsible for whatever happens.

If you cast a spell and the result is good, then by the Law of Threefold Return you will profit in some way from the spell. But if you perform a spell that is designed to hurt, manipulate, or harm someone else you will have to deal with the consequences of that spell. When you are performing spells the intention that you put into the spell is just as important as the words you use in the spell. So if you say positive words in the spell but have a harmful intention when you cast the spell any harm that comes from the spell is your responsibility.

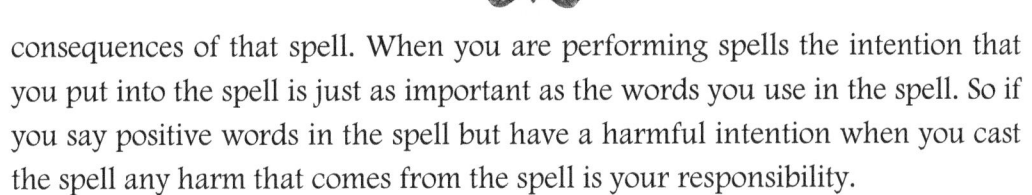

Faith Is Personal

You have noticed by now that there is a lot of emphasis on individuality in Wicca. That's because Wiccans believe that faith is personal. Your relationship with the divine should be one that you choose and one that you maintain because you want to, not because you are told you have to. Wiccans choose to follow the magical path because they are strong, independent, free thinkers who want to express faith in their own way. When you practice Wicca, everything becomes deeply spiritual. You see magic and harmony all around you.

That's why spells are really acts of prayer. Just like meditation can be prayerful because it strengthens your connection to the Universal flow of energy. Developing a personal moral code and a strong connection to the Universe is something that Wiccans do because they want to live on their own terms and Wicca supports and celebrates that. No witch believes exactly the same things as another witch, yet they recognize that they are all part of the same Universe.

Give Reverence to Ancestors

Wiccans believe that the cultures and people who came before have a lot to teach and should be acknowledged. Both personal and cultural ancestors are looked at with respect and honored at feasts. Wiccans believe that much of the knowledge and wisdom passed on from generation to generation is what makes it possible for Wicca to exist today. A lot of the magical lore and knowledge from the past is studied and used today in modern Wicca.

Wiccans often will include their ancestors when they give thanks to the deities not because they think their ancestors are gods and goddesses but because they believe that their ancestors were wise and powerful.

Wiccans also believe that the elderly should be venerated and respected for their knowledge and life experience. The Crone, which is one of the faces of the Goddess, celebrates the wisdom and power that come with age.

Priests and Priestesses Are There to Guide

Even though Wicca is a religion that has no hierarchy there are Wiccan priests and priestesses. But they are not officially sanctioned by any council or hierarchy. Within a coven, a priest and priestess will be chosen to play the role of the Horned God and the Goddess of the Moon during Sabbat ceremonies. Coven members may take turns playing these roles or it may be the same priest and priestess each time.

Priests and priestesses are Wiccans who have spent years studying magic, casting spells, and studying other topics like herbology, aromatherapy, divination and many more. They are given their titles by the other members of the coven because they learned in the ways of Wicca. Anyone can become a priest or priestess if they put in the time and effort to advance their skills. Some covens may not have priests or priestesses because they are not required in Wicca. But some covens prefer to have the wisest and most educated witches in the group act as the priest and priestess to guide and counsel the other members of the coven.

Chapter 2: Fundamental Wicca Tools

Like most other religions, there are various tools and objects used for ritual purposes. They are used to summon deities, get rid of negativity and direct energy with our touch or intentions.

Most people already associate a broom, a cauldron and a magic wand with witches. Although they have their place in the Wiccan world, only Wiccan understands the real power associated with each other.

If you are a beginner, you do not need to spend large amounts of money on specialized items.

These tools are symbolic, so you can use whatever you want. You will find some of the tools you will feel more comfortable with the energy in you and your device. This tool would be designed specifically for its use and for you.

To work with these tools and become familiar with their abilities, how you add energy, you will find that they become obvious and second nature. It can be pretty hard to get, but you.

Once you get each tool, clean it thoroughly to eliminate all associations and energy.

Dry the tool, then bury it for a couple of days to remove all the energy that has been left.

Dig p and clean. Now he's ready for your magic. You can choose a wedding ceremony for each tool if you want.

2.1 Broom

The broom is used in magic and rituals. Sacred to both the goddess and God. Of course, witches cannot fly with a broom. The witch hunters invented this story to show their alliance with the dark forces. If this could be achieved, it would be supernatural and would consider the devil in the eyes of witches.

The broom is used in Wicca today. Before the ritual, the area inside or outside can be swept away with a magic broom before the altar is built. Scanning is more like physical cleaning. The broom does not even need to touch the floor. Only by displaying the broom will remove the astral buildup to cleanse the area from the ritual. The broom is a cleaner, and therefore it is related to the water element. It can be used in all water spells, including Love and psychological functioning.

The ancient magical formula for making a broom is the ash disk (protective), birch twigs (cleaning) with willow (sacred goddess) binding. It does not matter what kind of tree or shrub you use. It can be small or large as you want. Do not forget to thank the tree for its sacrifice for you! Wiccan and pagan hand fastings often involve jumping over a broom during the ceremony.

2.2 Baguette

For thousands of years the wand is used to direct energy, draw magical symbols on the floor, pointing to the danger and mixing of the boiler. The wand is one of the first magical objects. Chopsticks are traditionally made of various woods such as willow, elderberry, oak, apple, peach, hazel, cherry and more. Some Wiccan measures from the elbow to the tip of the index finger and cut the wand to this size. You can also use peg, but I advise you to find and create one, rather than buy. The wand will come to you like most of your tools.

2.3 Censer

The censor is an incense burner. During the Wiccan ceremony, the censor holds incense for smoking. If you have not been asked for any particular incense for a particular ritual or charm, choose yours. Most Wikileaks prefer granular incense but sticks and cones will be enough. Ghosts are sometimes invited to appear visible in the smoke of the censor during ceremonial magic, but not in Wicca. Wiccans often report seeing a goddess and God in rising smoke. When performing a Wiccan ritual inside, you need to use incense, while outside you can use fire. The censor represents an air element. The censor can be used for fumigation and blurring, purification, increased potency, trance as states, exile of evil spirits, encouragement and acceptance of spirits

2.4 Boiler

The boiler is an ancient container for cooking and preparing infusion. The boiler is very mysterious and dipped in a magical tradition. Wicca sees the cauldron as a symbol of the womb of the goddess. The symbol of the element water, reincarnation, immortality, inspiration and the essence of femininity and fertility. This is the main contact point during ritual the boiler is used for burning, fertility magic, moon magic, preparation of herbs and potions. Boilers can be found in any size, from a few centimeters to three meters. Ideally, it would be made of iron with three legs. Most of today's Wiccan, who lives in the city, uses their own pots, pans and kitchen. Don't look too hard on the boiler, it is quite difficult to find, but if you need is to be patient and the goddess and God you can make sure that comes to you.

2.5 Athame

Athame represents an element of fire or air according to tradition. It is used for ceremonial purposes with male energy and symbolizes the animus. The most important tool in the collection of witches and should be sought with conviction. It would be better to find or get it than to buy it if you noticed it in the flea market, etc. And you knew you had to have it. There are nice letters, open them. Athame is used to mix, write, charge, consecrate, raise, draw lines to make choices.

2.6 White Knife for the Handle

This knife is purely practical, and not a ritual with a knife. It is used for cutting wands, herbs, ROPES and signs in the candles or wood, etc. must be separated from the rest of the family and used only in preparation for rituals.

2.7 Crystal Ball

When you take a closer look at Crystals from different directions you will begin to see the Witchcraft energy of these stones. They have been used as a talisman and to make jewelry for many years. These stones create an aura of the stone being a symbol of creativity, representing the living power of the Earth and infinity.

Crystals are used for their healing powers and their ability to increase the energy in physical spaces. They are also used as a source of alternative healing.

Crystals in the new age and Wiccan circles are used to mean an array of solid minerals. A substance that is inorganic in nature and formed when the geological processes take place underground is called a mineral. Every mineral has its own composition and energy that makes it unique. Every Shaman, Witch, and healer know the energies that are present in different mineral stones.

The regular molecular structure that is formed by a mineral stone that creates a surface that is flat informs what we know to be crystals. The popular crystal is the clear quartz. True "crystal balls" are said to be formed by clear quartz. Other popular crystals are the amethyst and rose quartz. Interestingly, known stones such as the lapis lazuli, bloodstone, and jade are formed by the combination of several stones and are not regarded as true crystals. Amber and jet, which are also considered to be "crystals", are apparently organic substances that have been fossilized. It is for these reasons that to enjoy the gifts of the earth stones and crystals have been used in the place of each other. One of the known ways of practicing Crystal Initiation simply is by charging a stone with an intention and having it with you as the day progresses. Crystal spell is cast by individuals to be used situations that seem challenging. Such situations could be those that require communicating something important as well as situations that require people to draw agreements thereafter.

Lapis Lazuli is a crystal stone that is referred to as "a stone of truth." The name is derived from Persian and Latin and it means "blue stone." The Lapis Lazuli helps with effective communication with others and yourself. Blue as a color symbolizes the throat chakra whose association is the expression of one's true voice. Negative thoughts and words from other people can also be thwarted by the Lapis Lazuli. The stone sends the negative energy back to its senders. Having a Lapis Lazuli that is charged enables one to be confident and have the general peace of mind in a conversation that might be challenging. When charging a lapis stone, if one puts either amethyst or clear quartz, the lapis will receive an energy boost.

To cast this spell one would need one piece of lapis lazuli stone, 1 yellow or white candle and 1 or more optional pieces of either amethyst or clear quartz crystals
Instructions are:

If using amethyst or crystal, place it first at the front of the candle while lighting the wick. Take the lapis lazuli stone and place it in both of your hands, with your eyes closed, take in deep breaths. Take a moment to visualize feeling a sense of relief after having a potentially challenging conversation. After that, visualize the positive energy that you experience while visualizing the result of the conversation and feel it flow into the stone.

Once you get a strong feeling about the stone being charged enough, take it and place it next to the amethyst or clear quartz if you were using one of them and leave them by the candle as it burns for the next one hour at least. Once this is done, your stone <u>is now able to guide you in any potentially charged conversations.</u>

Crystals and stones have powerful energies and are the reason why they are used in initiation. The amethyst enables one to have a clear purpose and is violet in color.

The **bloodstone** is green in color and has gold or red flecks has energies that promote prosperity and physical healing

The carnelian crystal is used to thwart negative energies away and is either orange or red in color. It also enables one to be courageous.

The **citrine** has magical properties of renewal, useful dreams and is yellow in color.

The **hematite** is either grey, black or grey and has the magical properties of aiding with problem-solving and also strengthens one's willpower. Jade is a black crystal that has the magical properties of protecting one from negativity and helps during the transition of grounding and centering.

The blue or dark blue lapis lazuli has the magical properties of divination and altered consciousness.

The malachite is a green crystal with bands of dark black and green and has the magical property of aiding with emotional courage during a person's significant transition and enhances spiritual growth.

The moonstones are usually either a pale blue or white in color that has the magical properties of enhancing the reception to initiation, creativity and is supportive of intuition.

The quartz crystal is clear or white in color and has the magical properties of promoting spiritual growth, healing, and clarity.

The rose quartz is pink in color and has the magical properties of enhancing friendship, love, and emotional healing and wellbeing.

The tiger's eye has the magical properties of energy and protection and is brown, tan or gold with bands of black in color.

2.8 Herbs

The plant kingdom grew in the earth dating back to millions of years ago before human beings had evolved into what they are today. Herbs are known to be the oldest form of healing that enhances both the spiritual and physical wellbeing. Different plant species were identified and used by shamans and healers in the old days. This dates back the origin of herbal initiation.

Physical healing was initially carried out alongside rituals and prayers. This was before physical healing was separated from medicine. A patient would be given herbs to drink and an invocation was then made to the spirit to enhance healing. In today's world, drinking herbs can have spiritual, emotional and nutritional benefits to one. This is modern initiation. The craft of herbal initiation is considered to be highly rewarding to a witch.

Plants embody the four classical Wiccan elements. A seed is first planted in the soil; minerals in the soil are to enable the creation of life in the seed. Sunlight is the other aspect needed by the growing seed that facilitates the conversion of carbon dioxide to oxygen, which determines the quality of air. The air generates wind, which leads to the branches and leaves of the growing plant. Water is also needed for the growth of the plant. This process elaborates the four elements earth, water, air and fire to be essential in the growth of plants. According to the belief Aristotle who is an ancient Greek philosopher, plants have psyches, which are the spirit and soul aspects of a human being. This belief is shared by witches and Wiccans. Modern scientists are on the verge of discovering the consciousness of plants

Plants are able to pass information to each other hence realizing communication. Trees and plants in the forests communicate on the formation of their roots with fungi. This network of fruit allows for the nutrient to be shared among the plants protecting each other from the lack thereof during their growth. In addition, plants can warn each other from pests. For instance, when a plant is bitten by an insect, it generates chemicals that protect it from the attack ad prompts other neighboring plants to do the same for their protection. Such discoveries showcase the intelligence of Mother Nature and this explains why witches desire to tap into this magical energy. Growing a personal herbal garden keeps one in touch with nature and the four elements. You will stay in touch with life and death cycles in addition to other aspects that are lifesustaining such as some insect. Furthermore, growing your own herbs ensures that you charge them during their entire development. Herbs can be used in the creation of magical crafts such a dream pillows, spell jars, sachets, poppets, and other charms. You will find that some people prefer and enjoy making their own oils and incenses using herbs strengthening the magical powers of their crafts. Kitchen Craft is making magical tea, potion, tinctures, and baked foods among other foods. Herbs are used in, bath spells, candle and crystal initiation. Dried herbs are smudged to purify physical spaces a practice that is also done in modern contemporary witchcraft. During the sabbat rituals, some Wiccans use some herbs to cast a circle. Other Wiccans use herbs as a way of worshipping their deities such as the Dianic Wiccans who use a lemon balm to honor Diana the goddess. The fascinating thing about herbal initiation is that you can begin already with herbs that are in your kitchen.

Herbs are distinguished from other types of plants due to their specific characteristics. Herbs are defined as any plant that can be used to the benefit of human beings. Its benefits can be experienced when cooked, used as medicine, like fragrance, clothing as well as any spiritual work. Some trees, shrubs, vegetables, grasses, flowers, and fruits can also fit into the definition of herbs by cooks, witches, shamans, and healers. Both herbalists and witches agree that plants that are either poisonous or not to the human being are still considered to be herbs. An example of herbs that are poisonous to the human body includes henbane and belladonna. It is agreed that both types of plants simply have different relationships with the human body. One needs to take account all knowledge available concerning toxic herbs as they start out in herbal magic. In the case of a toxic herb required in a ritual, it is best to simply substitute them with other non-toxic herbs as a beginner.

There is a lot of information available on herbal initiation something that can be very overwhelming for a beginner. One is then advised to begin by knowing the magical properties of a few herbs at a go while developing a relationship with the energies the plant kingdom. Encouragingly, a number of herbs to start with are available in your local grocery store. We can start by learning a simple herbal initiation spell that enables one to open love into their lives. You will find that a number of people are interested in attracting love into their lives but are unknowingly blocking these opportunities. This herbal initiation tackles the unconscious blocks and any other underlying issues that are blocking love.

This spell can prove to be emotionally overwhelming once you start it out, but it is important to note that it is worth the effort.

One can make charmed herbal sachets to carry around in the pocket or purse. It is advisable to use a tiny drawstring bag that is made from silk, muslin or cotton. If you are handy then you can definitely saw your own drawstring bag using needle and thread or simply use a piece of cloth and a ribbon to make a charm bundle.

Herbal initiation can also be used in combination with candle initiation. The ingredients to be used are 6 whole cloves, 1 teaspoon of lemon balm, St John's wort, rose petals and dried mugwort. A small bowl, ¼ cup of chamomile flowers and a pink candle are also required.

Once you have all these things you can collect them and place them on the altar of the surface you will be using. Next, after you light a candle take time breath in and out calmly to calm your mind. Put the lemon balm, mugwort, chamomile and set john wort in a bowl and gently mix them with your fingertips. Put the mixture into a sachet, add the cloves, then the rose petals and then close the sachet.

While holding the charm in the sachet, close your eyes and visualize your body immersed in white light and have the center of the light to be your heart drawing outside.

Let the candle burn out in its own time and then purposely have the charm very close to you at all times. At a certain point when you strongly feel that the purpose of the charm has been served, you may sprinkle it on the earth or bury it.

Some of the popular essential oils, herbs and incenses using by witches in initiation have the following properties:

Basil is used for thwarting negative energies and enhance loving vibrations.

Bay leaf is used for healing, strength, good fortune, success, money, purification and protection.

Chamomile is used to release someone from stress as well as foster love and healing.

Cinnamon is used for prosperity, luck, love, success and to raise energy vibrations in physical spaces.

Dandelion is used for interaction with the spirit world, to cast wishes and divination.

Elecampane is used to chase negative vibration, protection, and communication with spirit plants.

Hibiscus is used in lust, love, divination, and dreams.

Lavender is used to helping with restful sleep, healing, money, grief relieving, peace, love, happiness, clairvoyance, meditation, and longevity.

Mugwort is used to enhance psychic abilities, fertility and lust enhancer and in protection as well.

Nutmeg is used for protection, money, good fortune and prosperity.

Rosemary ensures restful sleep and is also used for love and lust.

Sage is used for wisdom, chasing negative energies, protection, and longevity.

Star anise is used for psychic and magical abilities, spiritual connection and good fortune.

Thyme is used in enhancing psychic powers, affection, and love.

Valerian dispels negative energies, is used for protection and purifies a sacred place.

Yarrow is used in enhancing confidence, promoting love, divination, and healing.

2.9 Essential Oils

Oils have been used by shamans, healers and priests for initiation and medicinal purposes. When fragrant plants were heated, sacred oils were made. Some of these fragrant plant matters were from flowers, barks of trees and leaves in oils made from seeds such as sesame, olives among others. **Cinnamon**, **myrrh**, and **frankincense** are some of the fragrant oils that are used in modern day craft. Other ways of making essential oils have been discovered over time with steam distillation and other methods using technology. Essential oils can now be derived from flowers, plants and citrus plants. There is also increasing curiosity around aromatherapy and its benefits of healing. Right now, there are a great number of essential oils available for use. In initiation, oils are used to complement the work of candle or crystal initiation. Witches use oils in the anointment of their tools of rituals as well as their bodies. Any initiation work can be enhanced by the use of essential tools.

Essential oils that have been derived from plants are used because of the magical energies of plants, which are now in liquid form, and the presence of magical properties in plants, which is in the composition of these substances. It is important to note that inorganic oils, unlike botanical oils, do not have these magical properties in plants. Although they might smell like the botanical oils, they do not have these magical properties. Although the inorganic has been successfully used over the years by witches, the strength of botanical is very strong

The essential oils also have a trick and that is the fragrance. The fragrances of essential oils play a great role in the mind. This is just an instinctive feeling that one gets after smelling a certain fragrance. The feeling could vary from happiness to relaxation. For instance, the fragrance of cedar wood and myrrh can quickly awaken your sense of smell very strongly putting your mind in a very different frame. This can also be achieved by using a blend of clove and lavender. The frame of mind that these scents put the mind in use the invisible power of the universe, therefore guiding powers, to achieve our intention. This demonstrates the direct link that botanical oils create between the physical and the spiritual realm. To release the right intention into the universe, you need to be in your right frame of mind. It is for this reason that incense is very important in ritual initiation. This frame of mind remains to be oblivious of what is mundane in the physical realm. Sacred places in the pagan and Wiccan traditions will have the smell of burning incense wafting in the air.

Essential oils enable one to connect with their higher self, to connect with deities and to focus. Scented oils are also very instrumental in this transformation of our reality. This is because as they are blended and charged with herbs, they become very potent with aromatic resources with charged magical powers.

You may observe that there is growing popularity around essential oils and something that has contributed to them being very expensive to purchase. If you intend to buy them, it is best to purchase them from food store. You may also make your own magical oils by blending 2 Or 3 different oils together or even more. The amount also varies in the number of drops to use. As a beginner, it is advisable to start small with the amount and the composition of the oils as well

To blend oils, you may begin by measuring the amount of carrier oil that you will need and pouring it into the jar you will use for your blending process. You may then begin to add drops of different essential oils at a time while swirling the jar and smelling the aroma as it forms.

If the blend is for a particular spell, you may set your intention by visualizing the aim of your initiation during the blending process. The following essential oil blend could be used in anointing your spiritual tools and the altar for your spell work or ritual.

Use 2 tablespoons of either 2 or more of these carrier oils: **grapeseed, safflower, apricot kernel, and jojoba.** Have the essential oils that you intend to blend. Have a clean blending jar that is well sterilized, a small funnel, brown or green glass bottles that will be used in the storage of your blend and small glass droppers.

Money-Drawing Oil:

- 4 drops patchouli
- 3 drops bergamot
- 2 drops cypress
- 1 drop lavender

Purification Oil:

- 5 drops juniper
- 3 drops cedarwood
- 1 drop lavender

Consecration Oil:

- 5 drops frankincense
- 5 drops myrrh
- 2 drops cinnamon

Blending is simply art that requires patience and frequent practice as well as experimentation. Provided you have visualized your intention, your blend will have magical properties even though at the beginning you might not get the desired scent you had hoped for. It is for this reason the practice is referred to as a Craft as you need to keep doing it every other time to get better. You can be assured that this is a very rewarding process.

2.10 Cup / Cup

Just a cauldron with a stem. It can contain a ritual drink or just water. You can sit on the altar, remember your blessing, wash it and periodically fill it when the water evaporates.

2.11 Bell

The sound of the Bell has strong effects depending on the volume, tone and building material. The bell is often used to summon the goddess during the ritual.

The bell can be used to avert evil and induce good energy. Hanging a bell on the door protects the House. Sometimes bells ring during rituals to mark the beginning or end of the spell.

Chapter 3: The Wicca Circle

You may or may not have heard of "circles" before in your explorations of Wicca. A circle is much like a coven in that it is a group of people coming together for the purpose of ritual worship and spellwork. It is also a big place of learning, both for newcomers to the Craft and for solitaries who are looking to find a sense of community in their practice.

This relatively new form of spiritual community has evolved out of a desire for less structure and less hierarchy than what is typically experienced in a traditional coven.

While you may see both circles and covens advertised in the same sections of online forums and directories, there are significant differences between these two types of Wiccan groups.

For starters, covens are generally exclusive, and often are not open to new members. You typically can't just arrange to come in and be a part of a coven. A circle is much more open, with fluctuating membership, usually allowing new people to come and go in order to see if it is something they enjoy. In addition, circles tend not to follow a specific tradition. Some do, and they may ask that only those who practice under their tradition, or else are willing to learn, join them, but usually they're fairly eclectic groups that come together from many different traditions and backgrounds.

As indicated above, circles are much more informal than traditional covens. Circles come together to practice the Craft, but without developing any hierarchy among members. No initiation is required, and there are no degrees to move through. There are no High Priestesses or High Priests. Attendance at meetings and rituals is not mandatory. A circle is more like a club, which makes many people feel more at ease and in control of their own spiritual paths. Of course, for some Wiccans, a "club" is a little too loose in terms of the bonds that can be formed through the long-term commitment involved in a coven. Having consistent membership creates a more solid group dynamic than might be possible in a circle. Nonetheless, circles can be an ideal way for solitary and eclectic witches to come together and discuss their religion with like-minded others, to have access to community for ritual and spellwork, and to keep learning as they pursue their path.

3.1 The Magick Circle

The magick circle is the sacred space where rituals and magick take place. It offers protection from unwanted influences and energies that are attracted whenever magickal, spiritual energy is practiced. The magick circle also amplifies any energy raised within it, making spells and rituals more powerful and connection with deity more immediate. Before you begin to cast the circle, be sure that everything you need is already within the space. This includes all the magickal tools required for the work at hand, including candles, herbs, spell ingredients, and your Book of Shadows, among others. Once the circle is cast, you should try not to break or weaken the energy force by opening or leaving the circle until it is formally opened at the end of the rite. There are multiple ways to cast a circle—no particular way is more "correct" than others. Below is a description of two ways to cast and open a circle: the traditional way and a quicker, simpler method.

Traditional Circle Casting

1. Ground and center: Root your feet to the ground and connect to Earth; breathe deeply. Extend your arms into the air and connect to the sky. Feel the energy from the Earth and sky flowing into your body.
2. Carve the circle: With an athame, wand, or your extended finger, walk around the circle clockwise three times, beginning and ending in the east while visualizing a sphere of light forming into a bubble and surrounding you.
3. With a dish of salt water, beginning and ending in the east, walk around the circle clockwise three times while sprinkling the water.
4. With smoking incense, beginning and ending in the east, walk around the circle clockwise three times while wafting the smoke.

5. Call the quarters: Beginning with the east, then south, west, and north, silently or aloud invite the Elements of Air, Fire, Water, and Earth into the circle.
6. State forcefully: The circle is cast.

To Open a Traditional Magick Circle

1. Release the quarters: Beginning with the north, then west, south, and east, silently or aloud thank the Elements and release them. An example would be: **"Thank you Element of (Earth, Water, Fire, Air) for your attendance. Hail and farewell! "**
2. Release the circle: With an athame, wand, or your extended finger, beginning and ending in the north, walk around the circle counterclockwise once, visualizing the bubble becoming thinner and sinking into the ground.
3. State forcefully: The circle is open.

Simple Circle Casting

1. Visualize yourself and your space in the center of a ball of white light.
2. Visualize the light circling around you, moving clockwise, forming a sphere that completely surrounds you.
3. State forcefully: The circle is cast.

To Open a Simple Circle

1. Visualize the sphere of light fading until it disappears.
2. State forcefully: The circle is open.

3.2 Creating a Circle

A circle is a great way to create personal space for performing rituals. It also protects the Witch from any external influence. As long as you are within the shield, then no negative energy can interrupt your ritual or influence you negatively.

Creating a ritual is not a complicated process. Here are the steps you will need for it.

3.2.1 Step 1

Make sure that you find a quiet place for this. On the other hand, if you already have an altar, you can create a circle around it. If you feel that the circle cannot go around the altar, then you can create a circle in such a way that two points meet at the altar. That way, your altar itself completes the circle for you. You have to be prepared for this process. This means that there should not be any interruptions while performing this process.

3.2.2 Step 2

Find the four cardinal directions using a compass. If you already know them, then skip right ahead to the next step.

3.2.3 Step 3

For each of the directions, place a representation of the elements that they are attuned to. We have already discovered that the north is represented by the earth element. In similar ways, find the elements for each of the four directions. As for what the representation of the elements means, it could be any object that could be symbolic of that element. Here are some examples that you can use:

Earth: crystals, rocks, branches, potted plants

Air: incense, feather, a bundle of sage

Fire: candles, an oil lantern or burner

Water: bowl or mug of water, seashells

3.2.4 Step 4

Now stand up and look to the east. Ensure that your breathing is calm and steady. If you feel that you might need to meditate before this entire process, then I have provided a simple meditation technique that you can use in the next section. For now, keep your mind calm and grounded in the ritual you are about to perform.

Facing the east, imagine that the wind is blowing all around you. In a clear, but soft voice says, "To the spirits of the air, I seek your guidance."

Slowly turn to the south. Imagine the sun above you, throwing its warmth and heat to you. As you can imagine the power of the sun flowing through you, speak these words softly and clearly: "To the spirits of fire, I seek your guidance."

Now turn to the west. Imagine the waves crashing against your feet. Imagine the feel of rain on your body. Imagine how the water feels on your hands. Then speak these words clearly and softly: "To the spirits of water, I seek your guidance."

Turn to the north. Imagine the feel of the earth beneath your feet.

Or imagine the sand slipping through your fingers. Or you could even imagine how the earth feels when you touch it (this might be easy if you have been working with plants or trees). Then speak these words clearly and softly: "To the spirits of earth, I seek your guidance."

Return to the original position.

Note that if your original position was facing any of the directions, then you can come back to it. For example, if you started the ritual by already facing the direction of the east, then you will end up facing that direction. This does not have any influence on the rest of the ritual.

3.2.5 Step 5

Sit down crossed leg or in a position that is comfortable to you and begins meditating. Imagine the power of all the elements flowing into you. From you, they are flowing towards the circle and then powering them.

3.2.6 Step 6

When you are done (ideally, you should have meditated for at least 5 minutes), stand up. You are now going to thank each of the elements for their assistance.

Look to the east and say in a clear voice: "To the spirit of the air, I thank you."

Look to the south and say in a clear voice: "To the spirit of the fire, I thank you."

Look to the west and say in a clear voice: "To the spirit of the water, I thank you."

Look to the north and say in a clear voice: "To the spirit of the earth, I thank you."

3.3 Magical Techniques Like Astrology, Tarot, Runes, and More.

There is a lot to learn about magick, but we will cover them in detail later. For now, I just wanted to give you a short introduction on what magick means in Witchcraft. The first thing that you should know about magick is that it involves timing. If you have been reading about Witchcraft or of Wiccan beliefs, then you might have read or become aware of the fact that the moon plays a vital role in rituals. This is not a rumor that someone conjured.

The moon is indeed important in Witchcraft rituals. However, the misconception lies in the fact that all rituals are performed at certain times of the year. While the effect of performing rituals under certain moon phases does help in boosting the effects of that spell or ritual, you can perform the ritual or cast a spell at any time during the year. On the other hand, certain rituals are made specifically for certain phases of the moon.

Essentially, there are two main phases of the moon. When the moon shifts from the New Moon stage, go through the First Quarter, and enters the Full Moon stage, then this phase is called the Waxing Moon. When the moon shifts from Full, Last Quarter, and then finally to New Moon, then this phase is called the Waning Moon. Think of it this way, when the Moon is increasing in size, then the phase is referred to as Waxing and when it decreases, it is Waning. These phases are related to sympathetic magick.

You take an object and resemble it to the ritual you would like to cast or the outcome you would like to have. In this case, the Waxing of the moon (increase in size) can be used to improve upon things. Would you like to improve the opportunities in your life? Would you like to enhance the love that you and your partner feel? Would you like to have more friends? Any ritual or magick that focuses on increasing, enhancing, improving or other related results use the Waxing Moon. On the other hand, you have the Waning moon. If you are aiming to reduce something, then this is the phase that is ideal for the ritual. For example, are you planning to reduce the negativity in your life? Are you planning to remove evil presence? Do you want to manage depression or other health issues? Then you can use this phase.

Each ritual is unique and can be performed during both phases, depending on how you create the ritual or what purpose you would like to achieve. For example, let us say that you have caught a nasty bug. You would like to remove it from your system using Witchcraft. You can do one of the following:

1. If you are in the part of the year where there is Waning Moon, then your ritual should be focused on removing the problem from your body.
2. On the other hand, if you notice a Waxing Moon outside, then you cannot wait for the next phase before conducting the ritual! It's not like the problem is going to take a vacation just so you can prepare yourself! In such scenarios, the alternative would be to **improve** your health. That way, you are simply focusing the ritual on working past the problem and focus on getting you better

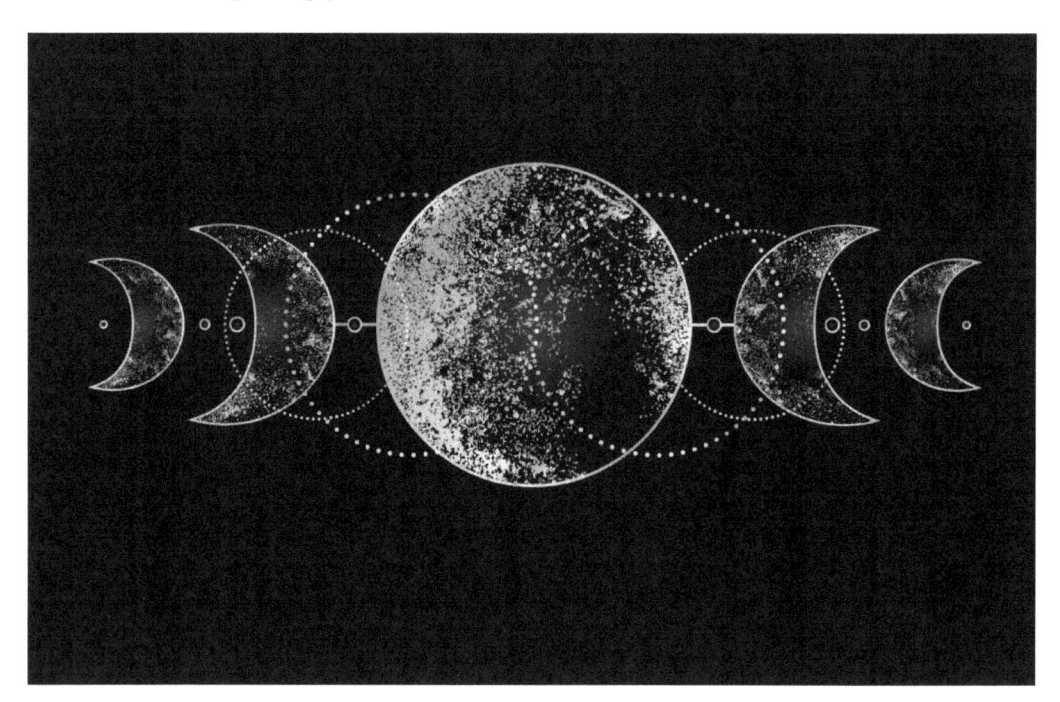

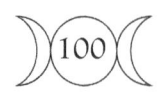

The phases of the moon play an important role in witchcraft ritualsThe second factor that you should think about is that magick involves feelings. When you want a magick to occur, then you must be sure about the fact that you want the magic to happen. If you would like to get better, you must want it with all your being. You cannot decide that you are okay with it one way or the other and hope for the ritual to work wonders. It is for this reason that magick is usually performed on the self rather than on someone else. You can control your desires. You can guide the magick to achieve its purpose. On the other hand, controlling someone else's wants is a tricky thing. Your magick might not work effectively on them because they might not want it as bad as you want to perform the ritual. They might have changed their minds or moved on from the problem.

This "feeling" that you have is a sort of "power" for the ritual. You can enhance your power by using chants and rhymes. When you chant or loudly speak a rhyme that you have created, then you are essentially reinforcing the idea of your desires. In similar manners, many Witches also strengthen their spells by performing dance rituals or even having sex. Each one serves a specific purpose, depending on the spell you are casting.

Thirdly, one important note to make here is that when you are performing magick, then you should have a clean body. You have to clean your body both externally and internally before performing rituals. Why? Because you are asking for the favor of a god or goddess. It would be nice to show them that you respect the rituals. Here are the ways you can clean yourself:

1. To clean externally, take a bath with salts (ideally sea salt, but in the absence of that, you can use bath salts or regular salt).
2. If you do not have a bath, then you can take a shower instead. However, make sure you try and use some kind of bath solution if you can get your hands on one.
3. To clean internally, make sure that you have fasted for at least 24 hours before you conduct the ritual. Abstain from the consumption of alcohol, nicotine, and other substances and sex.

Finally, and this is probably more of a guide than a rule. But before you perform any ritual, make sure that you ask yourself this question: Can your actions cause harm to anyone? If they can, then you shouldn't be doing it. No matter what happens.

Chapter 4: Wiccan Beginner's Ritual

Wiccan rituals are part of the fundamental core of practicing Wicca. Even within the diversity of belief and the personalization of practice, the Wiccan ritual has some basic elements that all Wiccans employ in common. The purpose of the Wiccan ritual is to bring people together (unless you practice Solitary Wicca) and to focus a particular energy into the world. There are many occasions for ritual, that of Shabbat celebrations, of course, but also of initiation ceremonies, life milestones (such as a wedding or partnership), and end-of-life respects. Most often, Wiccan rituals are held in private, though there are certain covens or groups that will perform rituals in a more public space in order to educate others about the belief and encourage more to join or participate. Even if you are practicing ritual in a solitary fashion, you are adding your unique energy and intention into the universe, and this is no less important than group gatherings or festival feasts.

As with all things Wiccan, there is no one set way in which to prepare and practice a Wiccan ritual, though there are some common elements that create a unifying sense of practice, especially to help the beginning practitioner immerse him or herself into the belief. Rituals can either be elaborate and bound by agreed upon rules within a coven, or they can be simple and ad hoc, depending on your intention and purpose. In addition, the content of a Wiccan ritual is often determined by the occasion for which it is constructed. Thus, a Sabbat ritual probably looks different than an initiation ritual, of course. Still, some common practice is brought to nearly every ritual, as explored step by step below.

4.1 Preparing Your Toolkit

As with nearly all religious ceremonies, sacred objects are used to enhance the experience, convey certain messages to participants or to deities, and to represent various intentions that are invoked during the ritual. Christian religions use particular vestments, depending on denomination, as well as altars and other symbols, typically speaking. Wicca is no different in this respect, and it too employs particular objects considered consecrated to the practitioners. These "tools," for lack of a better word, help Wiccans to focus their intentions and maintain spiritual energy. The difference between Wiccan objects used in ritual and those used in monotheistic religions is that there is an acknowledgement that the Wiccan practitioners themselves provide the energy and sanctification of the objects, rather than being wholly directed by some specific higher power. It is more participatory and shared, rather than authoritative. Because of this, most objects used in Wiccan ritual are not merely symbolic: they are also practical and can be used within the physical realm for pragmatic purpose.

Before you hurry off to acquire each and every one of the tools listed below, remember that you need none of them to actual start to practice Wicca. Wiccan belief is as much about tapping into a sense of spiritual oneness with nature, regaining a sense of the cyclical reality of the world, and learning to channel your own energies with intention; the tools are devices to help you do this. Acquire them a few at a time, as you develop your practice and as need dictates. In addition, not all objects that one uses during

Wiccan ritual are actual tools: the symbols discussed in the previous chapter also play a role; plates of offering or other symbolic decorations are often employed; crystals, stones, herbs, and other significant objects to Wiccan practice are also present in ritual displays. That said, the following objects are frequently part of a Wiccan's toolkit to help them practice ritual, channelling energy and intention and providing succour for the practitioner.

Chalice: this symbol of fertility, representing the element of water and the renewing energy of the Mother Goddess herself, can have several roles in ritual. It can offer any kind of libation, such as wine or ale or water, depending on the ceremony (it is most certainly used in a cakes and ale ceremony, ritual feast emphasizing gratitude and the good things in life). It can also stand empty to symbolize the openness to the flow of energy from the universe. There are many elegant chalices from which to choose, but any vessel with which you endow energy is worthy of a chalice. Just be sure the material is of the earth, no artificial plastic.

Wand: an oft-associated tool with witches, the wand is symbolic of the elemental power of air or fire. The object itself is not the source of power; rather, it is the conduit through which the practitioner channels her energy and makes real her intention. Traditionally made of wood (elder, oak, willow), a wand can be a homemade affair, carved by hand and consecrated with a gift to the tree that provided the wood. Natural material is preferred, of course, and if you live in an urban area, you can certainly seek out a wooden dowel to personalize and consecrate for your own.

Pentacle: this ubiquitous object can be found at Wiccan and New Age shops and is used to charge other objects with energy; other tools are arranged on it in order to elevate their maximum power. The pentacle can also be mimed in the air, a ritual sign of protection. As discussed in the previous chapter, the pentacle is representative of all four elements of the physical world and their unity with the spiritual, making this a particularly powerful object.

Athame: this is used to direct energy, either cutting away negative forces or encompassing the positive. Its masculine shape and power make it a symbolic representation of the god deity. It need not be particularly sharp, as the ritualistic ways in which it is used are symbolic rather than actual (no actual cutting but presenting the action—exceptions are made for kitchen work or herbal preparations).

Censer: the censer burns incense in order to purify the environment in which the ritual is practiced, as well as creating an atmosphere wherein the mind energy is focused on intention.

Candles: the candle is central to all Wiccan practice and ritual, as a symbolic element in its own right. Representing the element of fire, primarily, the candle also channels the energy of the bonfire (community), the torch (sight), and ritual offerings (gratitude). It has always been sacred to rituals throughout the Western world. In addition, the candle is one of the most powerful tools in a Wiccan's toolkit, as it transmits the message or request (the intention) from the physical plane to the ethereal one. The flame burns, transmogrifying the physical object into the spiritual intention, blending the elements of earth, fire, and air to carry messages from one plane to another.

Other: aside from the common items above, other objects often used in the Wican toolkit include the cauldron (where incense can be burned, offerings can be given, herbal potions can be brewed), the broom (to purify space, sweeping away negative energy), and the bell (to send clear messages into the ethereal plane). The bell, in particular, is used in religious rituals across the world, communicating faith or intention or congregation to those within the community.

4.2 Making an Altar

Once you have acquired your toolkit, you are ready to embark upon the symbolic centerpiece of Wiccan ritual, the altar. Before you begin to build the altar, however, you will want to purify the space and/or participants: this can take the form of "smudging," burning particular herbs (usually sage or lavender) to clear a space of negative energy, or in ritual bathing for those who are participating (this might be particularly useful for an initiation ceremony, for example). Long-time practitioners of Wicca might keep a permanent altar in their home or place of worship, but even then, the altar will be adorned differently depending on the ritual, the celebration, and/or the time of year.

As the physical focal point of the Wiccan ritual, the altar is crucial to the exercise, and it also serves as a central force in any number of celebrations and practices throughout the year: celebrating Sabbats and Esbats (full moons), practicing meditation, saying prayers, or creating spells are all activities during which the altar can be a focal point. If you don't wish to create a permanent altar in your home, you can certainly set one up outside in a private, secluded space, or you can construct a small, moveable altar that can be put away after a ritual or ceremony is over. Practicing Wicca outdoors is a preference for many, as it allows you to communicate more closely with nature and the spiritual.

There are no particular requirements when it comes to what the altar looks like, though it does need to have an accommodating flat surface upon which to place tools, ornaments, and other ritual items. Many Wiccans prefer a round shape, both because of its feminine and egalitarian associations and for its practical use in creating the sacred circle. Additionally, as with other Wiccan tools, the ideal altar is made of natural materials—wood or stone, not plastic or other human-made material. Other than these basic requirements, the altar can be made of whatever you have on hand, an underused desk or a coffee or end table. It is not necessary to purchase something new, though if you intend to use your altar with any frequency, it might be a good idea to find one that you can use continuously, rather than having to clear it up and put it away frequently.

Once you have the surface of your altar, be sure to adorn it with whatever colors and decorations you feel give it a magical aura— this is the goal, of course, to transform an ordinary surface into an extraordinary place in which your intentions are heard and your rituals are successful. You can change this according to the seasons, of course, using browns and golds during autumn and greens and yellows during spring; always be in tune with natural cycles when you can. The altar is also a place to keep energy channelling crystals or stones, images of deities or other symbolic representations, and candles. However, the main function of the altar during ritual is to hold your tools in some kind of thoughtful arrangement. As with all things Wiccan, this arrangement is mostly up to the individual practitioner, but there are a couple of standard arrangements that you can follow: first, a simple way to arrange your altar is to arrange all tools associated with the Mother Goddess (water and earth elements) to the left of center, while all tools associated with the Horned God or male deity (air and fire elements) to the right of center. Second, a more elaborate way of setting up an altar is to place the Goddess and God representations in the center with the rest of the tools arranged around them according to element and corresponding direction; that is, earth elements will be arranged facing north, while fire elements are arranged facing south, and water elements arranged to the west, with air elements arranged to the east. Again, many Wiccans will simply arrange their altar according to their own intuitive feeling, and you should feel free to do such, especially after you've had some time to practice and start to understand how energy works best for you.

The most important issue to remember when setting up your altar is that no one way is right or wrong, that no matter how large or small your area is, it is still meaningful. Indeed, you are the one to endow the space and the tools with energy and intention, so it should feel right for you. It should be a space of power, of energy, of serenity—and of practical use. If it's too crowded or if you cannot find what you need, then you know that it's not working as well as it could. In addition, each ritual need not be practiced on the same altar; a tree stump behind your home might serve particularly well for a harvest Sabbat, while your small home altar serves you better for daily meditation. The above are just some ideas to get you started.

4.3 Intentions and Support

In terms of the actual ritual itself, this is largely up to you and your group (if participating) to decide. After the circle is cast, as mentioned above, invocations are called for. Typically speaking, the Goddess and God will be invited into the circle first, followed by a recognition of each of the four elements and their contributions. Some ritual traditions also call for invoking the four cardinal directions. In yet others, a fifth element—Akasha, or Spirit—is also called upon. If you join a particular group, then they will likely already have their process in place, but if you are working on your own, decide what feels best for your intention.

Next, state your intention directly and clearly. Sometimes this will be quite simple, as for a Shabbat: "I am here to celebrate Samhain and to thank the Mother Goddess and the Horned God for a bountiful harvest," for example. Sometimes you will be asking for support, to help heal mind or body (see Chapter 4 for more details on this), or you will be practicing spellwork with a particular purpose in mind. Be clear and specific in your intention, invoking which of the elements, spirits, and deities you need to thank or for assistance. Once the intention is stated, the ritual itself can take many forms. There could be ritual singing or chanting, dancing or dramatic reenactments. For example, if you are performing a partnership ceremony or a Wiccan wedding, a dramatic reenactment of a spiritual union would be appropriate. Different groups have particular liturgical texts that they follow in order to best suit the intention or celebration. There may be offerings to hold up or to create within the sacred circle. If you are practicing solo, you may read from appropriate texts or chant your own compositions or perform acts of meditation or prayer. It isn't uncommon among certain Wiccan traditions to pray for the benefit of all of nature or humankind; the ritual dictates the boundaries of the intention. The "cakes and ale" ceremony is also a common feature of many rituals, wherein food and drink are ritually made or consumed or offered—or all of the above. Everything on offer is symbolic and intended to enhance the celebration or intention inherent to the ritual. Again, many groups will have enacted their own traditions for this sort of ceremony. In the following chapters, you will learn more about various ways in which Wicca tradition and ritual can benefit you—and others and the larger world—through typical practice. If your intentions are sincere and your actions genuine, then there is really no incorrect way of going about practicing Wiccan ritual. The more you understand about how each part of your daily life connects to Wicca, the more able you are to create a powerful mindset and positive energy to reverberate throughout the universe.

Chapter 5: Magickal Workings

In this chapter we take a closer look at magick and why it is an important aspect of modern Wicca. We also discuss some of the methods used today to cast spells to bring about positive change.

5.1 The Modern Witchcraft Journey

Spells, rituals, magick, and witchcraft are all important elements of a modern Wiccan's faith and practice. Each component is meant to strengthen the connection to the Gods and to the Higher Self, an individual's higher level of consciousness. Ritual devotion to the Gods and the observation of the Wheel of the Year and the moon phases will bring the higher state of consciousness needed to connect with the Goddess, God, and universal energy. Today's rituals almost always include raising energy to bring about change for the greater good: protecting and healing the Earth.

Participants of ritual experience a heightened sense of awareness, and ordinary actions and gestures become spiritually symbolic. Ritual takes on a specific meaning by taking Wiccan values and beliefs and enacting them. Ritual drama, such as plays that enact seasonal changes, like the harvest or the waning or waxing of the sun's energy, helps participants and observers focus on the deeper meaning of the ritual through a different lens.

5.2 Focus and Concentration

Before beginning any magickal working, it is important to prepare. Many modern Wiccans have clothing that they reserve specifically for rituals or casting spells, which can take any form or style that they wish. It is customary to first purify yourself spiritually by taking a cleansing ritual bath and then anointing yourself with an oil that complements the intention of the magick or ritual. To avoid distractions or interruptions, it's best to turn off the phone and television. Light some candles and incense and play some soft music. Allow thoughts of the mundane world to fade and focus on the magick or ritual at hand. Magick comes from a higher level of consciousness called the Higher Self. To access this level, one must learn to shift consciousness. The music, ritual bath, special clothing, herbs, oils, and incense are all ways to aid in moving from the everyday world into the world of spirit and magick.

5.3 Visualization

It's important for Wiccans to completely visualize their goal before beginning their spell or ritual work. The very first step in visualization is to know what you want. You must be able to clearly see the goal or outcome in your mind's eye. The second step is to see the goal already achieved. The third step is to see a detailed picture of the steps in the mundane and spiritual worlds that need to be taken to achieve the goal. Visualization puts into practice the Law of Positive Attraction, or "like attracts like." It is a beacon that draws your goal and everything you need to achieve it toward you. It activates the subconscious to bring forward ideas to achieve your desired outcome. It programs the brain to look for and recognize resources that can be used to reach the goal and builds motivation to take the necessary steps.

Here are some useful tips on successfully visualizing your goal prior to spell or ritual work:

- Spend a few moments every day in quiet meditation, "seeing" your life with the goal accomplished. Try to experience the outcome using all your senses: sight, sound, taste, smell, and touch.
- Create a vision board with pictures of your goal and use it as a magickal focal point.
- Write the goal on a piece of paper and keep it where you will see it several times a day.
- If applicable, take daily action to accomplish your goal, no matter how small that might be.
- Believe that your goal will be accomplished.

5.4 Sacred Space

Sacred space is simply an area designated to spirit. It is a place set aside, permanently or temporarily, for ritual, magick, meditation, prayer, and communing with deity. To create sacred space, first cleanse yourself with a ritual bath and dress in ritual clothing (any garment kept specifically for use during rituals and magick) or simply wear clothing you find the most comfortable.

Then ritually cleanse the area by following these steps:

- Smudge the intended space with smoke from a smoldering smudge stick or incense, beginning in the north and walking counterclockwise around the space.
- Spritz the space with a spray bottle filled with water and a few drops of an essential oil such as sage, frankincense, or lavender.
- Ritually sweep the space, visualizing the broom collecting and absorbing negative energy. Be sure to take the broom outside and shake it vigorously to release the baneful energy you collected.
- Sprinkle salt around the space. Alternatively, you can use a salt lamp to continuously cleanse the space, if you have one.
- Light a candle or sparkler and, beginning in the north, walk counterclockwise around the space.
- Visualize a cleansing ball of white light in the center of the room; "watch" it grows to fill the entire space.
- Maintaining the proper atmosphere is important to shift your consciousness into a higher magickal state. Light incense and candles, turn down the lights, turn off your phone, play some soft music, and allow your senses to become fully engaged.

5.5 Cleansing, Consecrating, and Charging

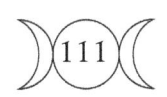

To consecrate something is to bless it for sacred use and to spiritually mark it as yours. Another word for **consecration** is **enchantment**. Cleansing and consecration are always done together, and your personal tools of magick should always be cleansed and consecrated before you use them for the first time. It's a good idea to start using your tools right away so the charge is "set" or bound to the tool. Keep in mind that the object in use must be purified of unwanted residual energy before it can be charged with new ritual or magickal power. Everything picks up energy from its surroundings, so it's important to "wipe the slate clean" before you use it in a magick circle or spell. Though it is good practice to cleanse and reconsecrate your tools on a regular basis, how often you do is up to you.

Many religions have consecration ceremonies that are performed only by their respective priesthoods. In modern Wicca, however, it is believed that every Wiccan holds the right to consecrate, because every Wiccan is considered a Priest or Priestess. The power to consecrate is inherent in every human being and is always effective if sincerely carried out. All it requires is for you to concentrate your intention and will, then beam that energy into the object to be blessed.

Book 4: Wicca Book of Spells

Chapter 1: An Intro to Wiccan Spells

The simple steps to casting a circle and invoking the energies and intentions of your craft will help you gain clarity and awareness with your work and your purpose. This chapter is a fun and easy collection of five, simple spells that you can use to get you started in your practice. You can use these spells as they are written but feel free to modify them to your liking and personal needs and preferences.

One item of note that you may find in your study and practice of Wicca is the Power of Three. Often in spells, you will notice an incantation "by the power of 3" or "3 times3" and this number correlates to a Wiccan rule of thumb that states whatever energy you are putting into the Universe will come back to you 3 fold, so make sure you are working with good intentions and not malice towards anyone. It goes hand-in-hand with the Wiccan Rede.

Banishing Spell

A banishing spell should always follow the Wiccan Rede that states, "If ye harm none, do as ye will." The intentions behind every spell you do should never be malicious or cause energetic harm to another. If you are needing to banish a person, do so lovingly or compassionately and allow the intention of your spell to do the work for you.

You will need the following:

- A sheet of paper

- A pen
- A fire safe bowl or container to put burning paper in
- Matches or a lighter

A few banishing herbs that you can choose from the following list: Angelica, broom, cedar, cumin, lilac, oak, onion, pine, rosemary, sage, salt, thistle, yarrow

A small bag, or bowl to put your herbs in on your altar. If they can be made into a bouquet, you can arrange them that way as well, otherwise, you can set them in the pouch or bowl.

Steps:

1. Cast your circle.
2. On the piece of paper, write what you are wanting to banish. Be clear and specific. You may be desiring to banish the unwanted energy left by your in-laws in your house or you may be trying to banish a person from bothering you all of the time. It could be you are also wanting to banish your anxiety, or nightmares. Whatever it is, state it clearly on the paper with the pen. (Using ink is better than pencil but you can use pencil if you have no pen around).
3. Have your herbs handy and you can use them to sprinkle over the sheet of paper in the bowl after you have read your words aloud or you can keep them ready to set on your altar after your spell.
4. Read what you wrote on your paper aloud. Saying it three times in a row is a good practice. You can then set it in the bowl first and sprinkle it with banishing herbs before setting it on fire and letting it burn. You can also use the herbs afterward instead of burning them with the paper.
5. As it burns, say the following words: By the power of 3 times three, I invoke the spirits and guides to come to me, Banish this negativity, From my home, my life, so mote it be!
6. Once the paper has burned, take the ashes and you can sprinkle them outside in the garbage or anywhere far away from you and outside of your home. You can even toss them in the street to make sure they are

not on your property. You can then sprinkle the banishing herbs on top of the ashes to seal the deal.

7. Go back indoors and close your circle and light a candle of protection on your altar. Smudge the area and yourself for extra clearing and cleansing.

Third Eye Opener- Psychic Spell

Part of the journey of practicing Wicca is to open yourself to your psychic and clairvoyant abilities. The more open you are, the better you can communicate with the energy of all things around you and invoke more powerful intentions. Your third eye is the place of your visions, dreams, and psychic abilities and this herbal spell can help you open it and keep it open.

Protection Spell

Protection is a useful way to keep yourself from attracting unwanted energies to you. It may be that you want to protect yourself from other people's energy, or you want to protect your whole house. Either way, the herbs and intentions in this spell can help with that.

You will need the following:

- Anise
- Basil
- Bay Leaf
- Black Pepper
- Cayenne
- Cloves
- Fennel
- Garlic
- Rosemary
- Salt
- Mortar & Pestle or food processor
- Bottle with cork or lid
- Black Candle Matches/ lighter

Steps:

1. Grind together the following herbs so they are mixed together like a powder: Anise, basil, bay leaf, black pepper, cayenne, cloves, fennel, garlic, rosemary, salt.
2. Put them in a bottle.
3. Cast a circle and "charge" your bottle of herbs with the intention of protective energy. Once you feel like you have set the intention firmly and clearly, you can end the invocation. ** NOTE: Charging is a way for you to clearly send the energy of a specific intention into something. You can simply hold the bottle between your hands and speak aloud your intentions with whatever you are charging, making a declaration of what the object's purpose is.
4. Close the circle.
5. Sprinkle herbs around the perimeter of your house. You can also wear them in a pouch around your neck, or sleep with them under your pillow. If you want, you can do a light sprinkling in the corners of your house as well.
6. Store what isn't used on your altar and use whenever needed.
7. Light a black candle of protection if you feel like you need that extra energy.

Money Spell

Who doesn't want a little extra money? When you need to draw abundance into your life, you need a little money spell to set things right. Casting a money spell has a way of helping you align with the energies of abundance and prosperity you are looking for in your life.

You will need the following:

- green candles in candle holders
- dollar bills (you can use coins as well, but bills work best)
- Herbs: basil, cinnamon, clove, ginger, nutmeg, mint, dill, patchouli (you don't have to use all of these herbs- you can use one, or create a blend of your choice.)

Steps:

1. Cast your circle.
2. Place the three dollar bills on your altar and sprinkle your herbs on top of each bill.
3. Place a green candle on top of each bill.
4. Close your circle.
5. Let the candles burn until they go out on their own.

Love Spell

We are all looking for love and a little love spell can help you open your heart to letting love in, as well as calling it to you. The love spells that are available in the world today are numerous and all very different. You can come up with so many different types of love spell and this one is a fun one to get you out under the stars.

You will need the following:

- Pink and/ or red candles
- Lighter or matches
- Rose Petals
- Jasmine/ Rose/ or Lavender incense
- Rose quartz crystal
- Sheet of paper
- Pen

** NOTE: This spell is to be performed at night when stars are visible in the sky.

Steps:

1. Cast a circle of protection and intention.
2. Light the candle on your altar and the incense as well.
3. On the sheet of paper, write down all of the qualities you are hoping for in a partner. Be as specific as possible. Read the list out loud in front of your altar. Fold the paper and set it underneath the candle holder.

4. Leave the candle and incense burning (make sure it is in a safe place) and take your rose petals and rose quartz outside.
5. Find a star that you are attracted to and hold your hand out, palm up, with the rose petals and rose quartz in it.
6. Imagine starlight from that star beaming down to your hand and charging and infusing the petals and the crystal. Think about the qualities that you wrote down on the paper as you continue to visualize.
7. Take the petals and the crystal back inside to your altar and say the following words as you sprinkle the petals around the base of the candle: Hear me as I call to you, Come to me, my love so true.
8. Set the rose quartz on top of the petals in front of the candle and allow the candle to burn. If you need to extinguish the candle overnight, you can relight it in the morning.

All of these spells are an excellent way to get you started on your journey with crafting rituals to help you align with your intentions.

As you advance in your work, keep playing with new versions of what you would like to do as you cast. In the next chapter, you will learn more about the power of nature in the practice of Wicca and why you need to devote your energy to participating in the rhythm and cycles of the seasons and the Great Earth Mother.

Chapter 2: Some Practical Spells

Sometimes, instead of yearning for romance and passion, we simply want to boost our happiness with a more fulfilling social life. Friendships are the bedrock of our young adulthood, especially, though when work and family become busy, we often find our youthful friendships falling away. If you have recently relocated and are looking for new social outlets, this is also a great spell for that. To reboot your energy in this arena, the following spell will help you bring new people and new positive energies into your life.

Before you even begin to amass the tools needed to complete this spell, spend some time thinking about what kinds of friendship do you want; the clearer your intention, the more successful the spell. Are you looking for a close, one-on-one friendship or a small, closely knit group? Or are you seeking a large, boisterous circle of friends to be regularly social with? What qualities do you find attractive in friends? What interests do you have that you'd like to share with others? The better able you are to pinpoint exactly what you're looking for, the better able you will be to direct this particular energy toward your spell. This spell is best practiced during the waxing moon, which represents increasing possibilities and abundance.

2.1 Spells for Friendship

Sometimes, we look around us and realize that people we thought were friends, were not truly friends, or that we have drifted apart from friends, and realize we need new connections—ones that will last. Wiccans tend to be introverted and sometimes have a harder time connecting with people. This spell is a little different than the spells we have covered, but it is not drastically different.

2.1.1 Charm for Spiritual Connections

This is more of a chant than a spell, so you do not have to cast a circle. You are merely putting out good thoughts in the atmosphere to find a deep spiritual connection with someone. These people can be friends or other loved ones. Spiritual connections are important because you need someone who sparks your soul. When you have the time, go into a solitary room, and shut yourself away.

Think about the type of connection you want and close your eyes. You want to find something deep within your interests, so keep that in mind. While you are imagining, the connection say this chant.

My heart my soul my spiritual friend come to me I welcome you in.

Say the chant three times and then open your eyes. You have completed the chant. Now go out there and talk to people. Soon you will find someone who sparks your very spirit. Be willing to get out there and find the person. This spell will also do its part and will draw you to the right people.

2.2 Spells for Relationships

Spells to attract happy and loving relationships into your life are brilliant ways of working. Always remember the Wiccan rede when working, and do not use magick to attempt to influence another's free will. The right person will come to you at the right time if you have confidence and approach your working in harmony and with love. Approach with a mindset of jealousy, control and anger, and you will attract those energies to you.

2.2.1 Common Items, Elements & Colors

Elements – Water for the emotions, Fire for passion.

Colors – Pink, gold, and red. Silver can be used to represent spiritual bonds of love.

Crystals – Rose quartz and amethyst for love. Ruby and garnet for passion.

Herbs and Oils - White sage for cleansing. Lavender oil for peace, harmony and self-love. Rose oil and bergamot for grounded love.
Jasmine and Ylang Ylang for passion.

Other Items - Flowers such as roses and carnations are wonderful for attracting more love. Representations of the Goddess and reminders of her Universal love are also beneficial.

2.3 Spell for Better Relationships

This spell can be used to harmonize your relationships. Remember to work on the material plane by communicating with your loved ones. It's not necessary to inform them specifically of your intentions. However, you must work in the spirit of easing tensions for everyone, not simply for getting your own way in arguments!

You will need:

- A white candle
- A large bowl
- Sea salt and sage
- A fluorite or jade crystal – both are excellent for inviting harmony.

Method:

1. Work during a waning moon
2. Cast the circle and call the quarters
3. Take your white candle and, using your Athame, carve the initial of everyone involved in your disputes, or simply write the word, 'peace.'
4. Place the candle in the bowl, and fill it with water. Place your fluorite or jasper crystal into the bowl.
5. Now, sprinkle the sea salt into the bowl whilst saying: "May disagreements be forgiven and negative energies dispelled. May water purify our relationships, and earth cleanse bad feelings."
6. Light the candle and say: "May light shine upon darkness. May our relationships be harmonious. For the highest good of all, so mote it be."
7. Wait until the candle burns to the point where the water extinguishes it, and then visualize peace and letting go of any resentments.
8. When the candle has burned out, thank the energies and dismiss them.
9. Take the crystal and place it in your living space if your spell is to bring greater harmony in home-based relationships, or carry it with you to help better and more harmonious relationships outside the home.

This method can easily be worked for others as well, by simply changing the words to 'their' instead of 'ours'. You may place the crystal in the workplace, or give it to the person you are working for to carry or place in their home.

2.4 Self-Love Ritual

Many people struggle with attracting the relationship they want because they don't feel self-love. We often attract outside influences that actually mirror how we feel internally. A perfect way to heal and attract love is to practice lifting your self-esteem with this loving ritual for the self.

You will need:

- Rose petals and lavender oil
- White sage and sea salt
- A pink candle
- A Rose quartz and some thin wire or cord.

Method:

Part A

1. For this spell, you will begin by taking a ritual bath. Ritual baths are amazing for cleansing and inspiring you, and this will put you in the perfect frame of mind for the second part of the ritual.
2. Run a bath and, whilst the water is running, put a few drops of lavender oil in, along with a handful of sea salt and a few white sage leaves.
3. Light your candle and get into the bath. If you can put on some calming music, that would also be helpful.
4. As you bathe, visualize all the negative emotions you have surrounding love being replaced with deep love for yourself.
5. Say out loud: "I cleanse myself of all negative energy. I connect with my divine being, made with infinite love. I am whole, complete, and I love and accept myself."
6. Repeat this phrase at least three times, and put as much focus and meaning into it as you can.

7. Get out of the bath and dress, and take note of the water as it empties. See all the doubts and worries you may have had about yourself drain away with the water.
8. If you don't have a bath, you can wash your hands and face in the scented water whilst repeating the invocation.

Part B

1. Next, go into your ritual space, taking with you the candle, your amethyst (or programmed clear quartz), and the cord or wire.
2. Cast your circle and call the quarters. Pay particular attention to water and the waves of emotion and love from this element.
3. Now, breathe in deeply and visualize yourself being filled with infinite love. Remember all your amazing qualities and forgive yourself for past mistakes. Then take your amethyst and begin to wind the cord or wire around it, until you have secured it tightly.
4. As you wrap the crystal, say: "I deeply love and honor myself. I am worthy of love, and I allow myself to feel and experience divine love."
5. Repeat until the crystal has been wrapped. Place the crystal under your pillow, or put it onto a necklace close to your heart center.
6. Thank the elements and dismiss them

2.4.2 Working for Others

1. You may use the oil and herbal / petal mixture in order to cleanse a representation of the person you are working for. You can use a piece of quartz and visualize them whilst holding it, for example.
2. Cleanse your representation whilst saying — "Beloved (insert name). You are a whole and complete being. You are worthy of love and feeling self-love."
3. Then, use your ritual space to wrap the crystal and invoke for your subject a feeling of divine self-love.
4. Give the crystal to them, or visualize the energy flowing to them before thanking the energy and allowing it to depart.

2.5 Working with Sex & Orgasms

A powerful way to work in any ritual is to use orgasms. We have included some thoughts here regarding the energies of orgasms and how they might be used. If you are planning on using this energy when with a partner, you must let them know what you are doing and why.

To not do this is to take their energy without permission, and this can end badly for you. There are other texts which discuss Sex Magick in more detail, and it is recommended you consult these before using magick with a partner in this way.

As a solo practitioner, you might use the power of your own orgasms to heighten spells you cast, especially love spells. The way you do this is important. There are two ways of having an orgasm and using the energy from it magickally. The first is to draw things to you, and the second it to project your will or unwanted things to the universe around you.

2.5.1 For the First, Follow This Method:

1. Lay down in a comfortable place and calm your breath.
2. Focus your intention on what it is you wish to draw to you. You may do this in your magickal circle if you are using it as part of your ritual.
3. As you begin to get close to orgasm, imagine the energy from your arousal to be working its way upwards into your body from your lower chakras. Imagine what you wish to be drawn magnetically to you.
4. At the point of orgasm, tense your muscles so that the physical sensation and energy feels as though it is directing inside of you, not outwards. Focus as strongly as you possibly can on a mental image of what you want (such as more money or better health).
5. When you have finished, it is particularly important to ground yourself with laughter and nourishing food.

2.5.2 Second Method:

1. For this method, begin as you did with the inward orgasm. However, as you begin to build the sexual energy, imagine it is flowing **from** you. If you want to rid yourself of a negative trait then imagine that trait leaving your body.

2. If you want to influence energy in some way (for example you want to project love and getting favorable circumstances out into the world) then imagine this energy leaving your body.
3. At the point of orgasm, attempt to 'push' your orgasm out of your body with your muscles as they contract. This might be a strange way of feeling them if you're not used to it.
4. Visualize the energy as strongly as possible, and then see it go out into the Universe.
5. Once again, take care to ground yourself with laughter and nourishing food afterwards.

Note: When you are working with orgasms, you may also add relevant crystals and colors, such as red candles or a ruby for passion.

2.6 Spell to Let Go of Old Love

Sometimes, we know the time has come to let go of relationships that are no longer serving us. It's not always easy, so a ritual focused on letting go and cutting those cords of attachment can be useful.

Please note that these spells should not be done in anger or to punish another person. If you are still holding onto anger or resentment, then it might be advisable to perform a self-love and self-acceptance ritual before you proceed.

This spell is to let go of energy, and to allow new things to come into your life. Therefore, you must be able to wish your old love well before you proceed.

You will need:

- Two red candles
- Silver cord
- Lavender Oil
- Rose quartz
- Sea salt

Method:

1. Cast your circle and call the quarters.

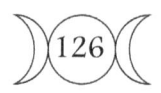

2. Take the two candles and tie them to one another with
3. silver cord. Visualize the person you need to let go of and the cords binding you both.
4. With the highest good in mind for you both, take your Athame (or scissors if your Athame is blunt) and cut the cord tying the candles together.
5. Say: "I release the cords between us. I thank you for your presence in my life, and I wish you farewell. May we both find love and peace. For our highest good, so mote it be."
6. You may wish to tie the cord three times and repeat, strengthening your intent each time.
7. Next, it is important to take good care of yourself, as severing these ties can be painful. Take the rose quartz and dab it with lavender oil.
8. Say these words: "I invite healing and love into the spaces now present. I forgive, both myself and (insert name). I let go and move forward with joy and love."
9. Thank the energies and dismiss them.
10. Go outside and bury the rose quartz, sprinkling sea salt over it before you cover it. Allow the earth energy to cleanse and take hold of any remaining negativity.

This is a highly personal spell that already involves working with another energetically (your old love). It's not recommended you work this on behalf of anyone else.

2.7 Soulmate Spell

Many of us search for our soulmates over our lifetime. Remember that many people have different ideas about who a soulmate really is. For example, some people believe we only have one soulmate. Another viewpoint is that there are many others out there who we are attracted to on a deep level, those who will encourage us to grow and find deeper love in our lives.

One of the advantages of this viewpoint is that it allows us to attach to the concept of infinite and healing love in a framework of abundance, rather than a scarcity model idea of only one soulmate, and that this soulmate is the only one who can complete you. Such a mindset often leaves us feeling hollow, as well as placing far too much pressure on one person to complete us.

Truly nourishing love doesn't leave gaps! We simply add to an already complete picture ~ like a circle that is continually expanding.

Use the following spell to attract such soulmates to you.

You will need:

- Silver ribbon
- Two pink candles
- A small heart. This can be a metal heart, or a heart you have made yourself from clay.

It is recommended that you make your own heart:

1. Simply take some modelling clay and form it into the shape
2. of a heart.
3. Next, use some silver paint (you can buy sprays or craft paint) to make it silver.
4. Add in some glitter-powder or small pieces of rose petal.
5. You will need to wait for it to dry, so do this 2~3 days before you intend to carry out this spell.

Method:

1. Wait until a full moon.
2. Cast your circle and call the quarters.
3. Sit inside your circle and take hold of the heart you have made. With one hand on the heart and another on your chest in your heart-chakra area, repeat these words: "My heart is your heart. Your heart is my heart. May we find each other and unite. For our highest good, in love and acceptance."
4. Next, take one of your pink candles and tie the silver ribbon around it. Do the same to the other candle, so the ribbon connects the two. The silver represents pure cords of attachment.

5. Light both candles and say:
6. "We are bound in love and acceptance. The pathway between us is forged. May we unite for our highest good."
7. Take each candle and carefully drip some wax from each onto the heart. Visualize the meeting of souls in love and unity as you do.
8. Extinguish the candles and thank the energies before dismissing them.
9. Place the heart under the light of the full moon.

2.7.2 Working for Another:

1. Use the same methodology. However, instead of speaking for yourself, speak these words:
2. "Two hearts as one. Found and united. May (insert name) and her (or his) soulmate find one another. For their highest good, in love and acceptance."
3. As you are weaving the candles, say: "Soulmates bound in love and acceptance. The pathway is forged. May they unite for their highest good."

2.8 "Spare Key" Spell for Spiritual Connection

Although we usually think of other people in the context of "relationship," we also have a relationship with our "higher power"—or whatever your personal term is for the force that moves through you when working magic. This spell focuses on strengthening that relationship, which is ultimately the foundation from which all human relationships stem.

While it may be becoming less common in today's world, it has long been the custom of many households to keep a spare key just outside the home, whether under the doormat, in a potted plant, or in some other hidden location. This is done as both a backup in the case of lost keys, and as a way of allowing relatives or friends access when the homeowner is away.

This spell draws on the energies of wisdom and trust that are inherent to this custom, as a way of honoring the benevolent forces working for you in the unseen realms.

By blessing and burying a key outside near your home (or in a potted plant indoors, if necessary) you are signaling to your higher power—whether it be a deity, a guardian spirit, or simply the benevolent energy of the Universe—that you welcome their presence and assistance in your home and in your life, no matter where you may be at any given moment.

It is also a way of reminding yourself that should you temporarily lose your connection to your spiritual center, you will always be able to find your way back in.

Depending on whether crime is a factor in your neighborhood, you may feel comfortable using an actual spare key to your home, but any metal key will work for this spell.

Some people like to use a gold key to represent the God and/or a silver key to represent the Goddess (using two keys is perfectly fine).

You will need:

- 1 key
- 1 white candle

Instructions:

Hold the key in your hands while meditating quietly for several minutes. Focus on that feeling of being truly connected to your true self and your higher power.

When you feel ready, light the candle and say the following (or similar) words:

"[Name of deity/spirit/higher power], you are welcome now and always in my home and in my heart. Let this key represent your access, and mine, to my highest self, from this day forward."

Pass the key through the candle flame very quickly three times (in order to protect your fingers, don't give it any time to become hot).

Then bury it at least 6 inches down into the earth outside your home, or in the soil of a large potted plant.

2.9 Herb and Candle Spell

Just as herbal baths and teas combine the magical properties of Earth and water, incorporating herbs into candle spells activates the synergy between Earth and fire.

Fire is the element of transformation, and in many spells, including the two below, the moment the candle is lit is considered to be the moment when the magic is sent out into the nonphysical planes.

Spell candles, tea lights, or votives are should be used for these spells as they will burn down in a reasonable amount of time. Be sure to use an appropriately sized holder.

2.9.1 Healing Love Spell

Not every love spell is about attracting a date or a relationship. Love has its difficult and even painful moments, and magic can be used for healing from these times. In fact, this kind of magic is often more powerful than any other. This spell is intended for recovering from a break up, but can also be used for healing a major rift with a committed partner.

If you work it for the second purpose, be sure to focus on healing your own feelings with your own power, rather than on something you want your partner to do or say to make it right. To do so would be manipulative magic, which will generally either not work at all, or even bring negative results.

Incense is used in this spell to help soothe hurt feelings and facilitate a peaceful state of mind. Some people are bothered by the smoke of incense. If this is the case for you, try an essential oil in a diffuser instead. (A few drops of oil on top of a wide-based lit candle can also work.

You will need:

- 1 pink or white candle
- Amber, frankincense, copal, or Nag Champa incense
- 2 teaspoons dried hibiscus flower
- 2 teaspoons elecampane root

Instructions:

Light the incense.

Take a few moments to breathe deeply with your eyes closed, focusing on what it feels like to have a sense of peace and feeling loved. You may not be feeling that way lately, obviously, but you can allow yourself to trust that you will experience it again. This spell is for speeding up the time it will take to get there.

When you feel ready, sprinkle the elecampane in a clockwise circle around the candle, saying the following words (or create your own affirmation):

"I heal the energy of this loss within myself, and release it to be transformed into positive energy." (You can substitute "conflict" for "loss" if this is for a conflict in an existing relationship.)

Then do the same with the hibiscus flowers while saying: "I raise my vibration to the level of highest love."

Light the candle, and say **"So let it be."**

Spend a few moments gazing softly at the flame.

Leave the candle to burn all the way down, and let go of any thoughts of the issue for as long as you can.

2.9.2 Money Attraction Spell

Basil and nutmeg make a powerful combination when it comes to bringing some extra cash into your life.

In the days after you work this spell, be careful not to try to figure out where the extra money will come from, or you'll get in the way of the magic's ability to work.

Money can come from all kinds of unexpected places. Go about your usual routine, and trust that you will see the results of the spell when the time is right.

You will need:

- 1 green or gold votive candle
- A teaspoon of dried basil

- A tiny pinch of nutmeg or cinnamon
- Rosemary essential oil or Prosperity Oil (see recipe below!)

Instructions

Anoint the candle with the oil by placing a drop or two at the base and rubbing it in with your fingertips, moving upward to the top. (Wipe your fingers on a cloth to remove any excess oil.)

Roll the candle in the basil so that a significant amount of it sticks.

Place the candle in the holder and say the following words (or create your own affirmation):

"From the endless stream of universal abundance, money flows to me."

Light the candle, then sprinkle the nutmeg or cinnamon lightly above the flame, so as not to put it out.

Leave the candle to burn all the way down.

Chapter 3: More Spells for Life Enhancement

Here are a few more spells for tackling life's challenges and making the most of the opportunities that come your way.

3.1 Good Luck Spell

Nearly everyone has had what many call a "bad luck streak," when things just seem to go constantly wrong.

It doesn't help that our mainstream culture tends to reinforce a belief in these bad luck streaks, while eyeing "good luck streaks" somewhat suspiciously. (The phrase "I can't believe my luck!" usually refers to good things happening, as opposed to unfortunate things.)

Moon phase: Any

Ideal day: Thursday or Sunday

You will need:

- 1 black candle
- 1 white candle
- 1 green candle
- Pinch of chamomile and/or star anise

Instructions:

Arrange the candles side-by-side with the white one in the middle.

Sprinkle the herb(s) in a circle around the candles.

Light the black candle and say **All bad luck away**.

Then light the green candle and say **All good luck to stay.**

Finally, say **Open my eyes and my ears to good fortune**, and then light the white candle.

Send out your intention to be more aware of **everything** that goes right in your life, no matter how seemingly trivial.

Try working this spell once a week for four weeks, and take notes during this time about what you observe. Record all the positive things that happen to you, and do NOT record any negative things. This is about retraining the brain to focus more consistently on the positive, so don't muddy up the work by including any details that don't support your vision of a lucky and charmed life.

When you repeat the spell, have your notes with you and spend a few moments in gratitude for what you have recently noticed regarding good luck in your life.

3.2 Courage Spell

This spell can help you approach any daunting task, whether it's a job interview, a medical procedure, or something more pleasant but still nerve-wracking, like a first date.

Its ideal day is Tuesday—the day associated with Mars, which gives it its association with matters of courage—but don't let that stop you from working this spell on any day you need to!

Moon phase: Waxing
Ideal day: Tuesday

You will need:

- 4 orange candles
- Clove oil (optional)
- 1 small object to "charm" (such as a crystal or other stone, a small piece of jewelry, or other small personal item)

Instructions:

Anoint the candles (if using oil), and arrange them in a square pattern. Place the crystal or other object in the center of the square.

Spend a few moments identifying a situation in which you have felt truly confident and courageous—you may want to do some brainstorming on paper to "dig up" a really solid memory.

Once you've got a visual, focus on it with all of your attention for a few moments. You are going to infuse the object you've placed in the square of candles with this powerful courage, so that you can draw from it later when you need to feel it again.

Light the candles, repeating this mantra as you light each one: "This fire of courage burns always in my heart."

Allow the candles to burn down, then keep your courage charm in your pocket (or wear it, if it's jewelry) whenever you need an extra boost of confidence.

3.3 Helpful Answers Spell

For those big, burning questions that just won't leave you alone. While it's often true that we can't know the answer to a question until we're absolutely meant to, you can ask the Universe to send you helpful information along the way. Just be sure you're open to whatever the answer might be—if you're too attached to a certain outcome, you might not be able to "hear" the truth when the spirit realm whispers it to you.

The answers may come in a dream, or in a moment of synchronicity in your waking life, such as a phrase spoken in a conversation with a friend or acquaintance.

Moon phase: Waning, particularly just before the New Moon

Ideal day: Monday or Wednesday

You will need:

- 1 yellow or gold candle
- 1 strip of paper, long enough to write your question on
- Crystal point, athame, or other ritual carving tool

Instructions:

Think clearly about your question and write it as concisely as possible on the strip of paper.

Carve one to three words that represent the question into the candle, starting at the bottom and working up to the tip.

Light the candle, and burn the strip of paper.

Allow the candle to burn down.

You should receive an answer within 7 days.

3.4 Psychic Attack Reversal Spell

Many resources on magic mention psychic attack, but unless you know other people in your life who a) practice magic and b) would actually work magic to hurt you in some way, you're unlikely to become a victim of an overt magical attack. However, because thought is energy, it's definitely possible to be undermined by the negative thoughts of others—particularly those who may be resentful or envious of us for whatever reason. These thoughts are also a form of psychic attack, even if the perpetrator doesn't intentionally mean harm against us. This spell helps you eliminate any effects of the negative thoughts and feelings of others.

Moon phase: Waning

Ideal day: Tuesday or Saturday

You will need:

- 1 black candle
- 5 garlic cloves
- 1 teaspoon honey

Instructions:

Arrange the garlic cloves around the black candle in the shape of a five-pointed star. Visualize the garlic absorbing any and all negative energy in and around your body.

When you're ready, say: "I release any and all negativity. I am protected from all harmful thought from all directions. I am healed from any harmful effects of the thoughts of others."

Light the candle and eat the honey.

When the spell is done, bury the garlic cloves outside.

Chapter 4: Top Tips for Spells

Spell tricks can range from essential pointers for the beginner to pieces of wisdom for the more trained charmer. As much as it may be, we could all do with a little help from time to time and it's far from hard to forget some of the things we learn along the way to becoming an accomplished and vital witch. So, I have assembled a tiring of some of what I consider to be the most important tips for spells that I have learned or that have been passed on to me and the expectation that you can find a use in them too! This way, no specific request:

1. One of the best spell tips I can give you in case you are just beginning is when you are looking for other people's spells to perform by going for the spell you are attracted to. This implies that you speak to yourself at the level of clairvoyant Association and will help you be ready to tune in to the correct forces when you perform it. Similarly, do not go for the maximum of out-ofcontrol complaints or more flashy claims. No spell should profess to have a chance to change your life in the medium term. In any case, this quiet, humble little spell could probably be to implement a little improvement that triggers opportunities that take you where you need to go throughout your daily life.

2. When you write your own, do close to them, you would be careful. Try not to hang up too much to try to duplicate another's style or techniques. Although it can help in the early stages to perceive how others work, you will be constantly gradually powerful in your spell work on the possibility that you can relate to your spell and see your qualities in it.

3. Use large devices. In the end, most witches break on devices made for reason. This can help with the atmosphere and environment of your elevated area or workspace and can also help as they are explicitly structured. So it is not essential and at random you find yourself with a connection to a specific object, at that time you stay with it for the necessary period of time. I had for example a huge bowl that I used for a cauldron for a very long time! The association is important in contrast to the thing itself.

4. Dedicate any space where you work consistently. Many witches argue that it is constantly essential for you to sanctify the area and the devices you use, but they disagree. In any case, it came to my list of 10 tips for spells because it is an extremely innovative service to instill the belief that everything is good and confidence in the workspace. You will feel that it is gradually Holy and "claimed" by you. The Smearing of lavender and Sage is feasible but simple.

5. Work with excellent ingredients on every occasion. More normal is better you will draw much more power from the resources of the world, for example. In the event that you use new flowers, be sure to cut them yourself on the luck you can.

6. Sixth of my advice for spells is to set. This is a botch for beginners largely and can emerge from being in a race on top to get started. Unfortunately, spells are usually not as beneficial as we would like and you will not have place running. You'll be a progressively powerful disaster if you find an example of putting yourself in the right attitude. Very well, you can take a relaxing shower surrounded by candles, using reflection or dressing in clothes that you feel give the correct energies. It could also be a combination of each of the 3 however review to find what is ideal for you.

7. In addition to the tips for spells number 6 above, you should at the same time not be in a hurry to see the results. I discovered spells that took a long time to work and ended up being greatly improved for me than I originally imagined! Trust superior wisdom at work and believe that the right moment is at hand.

8. Be reasonable. Great things can be achieved with the correct fate and a lot of hard work, determination and ability. In any case, do not try to duplicate things that you may have found on TV or in the cinema.

9. Work with the seasons or lunar cycles. This is connected with the incorporation of the energies that are around you, known to man. Everything is here to be direct, so why waste! You will understand how to have the opportunity to perceive the different energies around you as

you gradually become adept at drawing them and so you can design your spell in advance.

10. this might be my last advice for spells, but it's really one of the most important. Remember the evil person of Wiccan Rede. Try not to attempt to do something that could hurt others or attempt to change their freedom through and through. Be aware of your work.

Book 5:
Wicca Book of the Shadows

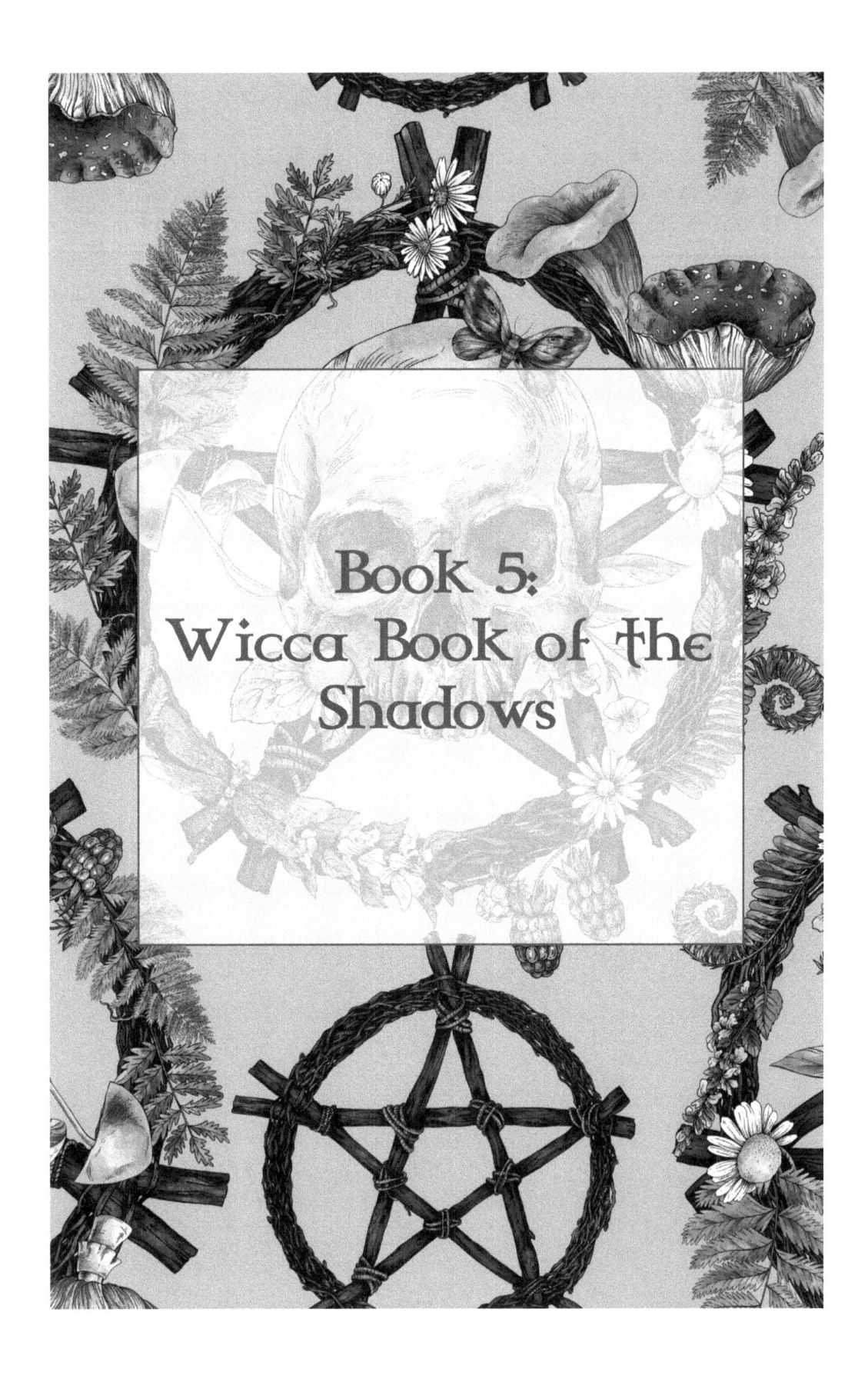

Chapter 1: History of Book of Shadows

As with most spiritual texts out there, there is a large debate as to when and how the book of shadows came to be. Some think that they were popular during the middle ages and were written in Runic alphabets to hide their meaning. Some people say that the Witches of middle ages were illiterate, and these books weren't written until the 14th to 15th centuries. Even during that time, they would have used the Runic alphabet to protect themselves from persecution and even death.

It does not matter how they got their start; they have been given several different names. The most famous mythological type of these books is called The Golden Grimoire, which is thought to be Merlin the Magician's book of shadows.

Inside the early books of shadows of the 1950s and 1960s, there weren't many rituals inside them. They would often include things like history, as well as an overview of the belief system of the Witches that used them. On occasion, some of these books might contain a small ritual, but there wasn't a lot of them to provide the practitioner with instructions on how to do a complete ritual from the beginning to the end. To be able to get rituals during that time, Witches had to be initiated in a tradition or make something by themselves.

In 1964, the first attempt to create a mass production of a book of shadows was made in a pamphlet form, and it was trying to devalue the craft. Allegedly, the pamphlet was from Gerald Gardner himself. It was published by Mary and Charles Cardell, who was a couple who liked to act like they were brother and sister. The Cardell's allegedly received their copy of Gardner's so-called book of shadows from Olive Greene, a disgruntled associate of Gerald's.

The Cardell saga is an odd one, and it's believed that Olive was a "spy" of theirs. sister. The Cardell's allegedly received their copy of Gardner's so-called book of shadows from Olive Greene, a disgruntled associate of Gerald's.

It was privately published and didn't go over too well in the witchcraft community. The Cardell's attempts at publishing the book of shadows turned out to be a flop, and the pamphlet was soon forgotten. Other books of shadows that were published did a lot better with the public, and many have been in print for several decades. We are going to take a look at some of the more popular mass-produced book of shadows. These have all changed the world of Witchcraft in their own right.

The very first book published that contained full-length rituals resembling parts of modern witchcraft was Mastering Witchcraft: A Practical Guide for Witches, Warlocks & Covens by Paul Huson. This book was a long cry from being a book of shadows, and many of the spells felt more like ceremonial magic than witchcraft. The book still felt familiar, however.

The book begins with an illustration of the Wheel of the Year before it dives straight into a bunch of spell work. He also had a bunch of invocations for deities like Diana and Cernunnos, pentacles, and familiar exclamations, such as "so mote it be." Most of the material during the first two-thirds of the book is very interesting but does not resemble much of Wiccan witchcraft.

However, during the last chapter, that changed.

During this part of the book, Huson begins to outline more than <u>just simple spells. He gives you ways to begin creating your book of shadows</u>. He also includes a couple of initiation rituals. His book was the first published version of The Charge of the Goddess, though it does vary from what most people are used to.

Even though Huson did take a huge step forward in published witch rituals, lady Sheba's book made the largest, most controversial leap with her book. Her book was titled Lady Sheba's Book of Shadows. She claimed that she was initiated into the craft during the 30s and that her book came from her initiation. The truth is, her book, as well as her initiation, came via proxy during the 70s. She later claimed that the Goddess had pushed her to publish the book that was likely full of oath-bound rituals.

Needless to say, it is an understatement to say that the Gardnerian practitioners were upset after her book was published. The existence of the book is still a touchy subject, even now. When the late 70s rolled around, Sheba had retired from the public eye. Even though her book was the first to show a ritual from start to finish, it still was not thought of as a complete book of shadows. It might have contained a lot of information about rituals, but it didn't give people any context about them. A book of shadows needs to be more than just a collection of rituals. It should be a source of information about the craft and give wisdom that has been passed from generation to generation.

The next book that was published didn't cause as much controversy. The Tree: The Complete Book of Saxon Witchcraft was published in 1974 by Raymond Buckland. It didn't break any oaths and was the first book for practitioners who worked alone. In history, Buckland is very influential among the Pagan world. He migrated from London to the United States during the early 60s. He began working with Gerald Gardner, and he and his wife were initiated into the Wiccan faith.

Even though his book did hold many similarities to the British Traditional Witchcraft, his Sabbat rituals were a lot different than Sheba's or Gardner's. Through his book, Buckland had come up with a new Wiccan path, which he called Seax-Wicca. This is still being practiced to this day. He added more to his book that Sheba's book had lacked. He gave information that explained how rituals worked. For many years, his book was one of the best places for people to turn to find information about Witchcraft. Samuel Weiser, in 1978, published A Book of Pagan Rituals. The information inside his book was originally created by The Pagan Way group, which is still being practiced. The information was passed through periodicals and magazines during that time. Their rituals worked in two ways. Their rituals were able to be used within an Outer Court setting. Outer Court was a training circle for pre-initiates that some traditions have. And they could also be used in a public setting where they were sharing rituals. Because most of the information was created for covens or groups, many of the rituals didn't have much in the way of context, but it also gave another huge lead in distributing ritual information. It was one of the first books to have the word Pagan in the title and not the word Witch or Witchcraft.

Then there's Doreen Valiente, who has been called the "Mother of Modern Witchcraft." She was one of the architects and writers of the modern revival. Valiente was initiated by Garnder in 1953, and she would end up writing most of the information for the Gardnerian Book of Shadows and several of the other books that it influenced. Doreen also released Witchcraft for Tomorrow in 1978. This was the first book on Witchcraft published in England that gave people full rituals for the Sabbats, as well as a selfinitiation ritual. This gave many people in Britain a way to get into Witchcraft that was the tradition coven structure.

Then, one of the most important Witchcraft books published in 1979 was called The Spiral Dance: The Rebirth of the Ancient Religion of the Great Goddess. Starhawk didn't just write a book about Gardner's Witchcraft and all of the other offshoots. Rather, it gave information about a new American West Coast Witchcraft. It was full of environmentalism, feminism, and all the influence of Victor and Cora Anderson. The latter two were the most influential teachers of Witchcraft in American history.

He didn't mean for this book to be a book of shadow, but it pretty much was. Its pages and the information they contained felt like they had been circle-tested. The book also seemed as if it had been taken right out of a real ritual that had to have happened at his home.

As the 1980s started, Steward and Janet Farrar published Eight Sabbats for Witches. It was full of ceremonies and rites for people who followed the Alexandrian Witchcraft path. There was a companion book released in 1984 called The Witches' Way: Principles, Ritual, and Beliefs of Modern Witchcraft. Both of these books had input from Doreen, and they all thought that the book was a great way to share the Gardnerian book of shadows. Some people say these books are a violation of their oaths. Valiente, though, assured them and others that they had permission to share this information. These two books would eventually be combined to create A Witches' Bible, and this would mark Farrars and Valiente's success at creating a book of shadows based on Gardner's teachings during the 50s. With the way it flows and is written, the reader knows that everything in the book has been shared exactly the way the creator of the rites wanted them to be.

Before the internet became the main way to keep in contact with the Pagan world, there were many Witches and other Pagans who stayed in contact through periodicals and magazines. Ed Fitch was a pioneer in this area, and his activities left a lasting impression on Witchcraft. He helped with the rituals of The Pagan Way, as well as putting together two "underground classics" that brought rituals to everyone. The Outer Court Book of Shadows and the Grimoire of the Shadows were private publications that circulated through the 1970s, and even today, that gave coven leaders a way to share rituals without feeling as if they were breaking their oaths. Besides those underground books, Fitch also created the magazine, The Crystal Well in 1965. In this magazine, he and Janine Renee share Sabbat rituals. What would become an influential book of shadows was first made public in 1989 and was called "Section III" in the Scott Cunningham book, Wicca: A Guide for The Solitary Practitioner. This book was very revolutionary because it was the first widely circulated Witchcraft book in the United States that used the word Wiccan in its title. Another reason it is so powerful was that "Section III," also known as The Standing Stones Book of Shadows, held complete information about magical oil, rituals, and spells. Cunningham's book served as an entryway into the Craft, and this is still true today.

Chapter 2: Creating a Personal Book of Shadows

Your own Book of Shadows (BoS) can be made from any materials that resonate with you. Each is as unique as the Witch it belongs to. Some are large, ornate, leather-bound books filled with parchment paper and only inscribed upon with quill and ink. However, a simple three-ring binder filled with notebook paper works just as beautifully. Ideally, you will always be adding to your BoS; keep that in mind when selecting a book or a method of organizing all the information.

Your BoS should reflect you. It should align with your style of practice, lifestyle, and it should motivate you to maintain it. You may want to spend time writing pages by hand, to bond with the book and imbue it with your energy. For others, printing out pages and adding them into the book is more fitting. Simply keeping the book on your altar will charge it with the necessary energy.

For the modern, technologically-minded Witch, keeping an electronic BoS might be the way to go. Maintaining a BoS on laptop, tablet or phone is extremely efficient. You can quickly and easily add, edit, and remove information. Multimedia information can also be kept in an eBoS—videos, recordings, links. You can decorate the book and pages however you like with the use of digital art. Keeping a space in a cloud like Google Drive, OneDrive, iCloud, allows for access from any device. Of course, there is much debate about bringing a mundane electronic device into the circle and utilizing it during magickal ritual. There is speculation that the electromagnetism can interfere with raising the proper energy. Additionally, there is the traditional belief of sacred space being a magickal place between worlds, a place not in the realm of the mundane. Taking care to carve out sacred space, get into the ritual mindset, and then cracking open your laptop that you use to delete daily spam and browse for dinner recipes could prove to hinder your magickal workings.

On the other hand, odds are that you're reading this book on a device. Our devices are quickly becoming part of us, and part of how we experience ourselves and the world around us. Bringing a device into the circle may feel like the most natural thing for you to do. Again, this is at the discretion of the individual Witch. If keeping an electronic BoS resonates with you, then feel free to include one in your practice.

What you include in your BoS is also up to you to decide. Wiccans commonly include the Wiccan Rede on their first page. You may also want to include a list of herbs you frequently use, and their properties, color correspondences, moon phases, the elements, anything you'll use in practice. Keep a log of your spells. Provide the step-by-step for each. Note the results and any impressions you get. Your BoS is the bible to your own path that you write along the way!

Chapter 3: Using Our Book of Shadows

3.1 Starting Out

You will need and possible approaches to creating your Book of Shadows, there are a few other considerations to address: how to compile the book, whether one book or more than one is best for you, why it's important to keep it safe and secure, and some 21st-century options for creating a Wiccan grimoire of your very own.

As always, remember that this will be **your** Book of Shadows, and it should be approached in the way that works best for you.

3.1.1 Keeping A Master Copy and Rough Drafts

Keeping rough copies of information for later entry into a master copy of your Book of Shadows is a wise approach, particularly for your first book.

This is a very important step for a lot of beginners because they may want to change parts of spells or rituals once they've had some experience. Adding and/or removing specific elements of ritual, spell ingredients, etc. is much easier to do in rough drafts than in a final copy.

Also, this way you can sift through and add different bits of information—such as the magical properties of a certain herb or an ideal blessing chant for a particular Sabbat - as you discover them, and then catalog your entries properly later on. If you plan on entering all kinds of information into your book and want to keep it well-organized while you work on rough drafts, you can use the multi-subject notebooks described above - that will help keep things in their place before you create the master copy.

A three-ring binder also works wonders because you can swap out the positioning of pages in order to keep things in logical order. Just be sure to get those little stickers that keep loose leaf paper from tearing out of the binder at random. Either way, a master copy is the "nice copy" that you can put in an elegantly designed cover (or many such covers, depending on your approach). These can be then used when you've hit your stride as a Wiccan and have amassed many spells and a wealth of pertinent data.

Master copies are also important if you work in a coven that allows you to keep your own book combining the rituals and spells of the coven with your own information. You will also find that there can be a lot of note-taking going on as beginners watch the High Priestess work with the other senior members of the coven during their first few times in the circle. These notes can be entered into your book too, if permitted by your group. (Remember, some covens forbid certain "information-sharing practices" because of privacy concerns.) So, as you can plainly see, having one book as a permanent home for your work after it's been perfected is very helpful.

It can mean the difference between a neat and organized Book of Shadows or a scribberidden, tattered, rough-draft type of grimoire. However, it's likely that you'll end up adopting your own version of continuing to use both types, since a Witch is never really done learning, no matter how practiced she or he becomes.

3.1.2 Keeping Multiple Volumes

In these modern times, with ever-shortening attention spans and constantly evolving ways of accessing and storing information, some practitioners of Wicca may struggle to make the best use of a single-volume Book of Shadows. It can be cumbersome to be wading through information pertaining strictly to coven work when you are really just looking to do a simple solitary sabbat ritual, and it makes little sense to have to thumb past pages of divination tool correspondences in a book you wish to only spellcast from at present. Depending on your preferences, learning style, and personality, you may benefit from keeping multiple volumes, or separate books for separate purposes.

Many Wiccans like to keep several books and divide them into categories. One book will be for spells, another for magical uses of herbs, a third for rituals, a fourth for divination, journaling—and so on. You can even color code each book, so that herbalism is a green book, for example, and rituals a silvery blue.

This method has unlimited potential for keeping your resources well-structured and organized. It also allows you to work until you have enough information in each to make a large grimoire on a particular subject or group of subjects. Of course, it's not necessary to keep multiple books, but it definitely helps when you've come to collect a huge amount of data across several subjects and want to be able to access it without pawing through pages upon pages of stuff that's irrelevant to that moment in time! And it's a great way to keep yourself organized and on the ball when it comes to working in the circle.

3.2 Magic Alphabets

Some practitioners like to write their grimoires in one of many magical alphabets. These alphabets are usually rooted in some form of ancient writing made for the purpose of protecting text from prying eyes—particularly those who would probably send someone to the gallows if they knew what was written on the page!

While we are now thankfully free of such dangers, some Wiccans find that there is magical value to the energy put into writing in a different alphabet that requires more time, care, and focused attention.

There are several older alphabets which we still have access to that are considered to be quintessential "magic alphabets."

Below is a look at a few of the alphabets Wiccans have used in their books of shadows.

You are bound to find a few ideas here for masking your work from unwanted readers without the need to cast a protection spell on your book. You can also use one or more of these alphabets to amplify spellwork that uses writing as part of the spell.

Of course, you're not limited to using an existing alphabet—if you're a "DIY" kind of person, see the suggestions below for making up your own!

3.2.1 Theban

Often referred to as the Witch's Alphabet, no one knows where Theban originated, but the magical alphabet was first read and translated in the 1500s. It's mentioned often in philosopher and theologian Heinrich Agrippa's de Occulta Philosophia, where he deduced that it was loosely based on Latin. Many Wiccans feel that this is one of the most aesthetically pleasing forms of ancient script out there.

3.2.2 Malachim

Malachim is another magical alphabet that was published by Heinrich Agrippa back in the 16th Century. It is derived from both Greek and Hebrew, and its name is similar to a type of angel in Judaism.

3.2.3 Celestial

Celestial is very close to Malachim in appearance and was actually created by Agrippa. Also known as "Angelic Script," it is considered by some to be the alphabet of the heavens, which came through Agrippa as a divine inspiration.

3.2.4 Numeric Codes

Numbers have very powerful symbolism and can be assigned in any order or arrangement to represent text.

You can follow the typical system, beginning with A to represent 1, or start at a random number like 22 and go from there. Just be sure to keep a key if you create your own system, since you might forget where you started later on.

You can also use traditional numerological correspondences— either the Pythagorean or Chaldean system—for letters, if you wish to skip creating your own code. These two systems are fixed, so you can rely on being able to translate your work any time, either through the internet or other print resources on numerology.

3.2.5 Slavic, Chinese, Japanese, Or Arabic

If you are fortunate enough to be bilingual, you may have the ability to directly translate other alphabet systems' characters into English phonetic sounds that can be used to make an alphabet. Better yet, why not write your book in your other tongue? If you're living in a mainly English-speaking place, the chances of someone translating it are slim, and you won't have to work so hard to write things down and read them back.

3.2.6 Homemade Alphabets

You don't have to follow any pre-established system when writing in a magical alphabet. In fact, sometimes the greatest power comes from an alphabet you create on your own. Think of it like speaking in tongues, which can be both therapeutic and make you closer to your creator. You can use symbols and sigils from alchemy, astrological symbols, shapes, combinations of dots, morse code, or anything else that comes to mind and makes sense to you. Again, just be sure to write down the correspondences somewhere safe for your own reference, should you decide to stop using it and want to look back at the sections or spells you wrote in your secret language.

3.3 Keeping Your Book of Shadows Safe and Secure

Your Book of Shadows is an incredibly important document. It is a religious book full of occult mysteries, your spiritual work, thoughts, feelings, and so much more. As a Wiccan, your Book of Shadows will have had a great deal of energy put into it, and it will serve as a very useful tool in all that you do with your religion and spiritual path.

As mentioned in the beginning of this guide, Gerald Gardner, the original coiner of the term "Book of Shadows", believed that a Witch's book was to be burned upon death.

Now, whether or not you arrange to have this done upon your final hour is a very personal decision. Some people don't agree that this is necessary in modern times where being Wiccan is much more socially acceptable.

Some Wiccans prefer to keep their books to pass down through the generations, while others haven't given it much thought at all. It's purely up to you how you want to handle the future of your Book of Shadows, but know that you cannot take it with you, so unless you destroy it yourself, it will be found by those you leave behind. Make sure it is full of positive material used for building yourself and others up, in the true spirit of "harm to none!" Regardless of what happens when you pass on, in the meantime you need to keep this precious book safe and secure at all times. It is not a child's plaything or your dog's chew toy. Your Book of Shadows should be stored with all of your other altar tools since it will usually be sitting on your altar during all of your work within the circle. It's advisable to wrap it in a soft cloth and keep it out of light in order to preserve it and keep its surface from getting damaged, scratched, or dinged by anything else in your cupboard or chest of magic tools. You will also want to keep it hidden in order to protect it from being glanced at by people who have no business reading it. This goes not only for children but others as well. This book is something sacred for you and those whom you grant permission to look within it. If you wanted people to peruse it for entertainment or as a novelty, it would be a coffee table book, rather than a Book of Shadows.

3.3.1 A Spell to Protect Your Book of Shadows from Prying Eyes

Here you will find a spell of protection for your Book of Shadows that banishes negativity while keeping its contents safe from harm and unwanted "sneak peeks."

You can perform this spell with an existing grimoire, journal, diary, or Book of Shadows, but it will also be of great help when you are about to begin a new one.

This spell is also very convenient and easy enough to do right after cleansing and consecrating your Book of Shadows.

You will need:

- Your Book of Shadows
- A silver or gold pen

Once you have cast your circle, begin by placing your Book of Shadows in the center of your altar. You will then take the pen and draw a sigil of your choosing on the inner side of the front or back cover (or both). This sigil can be a pentacle, an alchemical symbol, or something you have designed on your own, but it should represent protection, as well as divinity. (You can also pick two symbols, if you are doing both the inside of the front and back.) You might use a gold pen for a god symbol or the symbol of the sun, and a silver one for the moon or a triple goddess sigil. Keep in mind the loving, healing, and protective power of the divine as you draw your symbol(s) on the inside cover(s).

3.3.2 Wicca Grimoires in the 21st Century

Because we have so much technology at our fingertips in this, the 21st century, there are even more ways to compile a Book of Shadows than one could ever have imagined back in 1949. Like all things in this century, we are able to do far more with much less, and Wiccans now have an unbelievable amount of data we can readily access online. But some sources of information may be more useful than others, and each individual Witch will have specific interests and preferences. Perhaps you're more into electronic sources of information and don't care to work with physical paper and ink, but still want your own personal collection of Wiccan wisdom. Why not make your Book of Shadows on your computer or in an application?

3.3.3 Maintaining Your Very Own Book of Darkness

Creating as well as additionally preserving a Book of Shadows is never a demand for exercising Wicca, yet it can be a very helpful tool for a variety of reasons. For one, it's a method to preserve each of your essential information worrying your spiritual practices in one area. Most of Wiccans have, at the minimum a handful of books in their personal collections which include liked spells, routines, as well as likewise other understanding, however skimming them all to uncover what you're looking for isn't always the most trustworthy means to obtain factors done. As you create your technique, you can start recording the information you utilize one of the most in your Book of Shadows You can similarly examine aloud from it throughout regimens, as opposed to attempting to memorize everything all at as soon as. And also, obviously, it's an excellent location to tape tried-and-true spellwork for future suggestion, as well as information worrying your popular charming elements. Well, if you're a singular specialist, after that the products, order, as well as the appearance of your Book of Shadows is completely approximately you. It's also possible to get a dedicated empty Book of Shadows online.One practical referral, if you're the antique kind that still uses ink as well as paper, is to take into account holding off on including brand-new product up until you're specific of it. For instance, you can plan to document a particular necromancy or brand-new regular collection on different paper first along with try it out before devoting it to your Book of Shadows. But despite just how you choose to approach it, acknowledge that you can't obtain it inaccurate. It's your trip, and also the Book of Shadows is your taking a trip log, which you can remain to add to, deduct from, as well as change according to your extremely own internal advice.

3.3.4 Seven Things That Should Go in Your Book of Shadows.

Your Book of Shadows is possibly the most individual product in all the Wiccan products you have. There are no 2 witches that can locate the specific really exact same points in their Book of Shadows, that's just exactly how tailored it is. You could have a brand-new blank Book of Shadows, as well as likewise you are not sure of what to compose in it. If there is something else that you need to write down in your Book of Shadows that you are missing out on, or possibly you're just wondering about. Naturally, as a private, as it is, there are no absolutes along with challenging policies regarding what you must write in your Book of Shadows. What I am offering you right here is what you SHOULD CONSIDER composing in your Book of Shadows to improve your experience in your picked course, the Wiccan course. I can't count the variety of people who have actually said that their experience is a lot a lot more satisfying after looking back at the old gain access to they have in their Book of Shadows. Assessing just exactly how you have actually increased as a witch will certainly make you see everything with fresh eyes.Below are the standard things you must have in your BOS. Make note that after things 2 onwards, you can include your individual touches like reflections on a spell or a Sabbat. YOUR NAME I believe this is a given. It is yours, so you better place your name on it. You can compose it any way you want.

YOUR TRADITION, WICCAN REDE Your Book of Shadows also needs to state your beliefs. Are you a diverse Wiccan? Do you follow the Alexandrian path?

THE WICCAN REDE

The Wiccan Rede is what binds with each other all practices.

Unlike other religions with their several regulations and rules, Wiccans stick to the Wiccan Rede as well as the Threefold Law.

YOUR DEITIES

Create down your divine being's name, the pantheon he or she belongs to, and also what that divine being suggested to you, and so on

YOUR SPELLS AND RITUALS

This covers the spells you enjoy doing and also the spells you developed to spells you are anticipating trying. Create down your favored routines, the routines you on your own developed, as well as the rituals you are looking onward to trying. Include the ingredients, so you don't need to refer to a scrap of paper or that hefty book the following time you wanna carry out a spell or routine.

SABBAT ROUTINES AS WELL AS FOR YOUR SABBATS

List the Sabbats and also what each period indicates to you. Make a note of the rituals you such as to perform throughout each Sabbat you pointed out. Jot down just how you like to decorate your altar for every Sabbat.

CORRESPONDENCE CHARTS

In your Book of Shadows, compose down your natural correspondence chart, crystal chart, as well as candlelight shade communication chart. See, your Book of Shadows additionally serves as your recommendation product.

EXPERIENCES, REPRESENTATIONS, AND ALSO IDEAS

Your Book of Shadows additionally counts as your journal or journal. How else would certainly you see how much you have gone on your spiritual trip when you don't have anything that reveals your previous attitude and also awareness? Do not keep back on pouring your thoughts as well as sensations out considering that your Book of Shadows is personal, and absolutely nobody ought to have access to it. You can purchase an alternative to your candle lights, for your smudging bowls, for your church patens, and so on. Yet your Book of Shadows is not replaceable. You cannot go and also buy a new one to replace a lost one and duplicate everything that's in your old one. You additionally cannot replicate experiences that you wrote down in your Book of Shadows.

Chapter 4: The Whys and Ways Wiccans Use Their Book of Shadows

The modern Witch may have one Book of Shadows or a collection of them. There can be a master copy with tried-and-true information accompanied by a working document to record new "experiments," or a Witch may decide to put anything and everything into one massive book.

Regardless of the form it takes, modern-day Witches will use a Book of Shadows much like those who came before us.

Their pages consist of magical correspondences, recipes, spells, journal entries, poetry and music, rituals, sigils, and general notes.

They're an especially important part of a new initiate's time in the circle. This is because a newer practitioner will need something to refer back to for information that others already know by heart. Something like casting a circle may seem second nature to experienced Wiccans, but a beginner will need a guide for at least the first few forays into the circle.

Then there is ritual and spellwork.

Spells can be effective or ineffective, and they sometimes need tweaks or adjustments you would be unable to keep track of if you hadn't written the spell in your book for future reference.

In addition, some spells have elaborate wording and multiple steps, so it is much better to come into your circle with your trusty Book of Shadows in hand than to interrupt the energy by cutting out and then back in after looking up the answers to your questions.

One example of spellwork that almost always calls for a Book of Shadows is a form of enchantment, or "glamoury," which is much like a recipe you would use in cooking. The only difference is that you wouldn't be eating your creation, but using it to spritz on your hair or for washing your face.

These recipes are difficult to commit entirely to memory, and since this is fairly advanced magic, you want to be sure not to make any mistakes!

Almost every form of alternative spirituality and healing involves a journaling mechanism of some sort.

For example, there is so much to know about herbs and crystals: their magical, medicinal, and therapeutic properties.

Astrologers can appreciate this too because they would be lost without a lunar almanac, charts, correspondences, and ways to interpret the stars above us.

As you see, it would be pretty difficult to remember every single beneficial thing to know when practicing magic, and that's why every Witch can benefit from keeping a Book of Shadows.

Chapter 5: Modern Day Witchcraft and The Book of Shadows

When it comes to covens, the Wiccan Book of Shadows tends to function like Gardner's did back in the mid-twentieth century. These books traditionally contain rituals, spells, and information that is important to the coven.

Some covens follow the "original" Book of Shadows as passed down from Gardner's tradition, but may also keep an additional book specific to their own practice. There may be a record of the significant events in the lives of members of the coven, such as handfastings and births or deaths.

Often, and especially in covens that stick closely to "hereditary" traditions (like Gardnerian Wicca), the coven's Book of Shadows is shrouded in a lot of secrecy. There may be only one copy of the book, kept by the coven's High Priestess. There is a belief that these original books hold the most powerful spells and rituals, and must be guarded carefully from anyone not initiated into the coven.

In other covens, each member will have their own copy of the coven's Book of Shadows. Others will even allow for their members to keep their own personal, unique Book of Shadows, so long as they include the rites and spells the coven uses, for the sake of consistency. Their leaders may oversee the contents of it in some way, in order to prevent malevolent sorcery or other unwanted energies in the group's work. As you can see, there are all sorts of specifically prescribed practices that covens will follow, and because of the "group" orientation to Wicca that covens provide, they are by design more rigid in their approach than solitary practitioners are likely to be. By contrast, solitary practitioners have the utmost freedom in terms of how they create their Book of Shadows.

There is no High Priestess or coven telling them what to include or omit, which colors to use or what material their book should be made of, or whether they are allowed to have one at all. They can make one book, several books, or separate books for each area of expertise. They can also include other entries like poetry and drawings in their book that may not be directly related to magic but still hold a great deal of personal power.

It's important to note here that there are also Wiccans—both solitaries and covens—who shy away from doing spellwork at all, and only use their Book of Shadows for rites and documenting the events of each Sabbat and Esbat. They may have recipes for key components of their rituals, such as holy water or incense, but the focus here is on the formal elements of the religion and not on magic.

Conclusion

Unlike most other Western religions, Wicca is highly decentralized - there is no official sacred text, no central governing body, and this means there is no one way to practice the religion.

With this in mind, it is very difficult to create a truly encompassing beginner's guide to the topic, simply because different Wiccans will interpret the many facets of the religion differently - in some cases, **very** differently.

There is no right or wrong. As long as you keep the Wiccan principles at heart, and never intentionally seek to harm others, you can practice Wicca in any way you see fit. In fact, I would actively **encourage** you to seek out your own path.

One of the best things about Wicca is that your interpretations, views, and beliefs are highly flexible. When you are just starting out, you are encouraged to read and learn as much as possible, and so your initial beliefs are bound to be shaped by the guides you read.

Over time, when you begin to embrace Wicca in your daily life, you might have certain epiphanies that re-shape your approach to the practicing this religion. What you believe on day one, might be **very** different to your beliefs on day 100, which could be a world apart from your views on day 1,000. It can be a lifelong journey, and even after decades you will still find yourself learning new things. This is one of the many benefits of keeping your own Book of Shadows—you can literally track how your Wiccan journey has evolved over time.

Remember: nobody can tell you how to practice Wicca, and the religion can mean anything you want it to mean to you. While I have presented the information in this guide as "correct", I am in no way suggesting that it is the only way to practice Wicca. If you read other guides, there may be conflicting information. And when you read another guide to the topic, you will likely come across even more conflicting information!

That's just the way Wicca is. Even if you encounter some different opinions - even those completely opposed to what you have read in this guide - it doesn't mean one guide is right, and another is wrong: it just means the many different authors have interpreted different aspects of the religion differently.

I will leave you with that thought, as it is now time for you to start your own journey, and interpret the information presented to you in your own way. I have included a number of tables of correspondence at the end of this guide, which you should find helpful at some point in time. I have also included a number of suggested sources for further reading, as in the early days it is important for you to absorb as much information as possible on the subject.

I sincerely hoped you enjoyed learning about Wicca with me, as it is a topic close to my heart. It would mean a great deal to me if you continued on your path towards Wicca, but if you choose not to, I hope I have educated you on the belief system of the wonderful people who choose to practice Wicca.

Book 6: Wicca Candle, Crystal and Herbal Magic

Introduction

This book will still be of relevance to non-Wiccans—not all Witches consider themselves Wiccans, after all, and many practice magic without having a spiritual relationship with any deities. It's important to clear a few things up before we get started.

Although this guide is primarily aimed at Wiccans, not all Wiccans consider themselves to be magical practitioners—some only use candles to revere the Goddess and the God in their many forms, as well as the Elements of Earth, Air, Fire, Water, and Spirit.

Whoever you are, and whatever your beliefs, you are more than welcome here. However, it is worth pointing out that candle magic has Pagan roots—one trait found in just about any Pagan tradition is the belief in, and use of, the power of candles.

In this guide, you'll learn the basics of working with candles for magical purposes, including the reasons underlying successful magic, the best approaches to acquiring candles and preparing them for spellwork, and a selection of candle spells to try out on your own.

You'll also find ideas and resources for creating your own magic through the use of oils and herbs, as well as enhancing your work with an awareness of right timing by paying attention to the phases of the Moon and the days of the week.

However, no matter how much knowledge you acquire, it's really the practice of magic that leads to success. Be willing to try and try again, and you will ultimately find yourself with the ability to transform your life. Blessed Be.

Chapter 1: Wicca Candle Magic

One of the simplest forms of spell casting is through the use of candles. It is a form of magic which doesn't require the caster to perform any complicated ritual. It also doesn't require the use of any type of priceless ceremonial tools or artifacts. Basically, what this means is that candle magic is a type of magic that any average person can do.

Remember those times during your birthday where you made a wish and blew out the candles on your cake? The same theory applies. However, in this case, instead of wishing or hoping for something to happen, you're actually declaring your commitment.

Thinking about it more clearly, the blowing of the candle on the cake ritual is based on three key principles:

- Decide what you're aim is going to be
- Visualize what and how the end result would be
- Fully commit to achieve that result

1.1 The History of Candle Magic

Throughout the Middle-Ages, candles were being made in the same way as in Rome. The discovery of beeswax generated candles that burned cleaner and smelled more agreeable. But, beeswax candles were somewhat more expensive and more difficult to obtain and are mostly utilized in religious rites to mild holy temples and burnt as offerings to God(s) frequently accompanied by the refusal. The flourishing whale-industry of this 18th century led substantial quantities of whale-oil that was used to earn spermaceti wax and which substituted tallow and beeswax as the primary supply of candles. Like beeswax and bayberry candles, the candles made from spermaceti-wax burnt brighter, more equally, had a pleasant scent and didn't dissolve effortlessly within the mid of the year.

The industrial revolution, which came with the 19th century along with the disclosure of stearic-acid, which contradicted the wax, aniline colors, along with the creation of paraffin, introduced the very first mass-market candles in a variety of colors generated by machines. Further advancements in infrastructure, railways, and transport permitted for quality materials at a reasonable price to reach houses from across the city or even across the nation! No more did the ordinary individuals have to be made her or his possess candles or purchase them by a candle-maker on the off chance that they can promptly be bought from a commercial for a reasonable cost. As candles got to be cheaper and more effortlessly accessible, they got to be progressively more prevalent at the religious clinics of different societies such as **Hoodoo**.

The predominance of candle-magic not as it featured a coordinate relationship to get to quality candles at a sensible cost but in expansion into the commercialization of Hoodoo as early as 1940's with the distribution of these books as "The Ace Book of Candle Burning" from Henri Gamache and "The Direction Light to Control and Victory" by Mikhail Strabo. Starting around 1965 and continuing to the day, census information has demonstrated a tendency where blacks have started to come back to the south, mentioning improved racial relations and financial growth. Using their return to the southwest, many blacks exhibited a renewed interest in the spirituality of the ancestors. The access to the net in the mid-1990s and also this revived interest in most things emotionally set the stage for the beginnings of this Hoodoo Revival.

Together with that, humanity has come full circle. As our ancient ancestors lived in a universe inhabited by spirits, therefore we might realize that little has changed in this respect. As opposed to building fires from the jungle to push the darkness back and light how to love, achievement, health, and prosperity, now we burn candles to protect and guide us along life's journey.

Candle Magic is one of the kinds of magic. It is something and a candle. But, you might even add a couple more items to get your candle magic stronger, and much more successful. Candle Magic is historical, and it could be tracked back. Most people automatically believe candles to be religious; they influence our energies, our moods, even when we do not consciously know why or how. Candles are a part of our own lives, and they provide us blessings and gifts in various ways; this is the reason why we adore and use candles. And - feces are utilized in magic,

1.2 A Beginners Guide to Candle Magic

It said that candle magic is among the sorts of magic in history. Whether typically rectify, lights, balefires, and wheels, although it is certainly a fact that fire has been sacred to our pagan ancestors, who supplicated their deities not only with candles and admired. Given that terminating was the source of lighting besides the Moon and sunlight until recently, it's easy to understand the fire was a sign of energy that is sacred during our history.

That respect for this fire's energies has continued after the creation of lighting. Numerous religions presently proceed to from utilizing of candles, at the custom of lighting votive candles for intentions or whether religious services.

This recognizable custom is what makes candles Appealing. There's fair. We feel calm at ease, looking move, living light. Light a candle is among the simplest ways to start shifting from ordinary reality and linking with the hidden energies around us whether or spell work is in your plane.

1.3 Elemental Balance

The candle may be a well-balanced Representation of the Components. The wick additionally, the bottom of the candle represents the spoil component, which is imperative to maintain the flame equally grounded and ready to remain lit. The wax, which changes from a solid to a liquid and then to gasoline, represents the shape-shifting qualities of the Water Element. Even the Air Element, in the kind of oxygen, is imperative to keep the fire alive and is frequently made visible in the smoke generated from a burning wick.

1.4 Beginners' "Luck" in Candle Magic

For is truly an extraordinary starting point, and numerous Wiccans who practice magic are especially fond of the form. Simple, rich, and straightforward, simple candle charms can allow you to build and invigorate "charming muscles"--in other words, your ability to concentrate and direct your energy in your intention. It's the energy of the idea that lies under both the kinds of magic and the easiest. More especially, magic is the art of delivering a specific thought in the religious plane to be shown and came back to the airplane. For those beginning out, candles cause especially useful" messengers."

1.4.1 Herbs, Oils, and Sigils

By rolling up the anointed professionals prefer to follow up this Candle in herbs that are accompanying to include power. You can also Inscribe the candle using a couple of sigils symbols' body which compare to your objective. Consider experimenting by incorporating these steps at one time throughout a few spells to find out what resonates with you.

1.4.2 The Magic of Color

Together with their symbolic properties that are exceptional, candles let Us work together with the properties of color in a concentrated and direct way. For centuries, specific colors are linked with specific intangible attributes or events, such as love, fortune, riches, and passing. It appears that red has always been associated with passion and love --consequently of the center and the color of blood. The color green has long been related to abundance, as a result of predominantly green colors of Earth throughout the growing season. Using these color correspondences in candle magic strengthens the specific intention of this charm, and candles made only for this function frequently called "spell candles"--could be seen in only about any color.

1.4.3 Divine Communication

When the spell words have been discussed, and the candle has Been lit, people prefer to see dimensions, form, and the motion of the fire for indicators of this spell success. In certain customs, if the fire is high and powerful, the symptom is moving quickly, even though a low, feeble fire indicates not much spiritual energy has been spent in the reason. It said that when the wick produces thick or black smoke, then there is resistance to the job. Do not overthink these things, of course--you do not need to muddle the power you have sent out throughout the bout by trying too tough to find information only now. You might want to work many candle spells before getting your awareness of just how the wax and fires are all communicating with you.

1.4.4 Candle Magic: Safety First!

Most, if not most, candles spells, including permitting the candle to burn out all of the ways. And it is never an incredible thought. If you have to do this, make sure you set the candle in a sink or bathtub, far away from any flammable substances. Since these may be flammable Be careful as well when utilizing oils, and also, you do not wish to burn your hands! Ought to your procedure candle magic together with all the proper cautions, in addition to an honest and led focus--and with harm to no one, of course--you may see the achievement which will have you exploring the magic arts further. You will start by attempting this candle charm on the off chance that you prefer.

1.4.5 Choosing the Right Candles to Use

Many people who practice candle magic will most likely tell you that, similar to some of life's most important aspects, size really doesn't matter. The saying "The bigger, the better" surely doesn't apply in this case. In fact, making use of an over-sized candle may prove to be annoyingly counterproductive. The reason for this is because some candle-spells involve asking the spell caster to wait until the candle burns itself out before proceeding with the rest of the invocation of the spell. Therefore, making use of a tapered or votive candle is recommended.

There will also be cases where a specific kind of candle is required for a spell, such as a figure candle or 7-day candle, representing a specific individual. You'd be astonished to know, however, that one of the most famous candles that are used in the invocation of spells is the menorah candle. Menorah candles are usually sold in boxes in your local grocery store. They are white, unscented candles which stand about four inches tall—great for casting spells. One important thing to remember when using candles is always use a fresh, brand new candle for spell work—virgin materials. Never, ever use leftover candles from a previous spell work. Magical traditions believe that once a candle has been burned, it attracts vibrations from everything around it. It would be prudent to always use a fresh candle to have a positive or effective magical outcome. If you plan to invoke spells for different purposes, it would also be a good idea to have candles of different colors. Each candle color corresponds to a different type of candle magic. Below are some examples:

- Pink: Love and Friendship
- Orange: Encouragement and Attraction
- Red: Love, Lust, Courage, Health
- Yellow: Protection and persuasion
- Green: Fertility, Abundance, great financial gain
- Gold: Solar connections, Good business endeavors, great wealth
- Dark Blue: Vulnerability, Depression, anxiety, sadness
- Purple: Power and ambition
- Light Blue: Understanding, Good health and patience
- Black: Banishment, Negativity, restriction
- White: Truth, Purity, Tranquility
- Brown: Nature related (Earth and animal) workings
- Silver: Lunar connections, Reflection and intuition

Keep in mind that in some Pagan traditions, white colored candles are considered universal. What this means is that it can be used as substitute to any color.

1.4.6 Using Your Candle in Ritual

After you have chosen the right candle for the spell that you want to do, you'll want to apply oil on the candle before using it. This process is called "Dressing". What dressing does is it creates a psychic connection between the spell caster and the candle. Creating a psychic connection means that you're expressing your intent by projecting your own energy and vibrations on the wax of the candle before using it.

Dressing a candle requires using natural oil. Grape seed oil is preferred by many spell casters due to the fact that it has no scent. An alternative option is to make use of special magic oils that are usually found in metaphysical supply stores. Begin dressing your candle by rubbing oil from the top part, down to the middle part of the candle. Then, start at the bottom part, up towards the middle of the candle where you first left off.

There are some variations of this process, where coating starts from the middle of the candle and working its way to both ends. If particular candle spell requires the usage of herbs, just roll the oil dressed candle in the powdered herb until it is completely covered all the way around.

One of the most basic forms of candle magic involves using a small piece of paper that has the same color as the candle itself. The color of the paper and the candle will depend upon the intent of your spell. On this piece of paper is where you'll write your intent for the spell itself. As you write down your main goal for the spell, you must envision yourself attaining that goal. Think of the various forms in which your aim might come. Once you've written your aim on that piece of paper, fold it while still keeping your concentration on your intent. Some candle spell casters recite a little incantation in order to be more focused on their intent. The incantation doesn't have to be anything elaborate. A simple incantation expressing your intent would suffice. After folding the paper, allow one corner of the paper to catch fire by putting it into the flame of the candle. Hold the paper while it is burning until the last moment without getting your fingers burned. Place the burning paper in a cauldron or fire-safe pot or bowl to allow it to burn on its own the rest of the way. Leave the candle until it is completely burned out.

Once the candle is completely burned out, do not reuse it for later. Dispose the used candle immediately.

Chapter 2: Wicca Crystal Magic

The use of crystals and stones is absolutely indivisible from the practice of Wicca: these magical elements are utilized in nearly every ritual, in nearly every spell, in nearly every Wiccan home. Their properties are unparalleled in terms of creating and channelling the positive energies emerging directly from the earth, source of the Mother Goddess. Crystals and other stones are frequently used in healing rituals and to enhance the spiritual energy of particular spaces, as well as in a variety of Wiccan and other pagan forms of magic.

2.1 Earthly Magic, Spiritual Energy

Technically, crystals used in Wiccan magic are not all scientifically classified as crystals; they are a group of solid minerals that are categorized under the umbrella of "crystal" for ease of reference. Therefore, the terms "crystals" and "stones" are often used interchangeably, though there are some categorical difference between the two groups that will be explored later in the book. Quartz is a true crystal, the kind of ur-mineral from which all other crystals follow, as are rose quartz and amethyst. Other minerals used in crystal magic, such as lapis lazuli, jade, and bloodstone, are actually combinations of various elements and minerals, so they are not pure crystals. Nevertheless, all of these are used in Wiccan practice, and each has their own signature energy and purpose. Look to Chapter 2 for a comprehensive list of the most commonly used crystals and stones, along with their properties. These minerals are purported to have particular kinds of energy that emerge from their particular composition; most Wiccans report that they can literally feel the energy coming off of powerful crystals. It is, indeed, true that—even though crystals are made of inorganic, inert material—they can occasionally emit an actual electrical signal, called the piezoelectric effect, when subjected to pressure, or pyroelectric signal, when subjected to changes in temperature. Thus, it is not entirely inappropriate to suggest that these elements contain a spark of universal energy, a flicker of purpose. In any event, their uniquely geometric configuration, connection to earthly powers, and vibrant colors make them well-suited to Wiccan magic and other kinds of pagan practice—not to mention those phantom energy signatures.

In Wiccan belief, all energy is interconnected and meaningful, whether from organic or inorganic sources: the blowing of the wind and the rushing of a river represent energy just as much as conscious life forms do. Thus, crystals themselves make up a part of this universal energy. Additionally, since our thoughts—our intention—are also, in point of fact, **energy**, then we can channel that energy into tools such as crystals and stones to communicate said intentions to a different realm, that of the spiritual. We are creating the intention that is harnessed through the energy field of the crystals (and other magical tools) in order to create results of some sort. Debates still yet rage regarding the nature of consciousness: there are many even in the scientific community today who understand consciousness to be something independent of the material presence of the brain; that is, consciousness exists beyond our individual selves. Thus, when we use crystals, stones, and other Wiccan tools, we are projecting toward and communicating with this consciousness that is part of the fabric of the universe itself.

Crystals and stones are primarily associated with healing practice and with the ability to enhance positivity, creating a stronger flow of energy between objects and intentions. These objects have been used since the very beginnings of humankind for rituals and ceremonies. Think of the monumental Stonehenge structure, with its as yet undetermined potency; this is essentially a giant stone garden like one you might erect in your own backyard for power and protection. Think of the gem-encrusted paraphernalia of kingdoms and warriors and priests from ancient times to the present; this is not merely a presentation of wealth—though that is the standard, if incomplete, contemporary view—but an age-old belief throughout humanity that these elements from the earth contain and represent power. The association between crystals and magical powers have saturated even our popular imagination; the Indiana Jones franchise has repeatedly employed the trope, from the very first one (the staff of Ra requires a crystal to map the Well of Souls) to an overt connection in the last, the **Kingdom of the Crystal Skull.** This is, of course, only one example among many, but it is especially relevant because of the underlying thread of religiosity in these films. Historical references to crystals are found as far back as the Sumerians, and the ancient Egyptians made much use of crystals and minerals in their rituals as well— often as protective amulets, but there was also mineral use in make-up and other ritual adornment. The ancient Greece also made use of these elements—our contemporary word comes from the Greek for "ice"—and everyone from Greek sailors to Greek warriors used various stones for luck and protection. You can also find the use of precious metals and stones throughout Asia; in China, jade was one of the most, if not the most, important stones, with everything from musical instruments to body armor was made using jade. Indigenous cultures from Native Americans in the United States and Mexico to Maoris in New Zealand have used various crystals and stones for decoration, healing, and protection. It seems that the potency of earthly materials have been recognized by a whole host of various cultures across the ages.

Religious invocations of crystals and stones are also common throughout history, both in the East and in the West. Not only are precious stones of various kinds mentioned throughout the Bible and the Koran, but they also play significant roles in Hinduism and Buddhism. There are references to a throne made of diamonds on which the Buddha would sit to meditate—and one might infer connect to the universal consciousness—as well as the Kalpar Tree, in Hinduism, made of precious stones as an offering to the gods. In Hindu tradition, as well, the diamond is associated with thunder and the goddess Indra's great thunderbolt—earth and sky connecting. Rubies were considered good luck, as they represented flame that could not be extinguished. Undeniably, crystals and stones feature prominently in all major world religions, as well as smaller belief systems; their power has been recognized throughout the centuries. Thus, it is clear that, while many mainstream ideologies often lampoon the "New Age-y" vibe of crystal magic, ascribing it to fading hippies and other easily caricatured figures, they are very much missing out on the very real scientific evidence that reveals the hidden powers of inorganic materials and minerals of all kinds (think of pottery and the magnetic poles: the shift in the magnetism of our poles was discovered through the carbon dating of pottery). This is not to mention the greater understanding of how the universe itself works via the still new (in scientific terms, at least) field of quantum physics. Additionally, this mildly offensive caricature of crystal gazers also misses out on the very real history of the use of minerals and other natural elements to convey power, wealth, status, and a whole host of other very real human ideas and activities. Wiccans simply happen to be more enlightened and open to the possibilities that crystals and their ilk can provide.

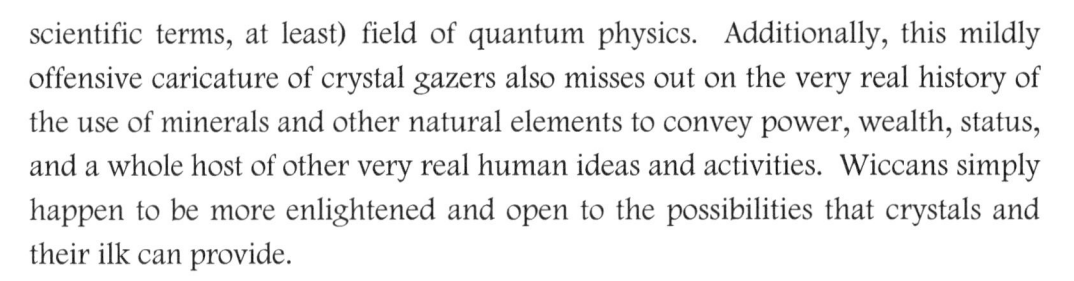

2.2 Traditional Uses, Purposeful Practice

One of the most common usages is to mark the sacred circle with either crystals or stones when embarking on ritual practice. Another is to honor the deities, as particular crystals and stones are associated with particular gods and goddesses. In addition, because of their inherent energy channeling properties, crystals and stones are often used to adorn tools, altars, ritual clothing, and jewelry of Wiccan practitioners—these aren't just pretty accessories but rather are potent additions. A Wiccan practitioner can also learn how to send a "charge" of intention to a particular crystal and simply carry it with her, to bring that energy with her wherever she goes. You can find crystals and stones in any number of places, from shops specializing in New Age philosophy or Wiccan practice to natural mineral stores; there are infinite resources online, as well, though seasoned Wiccans will suggest that selecting them in person is important. Choosing a crystal is a very personal event, as crystals give off that subtle energy; each individual is receptive to different energies in different ways, so it is quite possible to imply that the crystal chooses the Wiccan rather than the other way around (as in the Harry Potter wands, no? The wand chooses the wizard). This is why selecting crystals and stones in person is preferable. Not only is energy significant in choosing but color is, as well, with its own magical properties; the subtle color variations in crystals can only truly be seen close up. See Chapter 4 for advice on choosing and purchasing crystals and stones.

However, you decide to choose and use your crystals and stones, keep in mind some of the following general ideas for how best to utilize these magical objects in your daily Wiccan life and practice.

First, be sure to cleanse any crystal before you use it. Any residual energy that might not be to your liking should be wiped clean; start with a blank slate to get the most value out of your intentions. Many Wiccans sleep with a crystal near them, even under their pillow. Amethyst and selenite are said to improve relaxation and rest, so those are good choices for that particular usage. Some seasoned Wiccans also suggest that certain crystals can even assist in remembering and interpreting dreams, potent portents of things to come. As mentioned above, carry crystals with you. A select piece of citrine in your handbag or briefcase is an excellent was to travel with peace of mind, its protective powers always with you. Use crystals to boost the energies surrounding your activities, from the most mundane daily list of things-to-do to your journal to your list of spells and/or intentions. That is, keep your to-do list or your wish list or your intentions list—or all of the above—in a safe place with a crystal stacked on top. The energy from the crystal will suffuse your lists with intention and purpose, making accomplishment a foregone conclusion.

Crystals are also excellent cleansers, as well, not just for spaces but for personal usage. You can utilize crystals in the bath in order to promote calmness, for example, or seek out mineral scrubs to rid yourself of negative energy. For more details on this, see Chapter 9. Because of their intense energy, crystals are great guides: that is, use crystals to direct energy, literally, from one place to another. With your clear intention behind it, you can focus the crystalline energy to a specific point. Don't forget to seek out spells that help you charge your crystals with specific intentions and energies; they will need to be re-charged on occasion, too, in order to maintain potency. There will be guidelines for how to do this throughout the practical magic section of the book (Chapters 7-11). Speaking of the Practical Magic chapters, crystals can be used to make elixirs, to create talismans, to foster healing baths, to enhance candle and herbal magic. They can be used to promote love, to attract good fortune, to enhance harmony, to provide protection, to deepen inner clarity, to break bad habits, and to help you achieve goals— and more. They are truly indispensable tools within Wiccan practice. Finally, remember to enjoy your crystals: the positive energy with which you imbue them only makes them more powerful and you more successful. Crystals and stones are a significant part of the self-care that you deserve and cultivate with your Wiccan practice.

2.3 Cleansing Crystals

When you first start working with crystals, gems, or stones of any variety you need to understand that they have been part of the world much longer than you have. This means that it has picked up intentions from a variety of different places. Not only has it passed through a variety of hands during processing, it is likely that it has been touched but dozens of shoppers. Everyone that touches a crystal or a gem will leave traces of their energy on it.

When you are working with crystals or gems you only want your energy and intent to live within it. You absolutely don't want to deal with the thoughts and energies of others. So, what do you do about all that extra energy and the intentions of other people? You cleanse your crystals and gemstones before you start using them. While cleansing your crystals, gems, and stones may seem like a foreign idea it is actually quite simple. There are a variety of different practices that can help you achieve the goal of cleansing. An added bonus is that when you cleanse your crystals and stones it can actually help to cleanse your mind, body, and spirit, as well. It is important to note that crystal, gem, or stone cleansing is not something that is done once and never done again. The energy of these items can deplete over the course of time which will require you to cleanse and re-energize them. In addition, your intent for a specific crystal could change and this would require the cleansing process to occur again. If you have a certain crystal or stone that you work with frequently you may find that you are also cleansing it frequently. This is not a bad thing, in fact, it is going to work to your advantage.

Now that you understand the importance of cleansing your crystals let's take a look at a few different methods that you can use to accomplish the task. Keep in mind that there are a number of ways to do this and we are only outlining a few of the most popular methods that are available. Bathing your crystals or gemstones in sunlight or moonlight is an excellent way to cleanse them. Sometimes your objects will start to look dull and you can easily tell that their energy is depleting. By allowing your crystals, gemstones, and regular stones to bathe in the light of the sun or the moon for a minimum of four hours, you can accomplish cleansing.

You should actually take your crystals outside to do sun or a moon cleansing. This can be a bit difficult if you are working with large specimens; however, it will be extremely advantageous. Leaving them in your house and just putting them in the line of sunlight or moonlight may provide partial cleansing but it is never going to work as well as bringing them out and among nature. Oftentimes, when people use this method for cleansing, they do it about once a month. If you are moon cleansing, you will want to do it during the full moon. When the energy coming from it is at its highest.

When sun cleansing, you should still do it roughly once a month. Many find that doing it when the sun is at its peak for the day is the best time.

Another interesting way to cleanse your crystals and gemstones is to use other crystals. Selenite and Crystal Quarts are both known for having amazing cleansing energies and properties. Not only will they help with cleansing they can also help with adding energy to your crystals, as well as, promoting purification. It is amazing that these crystals can do this. Even more so amazing, is the fact that their own energy will not be depleted when they are used for cleansing, charging, and purification purposes. To accomplish cleansing through Selenite or Crystal Quartz you will need to follow a few simple steps. First, you will put your crystals or gems on a plate made of Selenite or Crystal Quartz. You will let them rest there for six or more hours. After this time has passed your crystal or stone will be ready to go.

Many people like to use these plates to cleanse the jewelry and amulets that they wear on a daily basis. You can cleanse them of negative energies that they have picked up throughout the day while you sleep. By the next morning, they will be full of new positive energy and ready to help you throughout your day. While most people prefer to use the plate form of Crystal Quartz or Selenite because it is easy to place things on, you can also use these crystals in their raw form. You may find it a bit tricky to place other crystals or gemstones on them, but some find that the energy is better because it has not been handled and changed.

Ultimately, both will work well, and the choice is up to you.

Returning your crystals, gems, and stones back to nature is also an excellent way to cleanse them. Just like us, these items do well when surrounded by the natural energies of the world. You can simply place them on the soil, or even better you can bury them in the earth. This process does take longer than the others that we have mentioned so far. You will want to leave them in the earth for approximately twenty-four hours.

Some like to submerge their crystals or gems in nearby water sources before burying them in the earth. This can help the cleansing process, but you need to be careful. Some crystals and stones are very porous, or they are salt-based. If submerged in water, you could cause damage to these types of crystals and stones. Knowing what you are working with is the key to using water for cleansing.

The last cleansing process that we are going to discuss is also one of the most popular. This is cleansing your crystals, gems, and stones with smoke. Smoke cleansing is something that dates back farther than pretty much every other cleansing process. It does an excellent job and comes with some added bonuses.

Most people prefer to use Sage, Frankincense, or Palo Santo to smoke cleanse their crystals and gems. The added bonus to these items is that they will make your house smell great and they will also help to cleanse your spirit. In addition, they are easy to get ahold of and you don't have to go far out of your way to accomplish it. To cleanse using smoke is pretty easy and can be accomplished in a couple of different ways. You can put your crystals or stones into a bowl and allow the smoke to drift into the bowl, covering them with the smokes cleansing energy. If you are working with large crystals or gems you can simply push the smoke toward it. You will want to work all the way around your crystal and gem. You can push the smoke toward it with your hands or with a hand fan. Either way, you will want to do this for several minutes or until you can see the life coming back to your crystals or gems. You will be able to sense it when the cleansing process has been completed.

2.4 Crystals and Intention Setting

Once your crystals have gone through the cleansing process there are some other steps that need to be taken before you start using them during spellcasting. Every crystal, gem, or stone has a variety of different natural properties that can influence the spells you are casting. So, it is important that you understand the item you are working on within the properties that it holds. However, there is another piece. You need to make your intentions known to the crystal, gem, or stone that you are working with. It is important to note that setting your intentions is extremely important. Understand that your intentions can change as you work with your crystals and it is simple enough to accomplish. When you are going to change the intention that you have pushed on to your crystal or gem it is important that you re-cleanse it. This will make changing your intention much simpler. Realistically, your intentions mean everything in the world of Wiccan practices. It is not only important to put your intention out there when trying to work with crystals it is also important during all types of spellcasting. Our intentions are what fuel the power behind our spells. The stronger your intention and the clearer it is the more successful you will be. Another reason that your intentions being pushed into your crystals, gems, or stones is important is due to the fact that they will be constant reminders. When you spend the time to give intentions to these items, every time you see them you will be reminded of them. This can help keep you focused and allow your intention to actually manifest.

Setting your intentions is not a difficult thing to do. There are a few simple steps that you can follow to accomplish this task. It is important to note that there are many different ways to set your intentions. We are going to give you an easy option to get you started. It really is going to help bring power to your outcomes and make manifestation easier than before. The power that crystals, gems, and stones bring to the table is really quite amazing. You will always want to start by connecting to and cleansing your crystals or gems. As noted, the correct crystal or gem for the job is the one that you feel particularly drawn to. The energy that it emits will affect you on a mental, physical, and spiritual level. Once you find the items that you are going to use it is important to cleanse away residual energies that may be on them. After you have cleansed your crystals, gems, or stones you will move on to intention setting. To do this you should hold the item in your hand and erase any negativity that may be burdening your mind. Oftentimes, people like to meditate or work through breathing exercises for a few minutes while holding their crystals.

This can be a good way to get your mind in the right frame.

When your mind is clear and calm, you will then focus on the intention that you wish for your crystal or stone to help you with. This can be something that will manifest over the long term or the short term. It is important to note that you should not be overly specific, and you really should not be going after materialistic things. These are much harder to manifest, and you will likely be disappointed with the outcome.

When you are focusing energies to manifest intentions it is best to work towards the things in life that you actually need. Going after things that you want will not usually come to fruition. This can be frustrating for some people but when you think about it really it makes perfect sense. We need to provide for ourselves in many ways. On the other hand, the universe will help give us the nourishment we need to keep our minds and souls healthy.

Now, when you are in a state of a calm mind you want to move your focus to your crystal. From there, you want to give it your intentions. You can do this by speaking your desires out loud and repeating them. In addition, you can repeat them in your head as long as you are maintaining focus on the connection of you to your crystal. Many people find repeating the words in their head to be a bit easier when trying to maintain focus. If you find that you are losing connection, or you cannot maintain focus while thinking of your intentions there is another way. You can write your intentions down on a piece of paper. When you do this place the paper underneath the crystal as you hold it and meditate. This will help to set your intentions. There are many people that like to push their intentions into their crystal while holding it over their third eye chakra. This chakra is extremely powerful and excellent in powering your intentions into your crystal, gems, or stones. Whatever method you choose it should feel comfortable. You should continue pushing your intention into the object until your body, mind, and soul all feel as if the intention was set.

Once your intention has been pushed into your crystal or gemstone it is important that you keep it around you. Many people will choose to use smaller crystals or stones so that they can actually keep them on their person. You can accomplish this by putting them in a small pouch, purse, or you can even place your crystals or gemstones under your pillow while you sleep. This will help power the manifestation of your intention and also allow you to keep your focus on it.

However, if you are using a large crystal or stone this could be impossible. So, instead, you will want to spend some time near your crystal on a daily basis. Here again, it will allow you to reflect on your intention and continue to experience the energy that your crystal, gem, or stone has to offer. It will also help keep the intention fresh within the item you are working with.

It is important to note that you need to set your intentions into your crystals, gems, or stones relatively frequently. This is not only when your intention is changing but throughout time. That you are waiting for manifestation, as well. Some people like to do a ritual on a monthly basis to make sure that their intention is set. Doing this by the cycle of the moon makes it very easy. As you can see, setting intentions with your crystals and gemstones is very important and it is not extremely difficult. Taking a little bit of time to accomplish this task will make all of the difference in the world. It is as important as making sure the negative energies are cleansed away from your crystals and stones.

Chapter 3: Wicca Herbal Magic

3.1 An Introduction to Herbalism

There are many different accounts of not only humans but animals with cognitive functioning using herbs to cure ailments. The Tanzanian chimp cures worms with the pith of the Veronian plant. Humans of the area do so as well.

So, humans are not the only ones who are known to use herbalism. Cats eat grass to settle their stomachs if they have indigestion. The type of grass they eat depends on the area they live in, and what's available.

Now on to the human history of herbalism. Humans have used herbalism since there were humans on the planet. Back when the cavemen roamed the earth, herbs were all they had to cure the ailments that they had. If they chose the wrong one, that could be disastrous. Since the beginning of time, people have relied on herbs for cures for sicknesses. It wasn't until the last hundred years that we really got into modern medicine.

There are even real documentations that go back over fifty thousand years that show that people back then used herbs to cure sicknesses that arose over time. A lot of the herbs that they used then, we use today, though most of them are called by a different name, as plant names have changed over the season. Herbs are documented to have eased the passing of some people who were too far gone to save. And have even been known to stop the spread of yellow fever, if caught soon enough. Herbs were there throughout bouts of epidemics, the bubonic plague, the red death, so many other diseases have been combated by herbs until modern medicine came along and completely knocked them out.

3.2 The Importance of the Nature in Wiccan Religion

The American Council of Witches has comprised thirteen statements that accurately summarize what Wiccans believe and follow:

1. Wiccans practice celebrations are known as Sabbaths and esbats. These help them follow the rhythms of the natural world and revere the God and Goddess.
2. Wiccans recognize that as intelligent beings, humans hold responsibility for the Earth's creatures, and should take this responsibility seriously.
3. Wiccans recognize their ability to utilize magic makes them unique, and in possession of a power non-magic-using people do not possess. Despite this, they do not see themselves as "better" than other people and use their arcane knowledge with care.
4. Wiccans recognize the duality in nature of masculine and feminine, and know that one should never have power over the other; as they are balanced. Additionally, Wiccans regard human sexuality as a divine expression.
5. Wiccans recognize there are many "worlds," or planes of existence, such as the material world and the spirit world.
6. Wiccan has no hierarchy of power within its numbers. There are elders, priests, and priestesses, but anyone may attain these positions, and these positions are merely for the purpose of leading ceremonies and teaching others their knowledge of the Old Ways.
7. Wiccans believe witchcraft is the combination of the use of magic, living daily life in tune with the God and Goddess, and cultivating a lifestyle that reveres and respects nature.
8. Wiccans believe being a "witch" is an active choice. It does not come from lineage or parentage, but from choice first, then from devotion, focus, and hard work. Once you've decided to practice witchcraft, then you are for all intents and purposes, a witch.
9. Wiccans believe by living more in tune with the natural world and the energy of the universe, they can live a more fulfilling, happier life.
10. Wiccans possess no animosity towards Christianity or other Judeo-Christian religion—save for any agenda by these religions to convince others their faith is the only "true" faith, and by infringing upon the rights and religious freedoms of the followers of other faiths.

11. Wiccans agree to cultivate and encourage peaceful debate among their communities, so Wicca as a unified but diverse faith may grow and adapt with the changing times.
12. Wiccans reject any concept of the Christian devil, as well as the concept of absolute evil. Wiccans do not seek to gain power over others and abhor the abuse of power through magic.
13. Wiccans believe Nature itself provides the knowledge, wisdom, and tools necessary for humanity to live a fulfilling, happy life.

Wiccan Practices

Wicca has many rites that mark different milestones in a person's life. They are not mandatory, but when celebrated, the community comes together to support the person being honored.

Wiccaning, or Naming. This ceremony can occur at any age, but is usually undertaken before a child reaches puberty. It is a way to introduce a child to the Wiccan community; often, new parents will have a Wiccaning to celebrate the arrival of their infant. A Wiccaning is like a baptism in that it brings the person closer to the community, but it is not indoctrination, nor a guarantee the child will pursue the Wiccan path. Wiccans believe every person's faith is their own to choose, even if that means choosing none at all.

Handfasting. Handfasting is performed when two people want to officially symbolize their romantic union. It is not a legal marriage, although many couples will have a judge officiate that aspect of it, then have a Wiccan high priest or priestess perform the handfasting ceremony. During a handfasting, the couple clasps hands and has their hands loosely bound with a ceremonial cord.

Some couples also opt to perform the ancient ritual of "jumping the broom," for good luck in their union. The words "remain together as long as your love shall last" are usually spoken.

Handparting. Unfortunately, some unions come to an end. There is no shame or guilt in a handparting. It is a ceremony in which the soon-to-be parted couple show their respect to each other, as well as gratitude for the experience of their love. The ceremonial cord is either untied or cut with a ritual knife. The couple may each choose to keep the remnants of the cord to remember their past together.

Croning, or Saging. In Wicca as in other pagan faiths, elder community members are especially adored. Croning, for feminine persons, or Saging, for masculine persons, recognizes that witch's contributions to the community, as well as their experiences in life. It is a way to honor an older coven or community member.

Additionally, a younger person may be croned or saged if they have survived—or are still battling—a serious injury or illness. Such experiences usually impart wisdom much greater than a person that age will possess, and the community recognizes this and gives honor to the individual. A croning or saging may also help prepare that person for the inevitability of death, and ease them into the peaceful, accepting state of mind one might need to embark on that journey.

Ethics

Wicca's system of ethics is fairly simple: do what brings you to delight in life, so long as it doesn't harm anyone or infringe on another person's rights. Wiccans do not discriminate against other people, period. All genders, sexualities, sexes, races, ethnicities, and backgrounds are welcomed to the fold. As far as casting magic spells is concerned, these ethics carry over into this topic as well. Responsible witchcraft means that a Wiccan will never cast a spell to exert influence, intimidation, or power over another person. If faced with a difficult situation, they may instead cast a spell to help foster peace and better communication. They might choose a spell for self-control, or for self-empowerment. They might cast a spell to bring about opportunities for positive change. There are many options in life to help us live happily and positively. In Wicca, it is believed that those options should never be the subjugation of another human being.

Chapter 3: MORE

On any witch's altar, all or some of the following magical tools might be present. We call these tools "magical," but it is accepted that the tools are more accurately conduits for their own magical power. The human subconscious mind works better with symbols and imagery than it does with words and descriptions. We might speak words when casting a spell such as, "I send my intention out into the universe, that I will be done," but if we add the action of our hand holding a magical wand, outstretched towards the heavens, we've then combined the power of our conscious and subconscious mind to create **magic.**

The magic, therefore, is within us. Humans create tools not to do the work for them (robots and machinery notwithstanding) but to **help** us do better work.

Tools should always be cleansed of lingering energy when first acquired or purchased. You can accomplish this by **smudging** or using sacred smoke, with sage, Palo Santo wood, cleansing incense, or rosemary. Tools can be blessed and consecrated beneath a full moon's light, and many witches place their tools and crystals beneath the moon every month to do so.

The Pentacle

The pentacle is a disc engraved, carved, or inscribed with the symbol of a five-pointed star, also known as a pentagram. It is symbolic of both the five magical elements, Earth, Air, Fire,

Water, and Spirit, as well as the Horned God and the wild, natural world. A pentacle is a lovely addition to a Wiccan altar; it reminds us of the forces of magic that naturally occur on Earth and within ourselves. It is a symbol of potential and power for a witch.

Wiccans and other pagans often wear jewelry with pentacles on them. This is both a statement of pride and defiance for many. Additionally, the US Army made the decision to recognize Wicca as an official religion and has since inscribed pentacles on the headstones of Wiccan soldiers who lost their lives in service.

The pentagram can be used in magic, as well. There is an invoking pentagram, as well as a banishing pentagram. The former is used to bring something we desire closer to us, and the latter is used when we wish to be rid of something or its influence. This concept is similar to choosing to cast a spell during the waxing or waning moon; each time has its purpose, and our spells should align with that for maximum efficacy.

The Athame

The athame is the ritual knife used to symbolize the energy of the God in the ceremony. It is usually a silver, double-edged blade with a black handle, but a wide variety of athames are available for purchase. Some are even crafted from stone or crystal. Typically, the athame's blades are kept dull. In the ceremony, the athame will often be placed within the cup or goblet to symbolize the union of the God and the Goddess. An athame should never be used for mundane things like preparing food.

An athame can also be used for casting a circle when one points to the four directions/elements.

The Goblet

The goblet, also known as the cup, or chalice, symbolizes the Goddess in rituals and on the Wiccan altar. It is classically made of silver, as this metal is sacred to the goddess, but goblets have been crafted of wood, pewter, brass, gold, copper, ceramic, marble, and other minerals. Some are encrusted with gemstones.

Others are humble and plain.

The goblet is passed from person to person with a libation of wine or grape juice during the closing of a coven or community's Sabbath ceremony, while each person says to the next, "May you never thirst." This is accompanied with a loaf of bread or plate of other food, along with is spoken, "May you never hunger."

A goblet can be a wonderful way to enchant herbs or water beneath a full moon's magical light. Using the moon to infuse magic into an object or liquid is a common practice in Wicca and other pagan faiths.

The Wand

The wand is considered an extension of the Wiccan's magical energy. It is connected with the element of Fire. A wand can be hand-crafted from a stick found in the forest or purchased. Like any newly-acquired tool, a wand should be spiritually cleansed before it is used. Traditional wands are made from oak, ash, birch, or willow, but wands can be made of any material. Bamboo makes excellent wands, because of a written sigil, spell, or blessing can be rolled and slipped inside the wand, and a crystal can be set in place at the wand's opening. A wand, like an athame, is often chosen to cast a circle with by pointing at the four directions.

The Cauldron

The cauldron is perhaps one of the most iconic symbols of witchcraft. When in ancient times, healers, herbalists, and village elders were turned to for help with illness, fertility, and injuries, the cauldron was an important tool, used to craft batches of herbal remedies.

Today, cauldrons are quite expensive, though fortunately, our magical use of the cauldron requires only a small replica of the original, large cast iron pots. Still, even a small, hand-sized cauldron will cost a pretty penny. It is not required (nor is any tool) to cast magical spells, but it is useful in mixing herbs, as well as filling with water to use the surface in scrying and divination. If a cauldron is beyond your budget, a black ceramic or glass bowl will work just as well. Some witches opt to have their mortar and pestle double as a small cauldron.

The Besom

The besom, or broom, is the most recognizable icon associated with witches. It is showcased in modern Halloween décor and in countless illustrations and cartoons. The idea witches rode brooms through the air was represented by Shakespeare when he wrote that the three witches in his play "Macbeth" would do just that. Broom-riding is likely an allegory for shamanistic astral projection, usually brought on by the consumption of hallucinogenic plants for the purpose of divination or journeys to the spirit world.

Today, the besom has a much more humble purpose, but no less important. Wiccans and other pagans use the besom to spiritually "sweep" negative energy from a space. Just like mundane dirt and dust, negative energy collects as we live our lives, and as we bring the energy from the outside world into our homes, rooms, and altar space. Sweeping from the interior of a home out the doors cleanses a space of stagnation and negativity, so magic can be performed there and a peaceful life lived.

Mortar and Pestle

Not typically recognized as a magical tool, the mortar and pestle nonetheless are an essential tool for herbal magic. The act of grinding and crushing the herbs to release their energy and mix them with each other can be combined with spoken words or imagined scenarios in which the magic is taking place; grinding the pestle sunwise (the Wiccan way of saying clockwise), will bring what one desires closer, while grinding the pestle widdershins (the Wiccan way of saying counterclockwise), will reduce the influence of something or drive it away.

Book 7: Wicca Moon Magic

Chapter 1: The Wiccan Moon

1.1 An Introduction to Wiccan Moon

This book is an introduction to Wiccan moon magic for beginner practitioners or those interested in the idea. Perhaps you've dabbled in magic already or just have a feeling that it would work for you. This first chapter will go over the basics of Wicca in general, and the next will focus on the magic of the moon. After that, we will dive straight into the magic itself. To begin, let's answer some questions that you likely have if you're new to the practice. If not, feel free to skip ahead.

1.1.1 Am I a Witch?

As simple as it may be, you are a witch if you practice magic. Not all Wiccans practice the craft of magic, and not all witches practice the traditions of Wicca. However, Wicca does have certain rituals, spells, and practices that apply to it. If you feel that you may have some magic in you or notice things like fledgling psychic abilities, you aren't automatically considered a witch. To become one, you need to actually practice the magic. If you have some talents that are relevant, you can pull from them and grow them. If not, you can still get started.

Anyone can be a witch. It should also be noted that the term "witch" is used for all genders in Wicca. There are certain qualities that those inclined toward magic tend to share. Witches are often very sensitive to emotions and moods, have a strong intuition, possess high creativity, often get lost in meaningful thoughts, and have an intense personality. Even if these don't fit you now, practicing witchcraft will hone some of these characteristics. Not all witches share these traits, however. They are a varied and diverse group.

If you're interested, you can find many quizzes or tests online that will tell you what "type" of witch you are, what element resonates with you, and hundreds of other details based on your answers to questions. These can be fun and may give you a little insight before you dive into witchcraft. Don't take them too seriously, though; you can still do whatever you want. If you've picked up this book, you probably already have a bit of affinity for the moon or are fascinated by it. That alone is a great place to start. If you're drawn to something, listen to your intuition. It will lead to wonderful things.

1.1.2 What Is Wicca?

Wicca as a religion is considered a Neo-Pagan practice that has traditions based on the Earth. There are two main deities— a God and a Goddess. The principles are based on respect for the Earth and rules of conduct prohibiting Wiccans from harming anyone, called the Wiccan Rede (pronounced as reed). Religion is more of a technical term than anything— Wiccans can be of any belief, ritual, or practice, and there is a huge variety among them.

The religion of Wicca dates back far before Christianity and Roman rule. Its ancient traditions have always been focused on Earth and nature and the four elements found there— the element of earth, air, water, and fire. Some also believe that a fifth element exists, that of spirit, or Akasha. Wiccans do not build temples as other religions since nature is considered the perfect temple. Outdoors among the elements is the best place for gatherings, rituals, and spells. The God and Goddess that Wicca focuses on represent the duality of the world; it is both masculine and feminine, and neither is more important than the other. They depend on each other to maintain balance. The same applies to nature.

There are some branches of Wicca that focus more on the Goddess. Moon magic leans toward this, as the moon is a representation of the Goddess herself. Most Wiccans believe that the God, Goddess, and spirits can go by any name since they are the same Divinity, no matter what they are called. This opens the door to focus on any deity of your choice or none at all. It is common to choose a deity that resonates with you, and there are several that correspond to the moon. In some traditions, you may hear the deities referred to as the Moon Goddess and the Horned God.

1.2 The History of Modern Wicca

Before the rise of Christianity, witchcraft or magic was practiced for thousands of years across thousands of cultures. Collectively, these are known as Pagan religions. As Christianity was established and accepted, Pagan religions were deemed heresy, and the propaganda spread said that it was associated with the Devil. Attempts were made to convert the Pagans to Christianity, and there were even efforts made to make it easy. For example, almost all Christian holidays today fall on the date of a Wiccan holiday rather than their actual historical date. That way, Pagans would feel more comfortable converting, or, rather, they could continue to celebrate their own holidays, while Christian leaders could claim they were converted. It wasn't long before witchcraft became punishable by death. Those who followed the Bible believed in its patriarchy and saw the powerful "wise women" of Paganism as evil. Gradually, Pagan symbols began to be associated with the Christian idea of the Devil. "Witch" became an accusation and, eventually, an insult. The stigma toward witchcraft remains to this day, though it is gradually lessening. In the 1950s, author and civil servant, Alex Gardner, published several books on the modern practice of witchcraft and its ties to the pre-Christian traditions. He had found a coven of his own and became motivated to share the philosophies with the world. Gardner is now considered the "Father of Wicca," though he referred to the practice as witchcraft or simply the Craft. He called practitioners themselves Wica (with one c), a term derived from the old English word for witch. The name Wicca for the practice itself came about sometime in the 1960s, though no one knows who popularized it.

Wicca is a unique blend of ancient and new traditions. It continuously evolves and has had different meaning throughout time. However, one of the core tenets is freedom, so these branching ideas are encouraged. Wiccans can worship any deity several, or none at all. Some view deities as divine forces, while others see them as symbolic archetypes. Gardner created a Book of Shadows that he shared with followers, but his intention was that everyone's can be unique, as they removed and added spells as they saw fit.

This flexibility has made Wicca more popular in recent years.

Some countries, including the United States, officially recognize it as a religion. There are still those who speak out against this or deem it as Satanic and evil. However, studies in the United States are showing that fewer people are practicing organized religions such as Christianity, where there are strict rules that are often used against groups of people. The culture, as a whole, is moving toward freedom of expression, love, compassion for others, and a focus on science. Wicca is a perfect example of this, and many practitioners are involved in science and technology. Modern Wicca exists in peace with other beliefs and scientific evidence.

Chapter 2: Rhythms of The Moon

2.1 Lunar Energy and Magic

Have you ever heard the saying, "it must be the Moon?"

Usually used in a joking manner to explain away any strange events or bizarre behavior witnessed when the Moon is Full, this phrase has much more truth to it than most people would believe.

Mainstream culture tends to laugh off the notion of Mooninfluenced feelings and behavior, but, as we saw in Part One, the Moon does have effects on people and animals. This tends to be most obvious during the days surrounding the Full Moon, whether we're noticing unusual behavior in our pets or children, or feeling ourselves to be abnormally "moody." But while you may already be aware that the "Full Moon effect" is not a myth, you may not realize that **all** phases of the Moon's cycle influence us on some level, however subtle it may be for those who aren't yet attuned to lunar energy. What does the Moon's energy have to do with magic? As multi-sensory beings, we are constantly interacting with unseen energies coming from every direction—from other people, from media, from the food we eat and the buildings we spend our days and nights in. Everything we interact with has an effect on our personal energetic makeup. We tend to focus on what we experience through our five physical senses—sight, sound, touch, taste, and smell.

2.2 Tracking the Moon

Before considering the relationship between the Moon and magic, however, it's important to identify the phases of the lunar cycle in more detail. After all, you can't truly take advantage of the opportunities that lunar energies present if you don't know what's happening in the sky when you're casting your spells! Let's take a look now at two different frameworks for describing and tracking the movement of the Moon as it orbits the Earth, and then we'll discuss the magical opportunities that each phase presents.

2.2.1 Light and Shadow

In the first framework, the Moon's cycle is tracked by its appearance in the sky. It begins as a barely-detectable sliver at the New Moon. Over the next few days, the sliver becomes larger and more defined, almost resembling the tip of a fingernail—this is called the Crescent Moon. From here, the Moon continues to grow—or "wax"— on its way to becoming Full. At the mid-point between New and Full, we see the waxing Half Moon, with the illuminated half on the right and the shadowed half on the left.

As the circle begins to be filled out with light, it becomes "gibbous," a word used in astronomy to describe the bulging appearance of the Moon during the days just before and after it's completely Full. Finally, when the circle is completely lit, we are looking at the Full Moon. In the days just after the Full point, the Moon is gibbous again, then continues to shrink—or "wane"— further back to Half. This time, the light half is on the left, with the shadowed half on the right. More and more of the Moon is covered in shadow as it wanes back to its Crescent point, and then completely disappears. This window of time before it is visible again is the Dark Moon. Once the sliver returns, the cycle begins again.

2.2.2 Measuring Time

The other way of tracking the Moon's cycle is to divide it into four quarters, spread out over roughly 28 days. Each quarter lasts approximately seven days, adding up to create what we call the lunar "month."

The first quarter begins at the New Moon and ends at the waxing Half. The second quarter runs from there until the Full Moon. The third quarter begins immediately after the Moon turns Full and lasts until the waning Half Moon, and the fourth quarter closes out the cycle through the Dark Moon, ending just as the Moon reemerges into New.

It's interesting to note that while the two systems are not technically in conflict with each other, in terms of covering the full lunar cycle, there is something of an asymmetrical "glitch" when you try to align them. The ordered, even-numbered quarter system contains 4 units, which doesn't quite align with the 5 major marking points—New, Half, Full, Half, Dark—of the older, somewhat looser framework.

This is because the quarter system doesn't actually take the Dark Moon period into account. In reality, the Moon takes 29.5 days to complete its orbit, which is a number that 4 doesn't divide into equally, so there's a slight "lag" during the Dark time between the fourth and first quarters.

Furthermore, the period of amplified energetic influence that the Full Moon exerts is much longer than the brief period of time when it's fully illuminated. In the Witching world, the Full moon phase is actually considered to be 5 days long—from the two days before Full, when the Moon is still gibbous, until two days after, when the waning is just becoming visible.

Some people go even further, designating a full week to the Full Moon. But for the purposes of working with lunar energies, it can be argued that the Full Moon phase begins and ends when you **feel** it beginning and ending. To some extent, the entire lunar cycle is a bit like that. Remember, it's ultimately about your personal intuitive perception—your sixth sense.

Nonetheless, the quarter system may be more appealing to some, as it can be easier to keep track of. In fact, many calendars note the beginning mark of each quarter. And it's particularly helpful when you don't have the opportunity to go looking at the Moon every single night. (In fact, depending on where it is in its orbit and your own sleep schedule, you may not be able to see it at night.)

The truth is, it really doesn't matter how you track the phases, as long as you're at least aware of when the New and Full Moons occur—these are, after all, the two most energetically powerful times of the cycle.

So if you're new to paying close attention to the Moon, start by paying attention to these two points. As you get into the habit of "tracking the Moon" in this way, you'll find yourself attuning to the more subtle, continuous rhythms of the various energies of the Moon's complete cycle. You'll also get a better feel for timing your magic to align as closely as possible with each lunar phase.

Now that the full cycle has been more specifically illuminated, let's delve into the magical implications for working in harmony with the rhythms of the Moon.

2.3 Magical Timing and the Lunar Cycle

For starters, as we saw in Part One, those who worship the Triple Goddess will generally call upon the appropriate aspect when working magic aligned with the Moon—the Maiden is asked for assistance in the waxing phase, the Mother at the Full Moon, and the Crone when the Moon is on the wane. Others may observe additional correspondences between the phases of the lunar cycle and the seasons, the Sabbats on the Wheel of the Year, and/or the growing cycles of plant life, which is the basis for so much of the symbolism inherent to Wicca and other forms of the Craft.

These systems can provide beautiful ways of further attuning to the Moon's subtle rhythms, as we will see next.

2.3.1 Seasons and Sabbats

Although it's the Earth's orbit around the Sun that is responsible for the turning of the seasons, the ever-shifting appearance of the Moon in the sky can be seen as a mirroring of the same cycle. For example, Spring is the time of new life and increasing growth, which corresponds to the Moon's waxing phase. The Full Moon represents Summer, with its explosion of vegetation and the flourishing of young animal life, while the Autumn corresponds with the waning phase, as plants die back and animals prepare for the end of the warmer seasons. The Winter, then, is represented by the Dark Moon, as all life waits for the cycle to begin again.

This system of seasonal alignments can enhance our understanding of the subtle distinctions between the various magical aims that are most appropriate at different points in the lunar cycle.

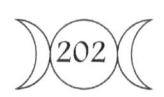

However, it's rather unevenly distributed in terms of the actual length of seasons—after all, Summer and Winter are just as long as Spring and Autumn, so in a sense it's disproportionate to grant them only a few days of the Moon's cycle while the other seasons get nearly two weeks.

But if you're willing to expand the framework and go deeper into the Wheel of the Year, you'll find that there's a much more evenly-spaced system that truly illuminates the alignment between the patterns of the Sun and the Moon. Using the eight Sabbats as a "map" of the Moon's travels, we can view the incremental shifts of the waxing and waning phases more closely, allowing for the "in-between" seasons to guide us into even more optimal timing of our magical efforts. One way to do this is to match the Moon's quarter marks with the solar Sabbats. For example, the Full Moon can be represented by the Summer Solstice (also known in Wicca as Litha) and the New Moon by the Winter Solstice (or, Yule).

This would place each Half Moon at an equinox point—the waxing

Half at Spring (Ostara) and the waning Half at Autumn (Mabon)— with the crescent and gibbous phases represented by the four Earth Sabbats: Imbolc, Beltane, Lughnasa and Samhain.

Then the days between Samhain and Yule, when the nights are the longest that they'll be all year, belong to the Dark Moon. (Of course, if you live in the Southern Hemisphere, these correspondences run in reverse—or counter-clockwise—with Yule being the Summer Solstice and therefore the time of the Full Moon, and the New Moon aligning with Litha, and so on.)

This system of Sabbat alignments works well for many Witches, but for those who live in northern climates with cold, long winters, it doesn't **quite** line up exactly with how the seasons are experienced. In these regions, the New Moon, as a symbol of the end of darkness and the beginning of new life, is actually more closely aligned with Imbolc, which is the Sabbat celebrating the first stirrings of Spring.

Therefore, many Witches align the Moon's quarter marks with the Earth-based Sabbats instead. This shifts the system by a halfseason, but still represents the overall timing and feel of the changes in the climate and landscape where they live. In this framework, the Full Moon aligns with the cross-quarter day of

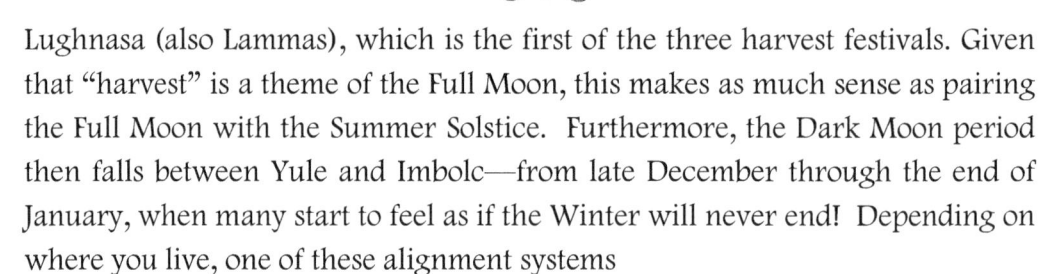

Lughnasa (also Lammas), which is the first of the three harvest festivals. Given that "harvest" is a theme of the Full Moon, this makes as much sense as pairing the Full Moon with the Summer Solstice. Furthermore, the Dark Moon period then falls between Yule and Imbolc—from late December through the end of January, when many start to feel as if the Winter will never end! Depending on where you live, one of these alignment systems

may make more intuitive sense than the other. Those who live near the equator, for example, may prefer the solar alignments, since the changes in seasons are not as noticeable as they are in the regions closer to the North and South poles. If you're seeking to draw romantic love into your life—or to reenergize an existing relationship—you know that the waxing phase is the best time to work. This gives you a window of two weeks.

But what if you want to narrow it down further? Take a look at the Sabbat correspondences and you'll notice that Beltane, a Sabbat associated with love and lust, falls at the waxing Half Moon. Why not choose this date, drawing on the bright, playful energies of Beltane as you send your magical intention for love out into the Universe? Of course, many Wiccans make use of correspondences between magical purposes and the days of the week. In this system, Friday is the most ideal for working love spells, which may or may not line up with the waxing Half Moon.

If the waxing Half does fall on a Friday, then you're looking at a truly stellar alignment for your particular goal! If it falls on a different day, then you will need to use your intuition to decide on the best timing for your love spell. As always when it comes to magic, do what works best for you.

Another approach is to simply incorporate the **feeling** of the corresponding season into your magical work. For example, in a spell for love you can imagine the delicious warming up of late Spring / early Summer—that promising preview of the warmth and lushness of Summer coming into full swing—and use the feelings created by those thoughts to fuel your magic.

And if you're the type to create your own spells from scratch, you can use the corresponding season and/or Sabbat as inspiration for deciding on ingredients.

For example, there are tons of herbs associated with romantic love, but which ones are at their peak during the Beltane season? Which are commonly used at Beltane celebrations?

Doubling up on your correspondences in this way can make your magic incredibly potent!

2.3.2 Aligning with Growth Cycles

Another creative framework for magical correspondences aligns the phases of the Moon with the stages of the life cycle of plants.

Although there is obviously a lot of variation between different kinds of plants—flowers, shrubs, trees, herbs, wild vs. cultivated plant life, etc.—a basic pattern is observed in the workings of the world of vegetation. With a few exceptions (like mosses, ferns and mushrooms), every plant begins as a seed. Given the right conditions of soil, water and light, the seed will root and begin to grow. As it reaches upward toward the sun, leaves begin to develop, followed by buds which become flowers. The flowers are pollinated—by bees, moths, butterflies, bats, or wind, depending on the species—which produces the fruit of the plant. The fruit contains the seeds that will start the next cycle of growth.

(Note that the term "fruit" is being loosely applied here and doesn't necessarily refer to something we would eat. A pinecone, for example, contains the seeds needed to grow new pine trees.

Nuts are also considered fruits in this growth cycle model.)

Once the fruit has reached its ripest point, it will either be eaten by an animal or drop to the ground. Either way, the seeds will ultimately find their way back into the soil, beginning the cycle all over again. Too often, beginning practitioners of magic will work spells for big goals and then sit around wondering why they didn't meet the partner of their dreams or become a millionaire this week. For one thing, the Law of Attraction—which is a big part of magic—states that you get what you think about, so if you're constantly focusing on how you still haven't seen your dream come true, that's exactly what you'll continue to experience. It's important to direct your thoughts to the manifestation **itself**, not the lack of it. More to the point, however, is the need to do your part in the co-creation of what you seek to manifest. If you learn to think of yourself as a magical "gardener," you will get a clearer sense of how and why your participation is a key component.

Whether we intend to grow flowers, herbs, vegetables, or trees, there is a balance between the actions we need to take, and the transformative processes that Nature alone is responsible for. We do the planting, the watering and nurturing, but the creation of leaf, bud, flower and fruit is all Nature's doing.

When our manifestation has fully culminated, it's up to us to either reap the fruit or let it over-ripen and drop to the ground. The composting remains of whatever we don't use are naturally designed to propagate new life the following season, but we can give this process great assistance and direction by tending the soil, weeding out what is unwanted, and preparing the garden for its winter rest. Furthermore, the growth cycle illustrates the role of **timing** in magic, not only as it relates to the energies of Moon phases, but also in terms of how manifestation actually occurs as it moves from the invisible plane to the physical plane. Just as each stage of the growth cycle has its particular purpose in the overall enterprise of plant creation, magical manifestation happens in stages.

Most often, the initial developments taking place are not visible to the eye, just as a seed takes root under the surface of the soil. And even as the manifestation begins to emerge, it may not immediately be recognized for what it is, just as most seedlings tend to resemble each other, no matter what species of plant they are. For those with untrained eyes, it takes some time before they've grown enough to be distinguishable from other plants.

The beginnings of our manifestations can be like this—a chance conversation with an acquaintance that turns out to be a tip on a new job possibility, or a run of what **seems** to be bad luck (a fender bender, a delayed flight) that puts us in the path of our next true love. Most realized goals can be traced back to a winding chain of actions and events that seemed unrelated or insignificant until the manifestation became clear.

So, if your magic is to succeed, it's not enough to simply plant a seed of intention. You'll need to nurture it. You'll need to be willing to leave your house, get out and meet people, and yes, maybe even buy a lottery ticket (though if you're convinced that your only chance at wealth is through a game with incredibly stiff odds, you won't be open to other, unseen possibilities).

You'll also need to practice being alert to subtle nudges from the Universe—i.e., your intuition—that may be trying to show you the seedlings of your intentions poking up through the soil.

Finally, you'll have to have patience, since no matter what actions you take, Nature works on its own schedule.

Be aware of the difference between what you can do and what is strictly up to the Universe and be willing to let the manifestation unfold according to divine timing. Of course, it's true that some manifestations **do** happen very quickly, just as some plants literally do spring up overnight. But even these still started out as tiny seeds, hidden from view.

Chapter 3: Lunar Phases

Witches and the moon are old hats. Witches have been dancing under moonlight since the birth of humanity, and so it goes without saying that if you are a practicing Wiccan or witch, you will find yourself in some connection or devotion to the moon and her vital energies and cycles.

3.1 Phases of the Moon

3.1.1 Phase: Dark Moon

Appearance: Invisible

Approx. Rising Time: Sunrise

Approx. Setting Time: Sunset

3.1.2 Phase: Waxing Crescent (New Moon)

Appearance: Slim crescent (facing right side)

Approx. Rising Time: Mid-morning

Approx. Setting Time: Mid-evening

3.1.3 Phase: 1st Quarter

Appearance: Half full (facing right side)

Approx. Rising Time: Around noon

Approx. Setting Time: Around midnight

3.1.4 Phase: Waxing Gibbous

Appearance: 3/4 full (on the right side)

Approx. Rising Time: Mid-afternoon

Approx. Setting Time: Earliest hours of the morning

3.1.5 Phase: Full Moon

Appearance: Round and full, complete

Approx. Rising Time: Sunset

Approx. Setting Time: Sunrise

3.1.6 Phase: Waning Gibbous

Appearance: 3/4 full (on the left side)

Approx. Rising Time: Early evening

Approx. Setting Time: Mid-morning

3.1.7 Phase: 3rd Quarter

Appearance: Half full (on the left side)

Approx. Rising Time: Midnight

Approx. Setting Time: Noon

3.2 Phase: Waning Crescent

Appearance: Slim crescent (on the left side)

Approx. Rising Time: Earliest hours of the morning

Approx. Setting Time: Mid-afternoon

Now that you have a general idea of all of the moon phase, you can see how their timing might affect different spells. The next section will discuss spells and each moon phase and how to incorporate them elegantly into your spells and rituals.

3.2.1 Dark Moon Magic

Some people will call the smallest crescent waxing moon a "new moon" and the invisible moon a dark moon. You will have to determine your preference in your own practice. This book will offer that the New Moon is the very first glimpse of waxing crescent moon.

This moon is a powerful banishment moon. It is not harmful to banish unwanted energies, but just be sure that you are in a mental state of "harm none" when working with this powerful moon energy. For those who practice harmful forms of magic, this moon would be the best for curses. However, that is against the Wiccan way of magic and will not be promoted here.

Consider the dark moon an apt time to banish that which is not wanted or is ready to leave but is still clinging on. Call it the "moon of serious banishment." Examples might include banishing addictions, negative entities or spirits, serious illnesses, and diseases. This moon has serious energy to help you clear and release the more difficult situations in life like cancer, a menacing stalker, and addiction to drugs and alcohol. If you want to banish your habit of drinking too much coffee or a needy ex who won't stop calling you for late night talks, you might find a better opportunity on a waning crescent moon. This is an excellent moon to look at your shadows, dig deeply, go beyond fear, and enter your cave of unwanted mysteries and miseries.

This is a superb moon time to work with divination and powerful soul searching.

3.2.2 Waxing Crescent Moon Magic / New Moon

A waxing moon is a growing moon. It is going from non-visible to fattest fullness. A waxing moon has magnetic energies that help bring things out into the open. This is building magic, such as growing something in your life, setting up a foundation and adding the walls, developing and building a business, growing your selfesteem, and growing your financial success. It is a moon that can bring things to us through the magic of building and growing. Call it the "growing moon" or the "self-improvement moon."

According to some practices, a waxing moon can be considered the best time to work on matters that pertain to the self, involving new beginnings, plans, projects, and relationships. When you want to conjure or grow some new positive energies in your life, like patience, compassion, or a brighter attitude, then this is a perfect time. This is a moon of self-improvement, bigger psychic openings, artistic and creative endeavors, beauty, absorbing knowledge or new learning periods, and meditations to ignite more passion and inspiration in all of your work.

3.2.3 First Quarter Moon Magic

The half-moon in its waxing phase is the time of attraction. You might even choose to name this moon "the attraction moon" to help you remember its benefits and powerful magic. The previous moon, the self-improvement moon, was about going within and bringing things to the surface; the attraction moon is about pulling desired energies from outside of yourself to you.

This moon is an excellent time for spells that involve things that you want to attract into your life. Typical examples are money, social and career success, and protection. Love is probably the most popular choice, along with money and success. This is a moon to attract people into your life, especially lovers and partners, but also friends, colleagues, clients, and even a pet or an animal companion.

If something has gone missing from your life, like a precious object or a wallet, you may cast a spell at this time to help you find what you are looking for. This is also an excellent opportunity to cast magic to find the house of your dreams if you are house hunting.

3.2.4 Waxing Gibbous Moon Magic

The waxing gibbous moon is getting closer to the full moon, and it is an energy-boosting moon to help you give some extra push to your goals and projects that need to make it over a finish line. It is the "boosting moon." It's all about reeling and going that final distance with what you have already set into motion and have been working on. When your work might be falling apart, stalling, stagnating, or is feeling flimsy, the waxing gibbous moon will help you push forward and through.

It is a good time for renewing strength, determination, and will power in all of your ventures and efforts and will help see you all the way through. Some examples of a situation where this is applicable are giving in to temptation on your diet, burning out from working hard on a major project for work, and starting to get distracted and lazy because you are tired and lackluster. Use the "boosting moon" for all of the spells to help you renew your efforts and keep going on.

3.2.5 Full Moon Magic

The most powerful moment of the lunar cycle, the full moon, is the time when the Earth is between the moon and the Sun, and the rays of sunlight are bouncing off the moon's face and reflecting fully back to us. It is in total alignment. This moon is an all-purpose moon and has such powerful energies it can be used as a constructive or "building" moon or as a destructive and releasing or "letting go" moon.

This moon is for your most important and powerful spells. It has the most energy of all the moons and will give any of your rituals and spells the direct power and influence that it needs to manifest your intentions and goals. This is for the moments of significant change in your life that need the magic of the full moon to help those changes occur swiftly and smoothly. You can plan any spell on the full moon, but consider this moon for your priority spells and incantations. What are the things that matter the most in your life, and how will you ask this moon for aid and support?

Any magic, meditations, purpose, or goals that are revolving around your openness to spirit, your psychic abilities, and development, dreams and divinations, and intuition are particularly enhanced at the time of the full moon.

3.2.6 Waning Gibbous Moon Magic

After the peak of the full moon, the waning begins. The waning energies of the moon are going to repel rather than attract energies, so this time will be the most important time to get rid of things, like shedding a skin. The waning gibbous moon is a good time for minor releases and banishment spells, general cleansing rituals in your home and workspace, and even for your energies that you may be carrying over.

You can cleanse personal objects, magical tools, and implements, your altar, and your car. This moon can be called the "Dusting Moon" as if you are just going around the place and dusting everything. Perhaps there is no significant buildup of unwanted energies, but it is good to do a maintenance check to keep things clear and open.

This can also be a good moon for closure with certain things, such as relationships that were not fulfilling for you or complicated business relationships that need to be let go of. This is a place for reflection and introspection. It is a nice time to take stock of how you are feeling about current matters in your life. Ask yourself some questions: what is affecting me the most in my life right now? How did my choices bring me to this place, and am I satisfied with those choices? What adjustments, if any, do I need to make moving forward?

3.2.7 Third Quarter Moon Magic

Call it the Waning Half Moon or the "Remover of Obstacles Moon." This moon can be beneficial with leaping over hurdles that present themselves on your path. Obstacles always appear at some point on our journey, and this moon can help you achieve an opening with your spell work to make sure that you don't stumble over the roadblock ahead. It is bursting away from anything that would set you off track or slow down your progress. Many people will use a third-quarter moon to help deal with temptations. After all, temptations can be a massive obstacle in achieving your goals. Working with this moon during your spell work would help banish the roadblock of temptation, whether it is on your diet or exercise routine or involving study or promotion. Use the "Remover of Obstacles Moon" to help you stay on your path.

Another way to use this moon's energy for a spell is when faced with transition periods. Whether they are purposeful or something that you have no control over, working a spell to aid with transitions at this time will have an even more powerful impact on your path.

3.2.8 Waning Crescent Moon Magic

The waning crescent moon is helpful in cleansing and clearing negativity from all parts of your life. This is a stronger banishing time, as it gets closer to the strongest banishing moon again— Dark Moon.

Whatever has been plaguing you that is annoying, concerning, or frustrating, (unless they are so serious that they need the Dark Moon), the "Banishing Moon" will help you. This moon will clear the decks of anything that needs to get going. It has more potency than the previous moon for this kind of work, so if you find that you need even more power for letting go of something, the Waning Crescent moon is an excellent time to cut cords, tie off loose ends, and bring hopeless cases to a close. This is also applicable when what you want is more than just dusting off but not quite banishing something seriously from the dark moon. It is a swift and benign ending with a Banishing Moon.

3.2.9 Best Ways to Use Moon Phase Magic

So, what happens when your magical needs don't always correspond with the best moon timing? This has certainly been known to happen, and you may not want to be waiting for the ideal timing to get going on your practice of a specific spell. So, how do you work around all of that?

This is when you can get creative and think outside of the box. An example might be if you are trying to lose weight. You can use each moon phase differently to help you with your goals. A Waxing Crescent moon will be ideal for helping you grow your will power and your energy to stick to your weight loss goals, while a Waxing gibbous moon will help you have those little triumphs over cravings of tempting foods. In a waning moon, you can cast magic to destroy or banish tempting foods that you know will be bad for your progress.

You get the picture.

Always consider what you are trying to accomplish, and then consider what the current moon phase can do to help you with that accomplishment. You may need to get your goal outlined clearly ahead of time and look at the moon phase calendar ahead. Your whole goal could be achieved in a deliberate casting that covers the entire lunar cycle. I guarantee that no matter what intention you are casting for, any of the moon phases will have strong, elemental power to contribute in some way. All you have to do is get creative with how you work through a moon phase. Let's use love spells as an example. Your overall goal could be to bring a soulmate into your life. You can use a Waxing moon time to call your soulmate to you, and variations of that waxing moon can be utilized to help you grow love within yourself to draw them closer and to empower the love that you will feel when you come together. You can also use the power of a Waning moon to help you let go of and banish any old cynicism or bitterness you may be feeling in your heart from older love partnerships. You can cast magic to release your wounds and heartaches and help you open more fully to love. You don't have to use an entire lunar cycle to cast multiple spells for one goal. You can simply time a one-off, specific spell throughout the cycle and fit it in where it feels appropriate.

If you are eager to perform a spell, and it isn't the right moon time for it, consider how you can dynamically utilize the current moon power to help you achieve your goals. There is always a creative way around it. Wiccans will also use planetary signs and signals, such as astrology, days of the week, and so forth, rather than just the moon's phase. You may find that utilizing the astrology of whatever sign the moon is passing through to help you out. Days of the week all have specific energies and are ruled by different planets, and you can use this kind of energy as well if the moon isn't right when you need it to be in a cycle for your spells. Not everything will line up neatly and perfectly every time, and so it is up to you and your practice to find the timing that will work best for you and your casting.

Fortunately, magic is not an exact science; it's more like creative art, like fine cooking, and so it will take some playful experimentation and practice while you get acquainted with the moon and her powerful resources better.

Chapter 4: The Triple Goddess

In most Wiccan traditions, the Goddess will take on a three-fold form that is called the Triple Goddess. She has three individual aspects that are known as the Crone, the Mother, and the Maiden. These are all in line with the Moon's phases while it orbits the Earth which are the waxing crescent, the full moon, and the waning crescent. These three aspects are representative of the three phases of a woman's life: before, during, and after her ability to have children. It also represents psychic abilities, mystery, and energy. You might see this symbol on headpieces or crowns of High Priestesses.

Even though a woman will go through these phases during her lifetime, every aspect of the Triple Goddess will have qualities that both female and male can relate to at some point in our lives. This three-fold Goddess can reflect all the complexities of the human psyche along with the cycles of death and life that are experienced by everyone who lives on Earth.

There are other ways to connect and honor the mother, maiden, and crone. Here are other meanings to the Triple Goddess symbol:

- Connection to the divine feminine
- Connection to all women
- Goddesses: Hecate, Kore, Persephone, Demeter
- Cycles of life, birth, death, and rebirth as the continuation of the moon phases
- Realms and planes: heaven, underworld, and Earth
- Origin Stories

The origin of this triple deity goes back to ancient civilization like the Celtic goddess Brighid. She rules over three critical skillings in the Celtic society, which is smith craft, poetry, and healing. The goddess Hera, who holds three roles in Greek mythology of widow, woman, and girl. These goddesses are possibly an inspiration for the book The White Goddess: A Historical Grammar of Poetic Myth that was written by Robert Graves.

Graves, who was a British scholar and poet, was writing at the same time as Gerald Gardner and other authors who were practicing a form of Witchcraft that we call Wicca. This book brought to life the cultures in the ancient Middle East and preChristian Europe who worshipped a White Goddess of Death, Love, and Birth and she went by various names according to the region they lived in. Earlier writers described a Triple Goddess and these included Sigmund Freud and Aleister Crowley.

Gardner didn't worship the Triple Goddess but other Witches during that time were drawn to her. Robert Cochrane has been credited as bringing her into the Witchcraft movement. It was in the '70s the Triple Goddess that we know today became the root of most Wicca forms.

Instead of being one deity that takes on different forms, the Triple Goddess is represented by three individual deities. Everyone is a different aspect of the Goddess. These might be borrowed from various ancient cultures. Some people worship the Hindu Goddess Kali as the Crone, the Egyptian Goddess Isis as the Mother, and the Roman Goddess Diana as the Maiden. These were rooted in the individual roles within each culture they were borrowed from.

Isis was a mother goddess of ancient Egypt.

Every aspect of the Triple Goddess can be associated with certain seasons or other natural phenomena along with elements of life and human characteristics. These associations could be used to call on the correct aspect of the Goddess during prayer, ritual worship, and magical work. These aspects might represent the cycle of birth, life, death or rebirth. Neopagans thought this goddess represents every woman in the entire world.

Followers of the Neopagan, Dianic, and Wiccan religions along with some mythographers and archeologist believe that before the Islam, Christianity, Judaism, and Abrahamic religions, the Triple Goddess was the embodiment of the Mother Earth, Gaia. There was a mother goddess who was worshipped under many names in the pre-Islamic Arabia, Anatolia, Aegean, and Ancient Near East. Neopagans claim historical antecedent on their beliefs. They hold that the Triple

Goddess precedes the nomads who spoke the IndoEuropean languages as well as in most of ancient Near East and in ancient Europe during the Aegean world.

The moon god Hubal of South Arabia had three other goddesses with her: the youngest was Uzza, "The Goddess" was Al-Lat, and the three cranes or Manat the Crone. Wiccans will sometimes work with the Triple Goddess in her true form but might look at a certain goddess such as the Crone, Mother, or Maiden even if there isn't any historical proof. One example is the goddess Hecate, who was first seen as three maidens when together or in later times as an old woman. Morrigan is another example. One more cross-cultural archetype is the three Fate goddesses. They were called Moirai in Greek mythology. They were called the Norns in Norse mythology. In Shakespeare's and Terry Pratchett's Macbeth, the Weird Sisters and the Wyrd Sisters are thought to have been inspired by the Fates. Neil Gaiman's The Sandman novels play on both the Maiden, Mother, Crone goddess and triple Fates with the characters of the Kindly Ones, Mother of the Camenae, and the Ladies.

The Celtic symbol triskele or spiral of life has been found at the Newgrange site in Ireland from the Bronze Age. This ancient symbol of the Celtic beliefs was used constantly in Celtic art for three thousand years. Celts think all life moves in eternal cycles that regenerate at every point. Celts also think that everything important will come in three phases, such as spirit, body, and mind along with rebirth, death, and birth.

The same spiral was later used in Christian manuscripts. The same triple spiral has also been used to represent the Triple Goddess in Neopagan religions. In the book Uriel's Machine that was written by Knight and Lomas, this triple spiral might be representative of the nine months of human pregnancy because the sun takes a quarter of the year to go from the equator to the poles and the other way around. During every three-month time frame, the sun's path looks like it forms a quasi-helical shape, which could be compared to a spiral. This means that the three spirals could be representative of the nine months and this gives us the explanation for the link between the triple spiral symbol and fertility.

The Maiden

This aspect is in line with the new waxing phase of the Moon. It represents the youth of a woman's life. This is her time to grow as reflected by the waxing moon as it travels toward fullness. In nature cycles, the Maiden is thought of as the season spring, sunrise, and dawn.

The Maiden represents carefree erotic aura, excitement, new beginnings, the female principle, expansion, inception, enchantment, new life, fresh potential, and beauty. In humans, she is their independence, intelligence, naivety, self-confidence, youth, and innocence. She also represents creativity, selfexpression, discovery, and exploration. Wiccans might worship the Maiden as the Celtic goddesses Brigid and Rhiannon, the Nordic goddess Freya, or the Greek goddesses Artemis and Persephone along with many others.

The Mother

During the full moon, the Maiden turns into the Mother and gives birth to the Earth's abundance. The season she represents is summer which is the most fruitful time of year since the fields and forests are flourishing with young animals growing into maturity. The time of day she represents is midday. Within the human realm, she stands for love, patience, power, self-care, stability, fulfillment, fertility, and ripeness, the fullness of life, adulthood, responsibility, and nurturing. She is the giver of life and she is associated with manifestation. The Mother is thought of by many Wiccans as the most powerful aspect of the three. It was the Mother Goddess that inspired Gerald Gardner's vision of the divine female. Some of the ancient Goddesses that represent the Mother at most Wiccan altars are Badb and Danu the Celtic, Ceres the Roman, Selene and Demeter the Greek, Ambika the Hindu.

The Crone

When the moon wanes and the night gets darker, the Crone comes into her power. Some early iteration called her "the Hag." She is representative of a woman's post-childbearing years. Her seasons are autumn and winter. She is associated with the end of the growing season, night, and sunset. She is the wise elder part of the Goddess and she governs past lives, rebirth, death, endings, and aging along with guidance, prophecy, visions, fulfillment, culmination, compassion, repose, wisdom, and transformations. She was feared for millions of years. She reminds us that death is a part of life just like the dark side of the moon is before the new moon. The Crone has been associated with the underworld and death like the Celtic goddess Cailleach Bear and Morrigan, the Russian goddess Baba Yaga, and the Greek goddess Hecate.

The Triple Goddess is a complex and diverse expression of the divine feminine. For anyone who worships her, she will give them consistent opportunities to grow and learn by connecting to her three aspects. It doesn't matter if you recognize her as an ancient goddess, or as a part of the Triple Goddess. You could just choose to honor the Maiden, Mother or Crone archetype. You might make a conscious effort to line up your worship with the Moon phases for a deeper and more rewarding spiritual connection.

Why You Should Use or Wear the Symbol?

You don't need to convert to Wicca or Paganism to enjoy this symbol. If you have been wearing it, it might be nice to know its meaning. Wearing this symbol could be a wonderful reminder that you are constantly connected to the divine feminine and all she represents. It is a reminder of the flow of life, birth, death, and rebirth. If you use this symbol in your sacred space or on your altar, it could help bring you that energy.

Chapter 5: MORE

So what is a Wiccan Symbol? Well, in simple terms, it's anything representing Wicca. There are four common categories that Wiccan symbols fall into. Those are items used when practicing Wicca, things that are linked historically to Wicca, symbols for the Gods and Goddesses, and symbols that have been adopted by Wiccans over the years. In this section I'll discuss some of the common symbols you'll run across and what they mean. This is by no means a complete list. I'm just pointing out some of the ones I think you should know starting out. You'll learn about much more during your future studies.

Ankh

Also known as the "Cross of Life". This has been adopted as a Wiccan symbol over the years but is originally based in Egyptian lore. The Ankh is a union of the God and Goddess symbols. Those being the oval of the female Goddess and the staff or cross of the God. It is meant to symbolize the universe's creative power.

Aura

This is the field of energy that surrounds things, especially living things. Everything either living or not living has an aura, as everything is made from energy. Many people perceive an aura as either light or color. Wiccans develop their abilities to try and sense these fields of energy.

Bat

These have become Wiccan symbols for a few reasons. Some of these reasons are because of their night time affinity. Another is because they use different senses than most to maneuver. Also, they are thought to have shamanic power in many circles.

Bonfire

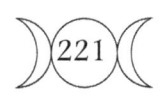

Things like bonfires represent the Fire element. Fire is considered to be the main transformative force in nature and represents Divine Light. Fire is normally invoked at most, if not every, Wiccan celebration. It's said when you jump through a Bonfire you are momentarily passing through a purifying flame. That means once you've passed through, you'll come out on the other end cleansed. Most Wiccans will often jump through the fire two times. The first time is to purge away the old while the second time is to empower all the new. Prior to jumping the first time, you declare or think of what you want to release from your life. Prior to jumping the second time, you set yourself an intention of what you want to bring into your life.

Cats

These creatures are often thought to perceive things that are beyond our own physical world. Cats are thought to be sensitive to many different types of energy and are seen as making a great companion to a Wiccan working magick. Many Wiccans believe that cats can protect a Wiccan while their working, while also acting as a messenger to the spirit realm. This makes them ideal familiars.

Circle

This is a prominent Wicca symbol. The Spiral of Life, Circle of Earth and Wheel of the Year are all based off the circle and the importance of nature's cyclical existence. This is why Wiccans often gather in Circles when doing spells, celebrations, and rituals.

Cloak

They have a symbolic function in Wicca. They are like Robes in that they cover us without being restrictive. This allows open space so that the Divine can enter. They also are great from a practical viewpoint as they can hide pockets carrying all your tools and implements.

Crone

This is a stage of life in women and one aspect of the concept known as Triple Goddess. The Crone is normally considered to be the Goddess of Wisdom. That's because she no longer sheds her wise lunar blood but instead keeps it within her body. Wiccans to this day still venerate the Crone. They have a perception of power bestowed upon them by years of knowledge and experience. Many Wiccans will actually celebrate when they go through Croning themselves, holding a ritual of passage once they've reached the end of menopause.

Divination

Most Wiccans perform some type of divination. These can include Scrying, Tea Leaves, Dowsing, Tarot Cards, and Palm Reading. In reality, Wiccans are constantly reading messages that are sent from the Divine. These messages come in sudden ideas, life events, feelings, and coincidences.

Dogs

Dogs, especially black ones, are heavily identified with Wiccans as their Familiars.

Dowsing

This is when Wiccans search for things that are hidden by using a crystal, stick, or some other form of tool. Dowsing is commonly used to find water, minerals, oils or anything else a Wiccan might need or be drawn to. Depending on what you're dowsing for depends on what type of tool you may need to use, For example, Willow works well for dowsing for water.

Energy

Energy work is a classic Wicca symbol. The idea of raising, shifting and directing energy is what Wicca is about in many respects.

Evil Eye

This one has become more and more closely associated with Wicca and Witches over the years. The Evil Eye comes from a myth about the Goddess Maat, and how her All Seeing Eye was able to tell a person's soul by just having a glance at them. Over time, this idea of telling and assessing a person's soul turned into cursing a person's soul at just a glance. Since receiving the Evil Eye is mainly seen as being given by a woman, the cures for the Evil Eye derive from symbols that are feminine or Goddess in nature. Those symbols include Black Cats, Cowrie Shells, and Kali's Black Pot.

Familiars

This is a popular Wicca symbol. Any animal may be a Familiar to a Wiccan. Some are more helpful in terms of practicing Witchcraft.

Animals closely associated as common Familiars are Cats, Bats, Black Dogs, Frogs, Snakes, Ravens, and Owls.

Feather

This is a Wicca symbol that represents the ability of flight, and our spirit's freedom to gain access to different realms. Feathers are most commonly used to represent the Air element when placed on a Wiccan Altar. One thing to note is feathers should always be purified or blessed before being used.

Frogs

In Wicca, these animals are known for their ability to move freely between worlds. That's because they both live on land and water. Wiccans relate to this because they live in both the spiritual world and mundane world.

Ghost

Ghosts symbolize the time of year when those who've passed can once again revisit this world. Wiccans are known for communicating with their loved ones even after they've passed much like in many other cultures and religions.

Goddess

Many Wiccans wear the Goddess symbol as she is interwoven with most Wiccan rituals and beliefs. People worship different Goddesses. For example, the Earth Goddess, the Moon Goddess, the Triple Goddess and the Star Goddess. There are hundreds of Gods and Goddesses to choose from. Each culture has their own rich history filled with different deities.

Grove

This is a small forest known as a traditional place of worship for Wiccans. This is often compared to a Wiccan cathedral. You have the trees acting as guardians, and under the moon and stars, you feel the Divine presence around you.

Herbs

Wicca is known for its association with nature-based healing. This is primarily done through the use of herbs, poultices, and different teas. Herbs play an important role in Wiccan spells and are often used as both magical and healing agents.

Incense

This is a Wiccan tool that also carries symbolic meaning. Smoke is representative of our intentions and prayers rising upwards towards the Divine. Certain scents given off by incense have the power to shift our conscious mind to the energy in plants. Incense is often seen on Wiccan altars representing the Air element.

Menstruation

This is sacred to Wiccans. The reason for this is that it is the magical and voluntary shedding of life essence, a woman's blood, without any wounds or harm. The word itself is derived from the word "moon". It's connection to one of the world's greatest powers, a woman's ability to give birth makes it sacred in many circles.

Midwife

Midwives have held a close association with Witchcraft for a long time. This is due to their ability to heal using both their skills and herbs. Midwives are also attendants to birth, the gateway from the realm of spirit to our physical world. They have the ability to change an outcome on whether a newborn is born healthy or dies during labor.

Mirror

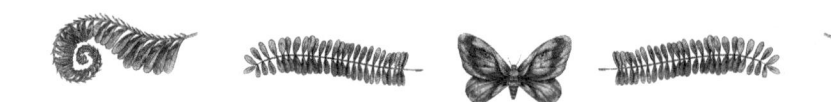

This is a Wiccan ritual symbol and tool. They are believed to directly reflect a person's soul. The mirror is representative of the Divine, reflected in a form we can see in the physical world. It is said that when one looks in a Wiccan ritual mirror they have the ability to see the God or Goddess that is within them. It acknowledges the belief that everything is the Divine.

This tool is often used in divination. For example, some look into mirrors to try and see into the future. It's important as both a tool and as a symbol.

Book 8:
Wicca vs Voodoo

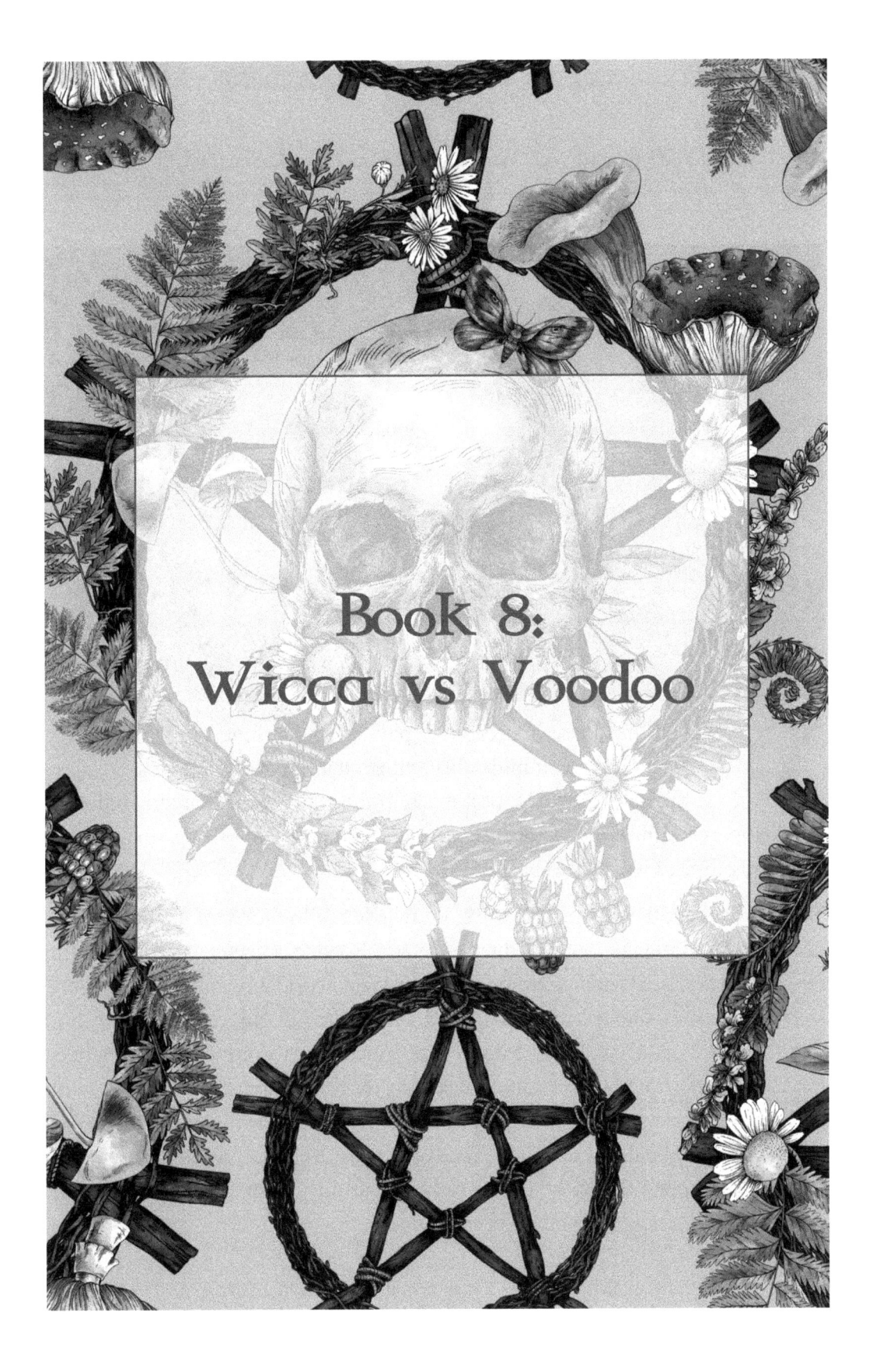

Chapter 1: Understanding Essence of Voodoo

When that sense of order is expanded to the philosophies of life and spirituality, you must also realize that the overwhelming power of the natural world, our space in the ecology of the food chain, the nurturing or harmful effects of flora on our state, and everything surrounding us in the physical world also take part in the hierarchy.

Thus, respecting the power of nature, knowledge of the force of a single root to heal or cause damage also becomes a part of Voodoo. Furthermore, when this sense of order is expanded beyond the physical world into metaphysical and spiritual realms, the spirits that passed on before us, ancestors of our own physical lineages as well as philosophical ancestors to our beliefs, practices, forms of Voodoo and other traditional religiospiritual systems, followed by saints and other notable spirits which possessed "power" in their physical life, as well as nonhuman beings—whether good or bad, holy or unholy, divine or otherwise—topped finally by deities, all form an up-down system of hierarchy which must be respected and revered.

Thus, in the end, every facet of Voodoo—from spirit possession to divination, and from its rituals, beats, rhythms, and spells to its forms of worship—revolves around understanding the relevance of the wisdom passed down to us without conceit, and appreciating the awesome chasm which lies between someone who is yet to embark on any path of spirituality with someone who has dedicated their life to it. This facet has passed on into the next state of being, and is transmitting that knowledge back down to us mortals with the added benefit of their unmatched experiences of the phases of living and dying.

Moreover, many Vodouisants consider this hierarchy so allinclusive that they don't differentiate between any forms of their own religion with those of others which may respect and honor elders and the order of the universe. This is why you may also come across many Houngans and Mambos, male and female Vodou priests respectively, who may also be initiated in the ways of Santeria (though they may hate to call it by this name, as this was a Spanish term coined by outsiders) and Candomblé, or many others who may not even differentiate between themselves and followers of other syncretic religions if the question comes to spiritual compatibility or to allow others uninitiated in their ways to take part in rituals or gatherings.

Lastly, unlike many other religions where spiritual help is preconditioned upon crossing their exclusive rite of initiation, Voodoo does not ask for seekers of knowledge or spiritual peace to meet pre-set requisites before help, guidance, or even future advice is offered by the spirits to other initiated practitioners in their name. Since everyone is part of the same order, anyone can access its benefits—however, perceiving said benefits yourself requires immense dedication.

Chapter 2: Preparing Yourself for Spells and Protection

I hope Voodoo is a new name for an amalgamation of immensely old systems which can be traced back at least seven thousand years in their making, if not more. However, unlike popular thought that mixing between faith systems somehow muddles up the original message and dilutes them down, Voodoo has only ever incorporated within itself beliefs that resonated with the worldwide wisdom of the ancients—that the Earth and its various component elements are not to be messed with; that there is an order to everything which cannot be ignored or surpassed, regardless of conceit or self-deception; that the soul isn't an energy which simply disperses after death, but retains its conscious form long enough to alter the workings of the world.

As an end result, Voodoo has taken the best of each system which encountered it in the past, and has expanded it till every practitioner within its folds can sharpen themselves to a honed spiritual edge depending on their intent, and yet not be able to even scratch the surface of the ultimate wisdom, nature, and understanding of Voodoo as a whole. In fact, any assertion that two practitioners would view Voodoo in the same way if they've had different teachers even in the same geographical neighborhood is entirely erroneous—much less if they were practicing it in different states or nations.

Even when Voodoo was under threat by Christianity in the beginning, it assimilated itself in a way that allowed it to nurture the same age-old bonds with Lwa and their previous beliefs—the only difference being that they equated each Lwa to a corresponding Saint, and took up their traditional prayers for said Lwa on the day attributed to that specific Saint. However, this doesn't mean that they weren't true Christians either, with Popes in the past as well having attended some positive Voodoo rituals, and commenting on the Christian piety of many Vodouisants. That was because the spirituality in this belief system was inherently strong enough to allow themselves to adapt and survive through their rituals, rather than feel insecure about their innate message being lost by adopting the mantle of a threatening religious system. What these seemingly segmented pieces of information is leading up to is this—throw away your notions that this is a spiritual form which can be easily entered, accessed, or even understood by someone unwilling to dedicate immense effort to the cause of unlocking its secrets. However, the spells and rituals may still be powerful enough for some uninitiated foolhardy dummy to cause damage to themselves and the ones they love, through misfired magic. Therefore, there are several preparations required to safely and successfully navigating these complex beginnings, without the hands-on help and guidance of a mentor.

The first thing which you need to understand is that excessive emotions and passions are a hindrance to practice, especially if you're a neophyte. In fact, those who try to break through this block with force of emotions alone may find themselves on the path of Bokors, and away from true Voodoo. That's because you need a calm mind to access the spiritual world, and an absence of ego and pride when conversing with spirits ages older and wiser, and infinitely more powerful than you. Therefore, the very first preparation needs to be engaging in meditative practices to control and overcome emotional turbulences. This will also help you understand and surpass petty fears and insecurities which may lead you down dangerous paths once you gain some proficiency in practice. As well, it will stop you from fighting when you engage in spirit possession after calling upon a Lwa. This is primarily because the main method of communication with spirits is by letting them inside yourself as the medium—though trust me on this, you're still light years away from attempting anything of that sort; said practices only being reliably invoked once you reach the level of priests, which means that you will already have had immense tutoring by Vodouisant mentors. However, it's a good foundation to build upon, and a great framework on which you can construct a positive experience and outlook as a Voodoo practitioner.

The next thing which you need to engage in, before attempting any spell or ritual, is self-purification. This is most commonly achieved through ritual bathing, using ingredients like sage, sandalwood powder, salt, mint, etc. in bath water. The biggest reason for this practice is to rid yourself of all residual negative energies which you may have picked up through touch or association while venturing outside, or even the same from your own surroundings—which is why burning sage at home before attempting any ritual is of primary importance. Other than purification before rituals, another great advantage of ritual bathing is that it can rid you of fatigue or emotional drains which may have latched on to you through outside sources or environments, and will give you a spiritual cleansing that will allow your own positivity to surface in everyday interactions.

The last preparation lies in the making of a Voodoo altar. Now, while you have access to Papa Legba, all the Ghede Lwa, and your ancestral spirits, beyond that the Lwa only respond to those for whom they may have an affinity. Since this differs from person to person, the only accurate way to create an altar dedicated to Lwa who **will** respond to you and will allow you to serve them, is by getting a reading from a mentor or another Voodoo practitioner. The Lwa only respond to people who have character attributes with which the specific spirits themselves can resonate, and so your reading will determine the way your altar looks in the end. Therefore, no, you don't choose the spirits which you serve as a basic practitioner, but rather the spirits choose if they will allow you to serve them.

However, for a **very** basic altar, there are very few requirements—since Papa Legba and the Ghedes are about all that are available to everyone right off the bat. All you need is a clean space—put a white table cloth on it for the Rada side as well as some black and red fabric for the space which specifically denotes Papa Legba, put a cross or crucifix in the center, arrange the symbols of your most beloved ancestors on the other side from the cross. Always have a bowl of clean and pure water, which is to be replaced as often as needed. Keep burning sage and purifying incense whenever you wish to pray to them. Present white flowers to Papa Legba's side, along with funerary flowers to your ancestors. Keep in mind that the flowers have to be real and changed as often as necessary to always keep them fresh. Make sure that the offerings of water and flowers are in separate vessels for each of the sides of your altar. Moreover, if you're creating a side on the altar for Papa Legba—as you always should—draw or recreate his **veve** symbol on a weave and place that at the altar. With this, your basic altar is complete. Aside from them, some of the other required tools are drums to create a conducive energetic atmosphere to incite the chosen spirits into visiting you. However, since you'll probably be a sole practitioner at first, search for specific music and chants dedicated to the spirit of your choice, and play that in the background to create the proper environment.

Chapter 3: Learning Basic Voodoo Spells

3.1 Healing Stone

This spell is meant to help relieve problems from physical ailments. This comes from old traditions and works on the principle of moving the disease or problem to a non-living object. In the past, people often believed that they could move their issues to an animal. For example, if they rubbed a toad over their body, their warts would go away. Don't worry though; we won't be using any toads. All you are going to need is a stone. The best place to find your stone is near a body of water, like a river, because a smooth, oval, white stone works best.

You are going to need:

- White stone
- White thread about 2 feet long
- A needle
- A piece of linen that is big enough to wrap your stone
- Matches
- White tea-light
- Nail

The best time to do this is during a Monday during a waning moon. Start by visualizing a giant white cross. This cross should be so big that it fills your entire room. Then, pick up the nail and carve a cross symbol into the tea-light candle so that the wick of the candle is in the middle of the cross.

As you light the candle, say: "Sick things are now burning, and disease is waning." Create a small bag from the piece of linen. Fold the linen in half and take the needle and thread and stitch up both sides of the linen.

Next, pick up the stone and touch the areas of the body where you are suffering from a disease or problem. As you do this, picture how all of your problems are moving out of your body and into the stone as a gray smoke. Continue to do this until you feel that you have done it for long enough.

Make sure you feel those words as you say them. Concentrate on the feelings of relief and joy that you are getting rid of your disease and are once again healthy.

Once you have finished, place the stone inside of the bag and then toss it into a natural and flowering water source.

3.2 Spell for Healing Sorrows

This is meant to burn away bad emotions or sorrows. This spell helps to support you in order to solve your problems in a magical way. Make sure you remember spells like this you can't solve all of your problems.

In the end, if you are feeling extremely sad and this spell doesn't seem to help, then you may need to meet with a medical professional to get more help. This spell can help you to name the problem and to focus on the solution.

You are going to need:

- The dried hull from five oranges
- Yarrow and dry mint
- Paper
- Quill and red ink
- Tea-light candle
- Lighter or matches
- Dry wood for a fire

You need to make sure that you have a quiet place to perform this outside. It is best done after sunset and during the waning moon.

Start by creating yourself a magic circle and then create a bonfire using the dry wood. Make sure that you have a safe place for the fire and that it won't catch anything on fire.

Start by visualizing a cross in a bright white light. Next, light your tea-light candle and then, on your paper, write down all of your problems that you are feeling right now. Pick up your dried mint and toss it into the fire. As you do so, say: "I am clearing you away." Then pick up the yarrow and toss it into the fire.

As you do, say: "I am free now." Then toss in the paper with all of your problems written on it.

Then toss in the dried orange hulls. As you do, say: "Only sweetness remains, my sorrow is away." Watch the first until it has gone out completely. Once it has burned out, you should bury the ashes as far away from your home as you can.

3.3 Money Magic Ritual

You are going to need:

- Two small pieces of coconut or wood
- Red wine
- Oil
- Bones
- Heart meat
- Candle wick
- A coconut

When you make this candle, you want to do so in a way that provides you with a strong connection to it. First, you will need to cut the coconut in half. You may have to have this done for you since an actual coconut is very hard. Then place three stones under the coconut to help stabilize it so that it doesn't end up falling over. It is also a good idea to place the coconut in the middle of a fire-proof tray with high sides just encase the oil ends up leaking. Don't take any of the pulp out of the coconut. The pulp is what helps to keep the oil from leaking out.

Next, take the bones and then push it into the heart meat. Sit the heart meat and bone into the coconut and then add in seven drops of the red wine on the top. As you drip the wine into the coconut, verbalize your wishes and call upon Legba.

Next, you will pour the oil over the heart meat and the bone. Make sure that you don't fill the coconut more than half full. As you pour the oil into the coconut, concentrate on Legba and your lamp. Take the sticks or coconut and place them over the top in the shape of an X. You can also attach them together like this using string or a candle wick. Place the wick between the wood pieces and very carefully place it inside of the oil. You want the bottom of the wick to be submerged. You can now light the lamp. The goal is to keep it burning until you have gotten exactly what you have asked for.

3.4 Banishing Spell

This spell can help you cut the link to your past. Your past can have an influence on your present life in negative ways. There might be some experiences you had in your life that still bother you. These can be harmful and can cause negativity to come your way. This could be childhood trauma, an accident, bad relationships, etc. There are two levels to this spell. The first is magical since we are influencing the flow of energy while cutting the link to our past so it can't get to us. The second is therapeutic since we are finding out problems, accepting them, and then letting them go.

You are going to need:

- List of your past bad experiences
- A cauldron of fireproof dish
- Scissors
- 8.25 inches black cord
- Dark blue candle
- Salt
- Lighter or matches
- Purification incense
- Charcoal disk in a fireproof dish

If you are familiar with Tarot, you can use the Death card for your ritual. This will symbolize the end of your suffering. Death has to come first, so new life can begin. Death clears a path for the new you.

The best time to do this spell would be on a Saturday during the dark moon. If the dark moon doesn't fall on a Saturday, it will be fine to do this on that day.

Ritual Preparation

The first thing you need to do is write out a list of past experiences that you want to get rid of. The best time to do this is the day after the dark moon. You will then work each day, getting your list ready. This means that you will be working on this list for 28 days. Each day you work on it, it is giving the ritual more power.

Each day while working on your list, you will say this to every experience: "I accept you as you are. Thank you for the lesson you gave me. From now, you have no power over me. You are free, and I am free. Goodbye."

You aren't going to feel anything at first. You might even feel some resistance. Just do it. Think about all the relief you are going to feel once you have done this ritual.

Continue doing this until the dark moon comes around again. Then, do the ritual. Once the ritual is over, you need to burn the list and put the ashes into flowing water.

Ritual

- Cast your circle using salt.
- Place the incense on the charcoal. Relax and notice how the smoke is purifying the room.
- Tie a know onto the left end of the cord. This is your past. Tie a different knot onto the right end of the cord. This is your future that is free from all these past experiences.
- Ask your higher power of love and light to come help you.

You have two options here about how to get rid of the connection between your future and your past. The first option is to take hold of your past in your left hand while you hold the future in your right. Hold the cord over the flame and allow it to burn the cord into two pieces. The second option is to use a pair of scissors and cut the connection between your past and future. Take a few minutes to see which one "feels" better to you.

Once you have cut the connection, place the knot that represented your past with your list into the cauldron of another fireproof dish. Light them and let them burn completely.

Sit down, relax, and meditate. Pray to your higher power. Thank them for their help.

To end the ritual, close your circle. If you live near a body of running water, place the ashes into the water. If not, find a hill and let the wind carry them away.

Chapter 4: Difference Between Wicca and Voodoo

4.1 Wicca

4.1.1 What Is Wicca?

Wicca is an eclectic faith focusing around gods, goddesses, and nature worship. A popular Wiccan writer name Gary Cantrell, says that Wicca is primarily based on "harmony with nature and all aspects of the god and goddess theology." The practice of Wicca involves nature control done via various rites to gain prestige, power, admiration, or other things that they want. It makes use of icons in its rituals and adheres to their own chronology in relation to Wiccan celebrations.

Its origins are in antique agrarian Celtic community. It is perceived as Neo-Pagan. There is no hierarchical clergy structure in Wicca. What is does have are priestesses or priests which equates to a position of leadership inside covens that contains witches. Wicca's diverse traditions have various requirements for obtaining positions of leadership. The well-renowned variations of Wiccan belief are Alexandrian, 1734, Dianic, Celtic, Eclectic, Dicordian, Georgian, and Gardenian. Wicca is also acknowledged as its own religion within the armed forces of different countries.

One of Wicca's standard ways of working creed is the teaching of karma and embodiment. Reincarnation's purpose is for the reincarnated individual to be taught lessons via the numerous lives it will lead. This process of rebirth is duplicated in multiple life spans until the spirit is enhanced. This enhancement is characterized by a spirit merger with the creator. The spirits are delivered back to whoever that Wiccan coven considers as Goddess or God. Karma, which governs the cause and effect law, does not reward or punish. Karma is considered by many as an all-encompassing law that reacts accordingly to any type of cause until dissonance is rooted out.

Wicca doesn't assert itself as the sole way but states that all faithbased religions are legitimate to the individuals who use them. It welcomes the truth that all forms of life are valuable, including animal, plant and human."

Typically, Wiccans refuse to acknowledge the devil's existence (They do not worship Lucifer/Satan). They do not perform group sex or any vulgar displays of sexual activity in their rites (although some Wiccan practices exercise nudity and sex not privy to the general public), no sex with animals, and no sacrifice of blood. In Wicca, casting spells to harm people is forbidden. They argue that moral absolutes do not exist, acknowledge nature's divinity, and aims to have a symbiotic relationship with nature.

Wiccans abide by two main rules. One of these rules is the Wiccan Credo that specifies that you can do anything that you wish as long as it does not harm anybody in the process. The second rule states that any kind of deed, whether good or bad, that you perform will come back to you threefold. This is pretty much selfexplanatory.

According to Wiccan belief, an all-encompassing life force referred to as "The All" or "The One" brought forth the female and male life aspects in this world. The Holy One, goddess or god, depends on the individual that you're conversing with, can possess various names. References to multiple deities from other beliefs: Buddhism, Sumerian, Egyptian, Christian, Greek, Hinduism, etc. can also be made. Wicca doesn't put much importance on giving names to a Wiccan's perception of God. A Wiccan may also consider its deity to be consciously aware of itself, while another Wiccan may not. Everything depends on a Wiccan's perception of whatever works best. Wiccan faith is solely based on self-design. Wicca acknowledges the fact that god can showcase distinctive traits in various ways to a diverse group of individuals. Therefore, Wiccans may have varied ideas of God.

Wicca is enticing for individuals who don't yearn or welcome absolute truths. A person has the freedom to find out their individual "path" in Wicca. To put it differently, they have the freedom to come up with a belief that best serves their desires.

It should be clear that Wicca is a faith of individual preference. This basically means you are free to create, formulate, and develop a religion that meets your personal wants and passions. Also, in Wicca you may attempt to manipulate your surroundings and other men and women by using spells and incantations. This blend of establishing a belief that suits your individual preferences and trying to affect others is very attractive to so many individuals.

4.1.2 The History of Wicca

In 1954, a retired civil servant named Gerald Gardener published a book titled, "Witchcraft Today". In his book, he disclosed that he had been initiated into an English coven, and was himself a practicing Witch—essentially outing himself from the broom closet. Since the mid-1500s, there had been a succession of laws in England, Wales, and Scotland governing Witchcraft. The Witchcraft Act of 1542 forbad the practice, stating it was a felony and a crime punishable by death. Almost 200 years later, the Witchcraft Act of 1735 replaced the penalties for **practicing** with penalties for the **false pretense** of practicing. For another 216 years, those who claimed to have magickal powers or occult knowledge of any kind faced charges of fraud and vagrancy. Gardener's courageous publication about Witchcraft being alive and well, despite centuries of persecution, came only three years after all laws against the Craft had been repealed. The response to his book from other underground Witches was enormous.

Having spent his life studying religion and magickal practices around the world, Gardener is credited with collecting historically ravaged and scattered beliefs, adding to them, and organizing them all into what we know today as Wicca. Through a revision of his coven's Book of Shadows—a book where rites and rituals are recorded—Gardener managed to provide the first guidebook for his Wiccan initiates.

In the 1960s, Gardnerian Witchcraft became the very first Wiccan tradition. Initiation into the coven was required. Covens were autonomous, but structured by a degree system in which only High Priestesses could form additional covens and initiate members. Gardener himself initiated many High Priestesses into his coven. In this manner, the Gardnerian tradition branched out into numerous covens, spreading Wicca across the United Kingdom and eventually into the United States.

It was customary for a newly-formed coven to copy the parent coven's Book of Shadows and to add their own discoveries, effectively advancing the information. Through this continuous modification of the central doctrine, several alternative Wiccan paths have been forged such as: Alexandrian Wicca, Dianic, SeaxWicca, British Traditional Wicca, Georgian, and many others.

The aforementioned Wiccan traditions still follow the convention of keeping their information initiatory and oathbound, meaning initiation into a coven is required to practice under those denominations. However, these days, the number of solitary witches that practice a form of Eclectic Wicca seems to exceed the number of formal initiates in more dogmatic forms of Wicca. This contemporary tradition is also known as Neo Wicca, and will be the focus of this book.

Securing together **all** forms of Wicca are the sturdy, common threads of Witchcraft and Paganism. In other words, Wicca as a formal religion may appear to be structurally loose and infinitesimally young in comparison to its Abrahamic kin. However, its roots, philosophy, and use of Witchcraft encompass over 30,000 years of aboriginal spiritual beliefs.

4.2 Wiccan Beliefs

4.2.1 Reincarnation

Just like many religions, some Wiccan's believe in reincarnation. Reincarnation is known as one's spirit or soul coming back after they have passed away and being placed into another living being whether it be an animal or a human.

Most of the time, the reincarnated comes back as an animal and the animal depends on how you lived your life during your years alive. Something such as a butterfly is said to be someone who has lived an extremely good life and done everything that they possibly could to live it the way that they were supposed to.

However, it is also believed that you are reincarnated to watch over your family. This can be either a blessing or a curse depending on how you look at it. Not all Wiccan's believe in reincarnation. If you believe in it is up to what type of Wiccan you practice as well as your own personal beliefs.

4.2.2 Afterlife

This is does not occupy a central place in the Wiccan religion. It is believed that everything that happens in a Wiccan's present life is more important than what happens in their next life because that is just a benefit from how they lived their life on this plane.

Many Wiccan's do not actually believe in the afterlife because they do not believe that the soul actually survives after the death of your body.

Depending on what you believe, there are different believes based on the afterlife. There is a Hawaiian religion that believes that the body has three souls.

Essentially, the belief of what happens to you in the afterlife is a personal decision rather than a religious one.

4.2.3 Animism

This is the belief that animals and plants as well as many other inanimate objects actually possess a spiritual essence.

This is more so a belief system that came from indigenous tribes but has been adopted by many religions.

Animism is said to be the most common foundational thread of indigenous people's spiritual or supernatural perspectives.

When you look at the Wiccan religion as an earth religion, they believe that everything has a spirt and should not be harmed. Hence why one of the rules of the religion is to do no harm to others. It is also believed that anything that has a spirit can be communicated with and animals can actually act as spiritual helpers or guides.

It is even believed that the earth has a soul and that her name is Gaia which is the ancient Greek goddess of the Earth.

4.2.4 Other Occult Systems

Polytheism is the belief in multiple gods and goddesses. Depending on which Wiccan sect that you belong to, depends on if you only worship the God and

Goddess or if you worship the multiple deities that are associated with the Wiccan religion.

Some of these are not actually viewed as literal entities but more as psychological constructs that exist within the human psyche. Some even believe that the Gods and Goddesses that they worship have physical forms and walk the earth amongst us unknown to anyone as to who they are. So, they believe that you are to treat everyone as you would want to be treated because

you never truly know who you are talking to.

When it comes to Mortality, Wiccan's believe that there is no true dogmatic or ethical code that that is followed by all Wiccan's universally. However, there is a code known as Wiccan Rede that actually is followed by most of the Wiccan's known as "and it harm none, do what ye will."

4.3 Voodoo

4.3.1 What Is Voodoo?

"Voodoo" is an indigenous West African religious and spiritual system that has been spread and disseminated throughout the rest of the world with the forced migration of Western African peoples through the Atlantic Slave trade that operated from the 15th to the 17th centuries.

Voodoo is an African term for "spirit," and this belief system essentially combines animism, nature worship, and ancestory worship, together with a belief in a Supreme Being and in spirits (also called Loas or Iwas) that actively intervene in the world of the living. Much of Voodoo practices and traditions are centered around the honor and reverence given these spirits, who are thus invoked for the guidance, wisdom and protection which they bestow upon the living.

While the basic philosophies of Voodoo seem simple enough, the evolution of the practice and growth of Voodoo throughout the years can be traced by following the fate of those West Africans captured and sold as slaves, and who were thereafter brought to America.

4.3.2 History of Voodoo

Not much is really known about the origins of Voodoo other than that it originated in Africa, and that its pattern of dissemination throughout the rest of the world, as well as its consequent evolution, is closely tied with the history of the Atlantic slave trade.

Some claim that Voodoo is an ancient spiritual practice, and is as old as humanity itself. A tall claim - but not so implausible when you consider that Africa is considered to be the oldest inhabited territory on earth, and according to most paleontologists, is also the continent from which the human species originated.

But Africa at present is a diverse continent consisting of 54 states, thousands of languages spoken, a great number of indigenous groups, and a wide variety of religious beliefs. Africa has a very long history of contact with other countries, many of which brought their cultures and religions with them. Some say that Voodoo originated in the Slave Coast of West Africa, specifically the country Benin (formerly Dahomey), but this is likely due to the fact that the Atlantic slave trade grew from developments in seafaring technologies that allowed European seafarers to navigate the Atlantic Ocean, thus bringing them into contact with societies and settlements along the West African coast, from what is now Senegal and Gambia to the Congo region. This promoted a new route for the slave trade from the African continent to the New World of North and South America.

At this time, the major religions of Christianity and Islam already existed in Africa - brought by the expanding civilizations of the early Roman empire and early Arabian Islamic Caliphates. These two major religions coexisted with the traditional African religions - including Voodoo. These days, the diversity of religious beliefs in Africa is still the same, although it is now mixed in with small smatterings of Africans who are Hindu, Jews, Buddhists, Confucians, and Baha'i. Many of the basic practices of Voodoo are traditional - utilizing a mixture of earth and spirit worship, animism, mysticism, ancestor worship, deities, as well as ritualistic practices.

It is estimated that some 10.24 million African slaves were brought to the Americas during the height of the Atlantic slave trade, some 3 million of which were exported out of the coast of Benin - and this lasted from 1650 to 1900, until the eventual abolition of slavery and the worldwide outlawing of slavery. This was later followed by voluntary migration of Africans as freed men, crossing the Atlantic in great numbers in what is now known as a new wave or cycle of the African diaspora. Whether slave or freedmen however, the Africans brought with them their culture and way of life, including their traditional religious practices, including Voodoo.

In fact, long centuries of enforced slavery and servitude to European masters in the Americas and the West Indies had created what might be considered optimal conditions for the embracing of Voodoo - and Voodoo has undergone its own rebirth as it is practiced today in different parts of the world. While in its original essence it is still being practiced today in its home ground of West Africa, Voodoo has evolved in the lands of the New World where it took new root among the displaced Africans. Part of it may have been due to the conditions of slavery itself, and the necessary secrecy of practicing a slave religion that was suppressed by many of the European masters. But part of Voodoo's evolution was also a result of syncretism - with Christianity and indigenous American traditions - and is a living religion practiced today in countries such as Haiti, Puerto Rico, Cuba, the Dominican Republic, Brazil, and Louisiana. Though it is certainly interesting to note that the growth, practice and development of Voodoo in each of these areas is quite different.

4.4 Voodoo Beliefs and Practices

4.4.1 Voodoo Rituals and Ceremonies

Rituals and ceremonies are huge when it comes to Voodoo. The religion is all about connecting with Lwas and the only known way that mortals can connect with them is through these specialized rituals and ceremonies.

Often led by Hougans (priests) and Mambos (priestesses) they are taught the process of summoning a Loa and Lwas.

Public rituals and ceremonies required lots of people. Not only the Houngan and Mambo participate in the events but hundreds of Voodooists are present as well, in Haiti when rituals are held in was known that people will go door to door alerting everybody that a ritual is about to take place. With that being said

Voodooists are very close to other Voodooists

Houngans and Mambos usually take charge in these rituals and their jobs consists of preparing and directing the ritual.

These rituals are usually held outside at night and the center will be a "Poto Mitan" which is a spiritual pole that connects the visible world to the invisible world. A Hougan or Mambo will then instruct drummers to repeat certain beats while the others will dance, sing, and chant while circling the Poto Mitan. Movement and noises are essential for these rituals, as it shows the Loas that there is movement and life among Earth and they are being called for.

To call on specific Loas, there must be specific things required such as specific chants, colors, objects and as well with the Loa's veve. A veve is a religious symbol drawn on the ground with cornmeal, sand, or other powdery substances that is used to call down the certain Loas.

After the daily chants and rituals, the Lwa will then showcase itself to the participants. They cannot be seen through the eyes of mortals, so the Lwa will need to find a human host, thus possession occur.

When the Lwa finds a human host, the host will showcase itself with certain behaviors in order for the practitioners to realize that a Loa was summoned. This means that the host will sometimes act like the Lwa from within the host.

After realizing the presence of the Lwa, it is then to begin the feeding or offering process. The Loa will then be presented with offerings and animal sacrifices must occur. The reason why is that the Lwas are too drained from their jobs and by taking the life of an animal it will restore their souls. Think of it like feeding or giving the Lwa a break for their services. By doing animal sacrifice during these rituals you will have a stronger relationship with the Lwas and make them happier.

After the Lwa is replenished, interaction will occur. Hougans and Mambos alongside its Voodoo practitioners will ask for advice or for blessings about a particular thing that they are needing or wanting. Almost always Loas will carry out what is being asked for as their job is to make sure people are just happy with their circumstances that they've created.

Lastly, the attenders of the ritual and the Lwa will exchange in goodbyes and leave to return back to the Vilokan or to other ceremonies that is being called for.

4.4.2 Voodoo and Healing

The central idea of Voodoo is healing people from illnesses and improving their own lives by these majestic spirits of Lwas. These healing activities contribute to the majority of all Voodoo activities. Voodoo Houngans, Mambos, and doctors participate in healing with herbs, faith healing (With the assistance of Lwas and other spirits) and, today even with modern medicine.

One of the most important reasons why spirits are summoned during these Voodoo rituals are to ask for good health and to heal the sick and the injured.

4.4.3 Voodoo and Catholicism

When West African Voodoo slaves were brutally forced to work on plantations in Haiti, many of their slave masters forced them to get rid of their original religious beliefs of Voodoo and to adopt Roman Catholicism instead. Though the slaves were forced to believe in the religion, they did not give up their own religious beliefs as well, instead they've merged both religions together into what is known as Haitian Voodoo. Voodoo and Catholicism have been closed to the same teachings and beliefs as one another.

As a matter of fact, Pope John Paul II has spoken about the Voodoo religion, quoting that it is a "fundamental goodness" because of the many people that have been healed from illnesses and injuries through this supernatural religion.

Many Voodooists are even known to have been baptized but are facing heavy criticism from the Catholic community for participating in Voodoo ceremonies. As of today, religious leaders are currently working together to bring peace and wealth to Africa, as well a clear understanding of beliefs.

Chapter 5: Elements of Voodoo

Throughout the years, Voodoo has proven itself to be an adaptable, growing, and evolving religion - a testament, perhaps, to the resilience of the Africans who were sold in slavery and who kept its practice alive throughout their servitude. But Voodoo is perhaps also one of the most misunderstood religions in the world - mainly because what little we know of it is based on what we have seen in films or read about in books. But all of it is fiction and their sole purpose is to entertain.

But while none of these fictional accounts presume to teach factual history, the impression it has made on the public mind certainly has been remarkable. Perhaps because Voodoo rituals are so rich in color, so different in context, language, and worldview from the main world religions, that people cannot help but be impressed by these selected presentations of what are really only small portions of this religion. These days, the word Voodoo raises images of zombies and dolls with pins sticking out of them - but this is only what media has conditioned our minds to automatically assume when we hear the word voodoo.

In this chapter, we take a closer look at some of the essential elements of the practice of Voodoo, its cosmology, and how it affects and influences the lifestyle and worldview of its practitioners.

5.1 Belief in a Divine Creator

Even before the arrival of the major religions of Christianity and

Islam, the Voudons believed in a supreme being or a divine creator which they call Mahou, or Mawu. This is a transcendent Supreme Being, the creator of the universe and the world. But this divine being does not figure prominently in people's lives. Probably because of his very transcendence, a person can only form a relationship with this divine being, in fact, through the intercession of spirits. Many of the practices of Voodoo faithful are thus centered around their relationship with spirits or the Vodun.

The god Mawu is omnipotent, but essentially aloof from the concerns of man. He is both unknowable and remote from worldly affairs. But Mawu delegated his powers to the Voduns or the spirits. In essence, the Voduns are Mawu's representatives on earth, and all acts of the Voduns are essentially attributable to Mawu. But his very transcendence keeps him inexplicable and incomprehensible to people, and so one cannot really find any direct worship of this divine being in Voodoo practices, save from scattered and vague references such as "God will act," or "God decides."

5.2 Vodoo Spirits, Animism, and Ancestor Worship

- Xêvioso (or Xêbioso) - the Vodun of the sky, and also of justice, and is represented by a thunderbolt, the ram, fire, and the double axe
- Agbe - the Vodun of the sea, and is represented by a serpent, considered a symbol of life
- Gu - the Vodun of iron and war, and metes out justice even to accomplices of those guilty of acts of infamy
- Agê - the Vodun of agriculture, forests, animals and birds
- Jo - the Vodun of air and invisibility
- Lêgba - the youngest son, and a Vodun who received no gifts because these had already been spread out among his elder brothers. He is therefore jealous, a wild card among the pantheon, thus he is considered Vodun of the unpredictable, of all else that cannot be assigned to the others, of daily tragedies and unforeseen events

These sons of Mawu also have sons of their own, each governing the respective Vodun facets of their fathers, and so the number of Voduns or spirits multiply, each governing specific aspects or facets of life and the world.

5.3 Belief in a Soul

Voodoo practitioners believe in the concept of a soul which can leave the body during dreams and spirit possession. In fact, there is an animistic side to Voodoo in which they believe that inanimate objects and natural phenomena such as rocks, trees, storms, etc., possess souls. These souls - whether human or otherwise, comprise the many Loa which are considered spirits, with whom

Voodoo practitioners nurture their connection, and through them, with divinity and the spirit world.

5.4 Rituals, Priests and Priestesses

The prominence and authority of the Voodoo priests and priestesses stem from their close connection with the spirits, and the honor and respect accorded to ancestors also yield tohereditary lines of priestesses. Thus, they are expected to perform many of the affairs for which people go to the spirits in the first place: healing, advice, and various solutions to life's problems. Voodoo priests and priestesses (Juju man or woman) practice an elaborate system of folk medicinal practices, and they also draw on the wisdom and ethical practices of the past through oral traditions of songs, proverbs, stories and folklore, many of which have been passed down through generations upon generations. Needless to say, magic and sorcery - with the aid of the spirits - is also practiced by Voodoo priests and priestesses.

This asking for help is sometimes accompanied by sacrificial offerings of chicken or sheep or the pouring of alcohol. In West Africa, human sacrifices ended almost a century ago, so these days, animals are tradionally sacrificed. There are also festivals or gatherings which are certainly partly or mostly religious in nature, and although the names of these festivals or celebrations and their purposes vary depending on the region and the traditions of the people celebrating them, the essence is the same: spiritual contact with the Voduns, and a recognition and celebration of the Vodun's power over matters on earth.

5.5 Talismans and Fetishes

Central to any Voodoo culture is a marketplace that sells talisman ingredients called "fetishes." The uses of these talismans or charms (also called "gris-gris") can vary from medicinal to spiritual powers, and a trip to a fetish market can yield an interesting array of ingredients such as stones, dried animal heads, animal parts, or elaborate statues that represent any of the diverse Voodoo gods. Voodoo shrines can usually be seen topped with various Voodoo fetishes, and these shrines would be placed strategically to protect family homes or areas, and food or wine are laid before these shrines as offerings to the Vodun spirits.

5.6 Sabbats and Esbats

Sabbats and Esbats are the time for regrowth, birth, or death of something. They are old traditions that have gone on for centuries, and thanks to our ancestors, they are the start of how our world works today. There are eight main Sabbats revolving around the sun; The Wheel of the Year starts like this:

Yule (Winter Solstice) On December 21st, 22nd, or 23rd, "Yule" - the winter solstice - starts. Normal people would call this Christmas, and it is the longest night of the year. The festivities of Yule originated back to the Norse people for whom this time of year was for feasting, merrymaking, and, depending on what was believed, sacrificing. The Wiccans celebrate by decorating a tree, caroling, drinking, and spending time with their loved ones. According to Julius Caesar, this was the time of year where the Druids would sacrifice a white bull and collected mistletoe for the celebration. In Wicca traditions, Yule is celebrated from back in the Celtic legend of the Holly King and the Oak King. The Oak King represents the light of the new year, and the Holly King is the symbol of darkness. The ritual is when the Oak King tries to take over the Holly King.

Imbolc/Oimelc - This holiday falls on February 2nd and is the first of the three festivals when the Earth starts to replenish the goods. Egyptians thought of this holiday as "the Feast of Nut". Nut's birthday fell on February 2nd and was seen as a mother figure to the sun God Ra according to the book of the dead. Nut took the form of a scarab beetle and, at the dawn of February 2nd, was known as Khepera. Ireland converted to Christianity, and the church allowed them to worship the goddess Brighid because the Irish found it difficult to get rid of their old gods.

Brighid is viewed as the woman aspect of the "maiden/mother/crone" cycle in Wicca and Paganism. The ritual consists of leaving a piece of their clothing outside for Brighid to bless the day before February 2nd. People put out their fire and make sure the ashes are flat and smooth. In the morning, there should be a symbol or sign that Brighid has left behind if she had passed by the campfire that was made. If the sign is there, Wiccans would then bring their clothes back inside as they would then have protection and healing powers thanks to the blessing of Brighid.

Ostara - Depending on which day the spring equinox falls on, this day start on March 1st, 2nd, or 23rd. This day is known as the second of the three spring festivals. The word **Ostara** originated from **Eostre,** who is the Germanic goddess of spring. It's the same day as the Christian Easter celebration, and also what we would call Easter, and at this time, the Jewish Passover takes place. This holiday is one of the "new" holidays for Pagans and Wiccans, because the Pagan Germans and Celts did not celebrate this holiday. The March Hare was a symbol of fertility and growth in the medieval cultures in Europe; this is because mating season happens in March for rabbits, and they all come out in the day when they usually only come out at night.

Beltane - The third of the three spring festivals falls on May 1st, and it has been celebrated for centuries. It means that summer is right around the corner. This is when fire rituals happen, and it stems back to the Greco-Roman religions. It is fertility month, and the Celts honored this date by giving their gods gifts and peace offerings. Their cattle had to walk through the smoke of the balefires for fertility and health blessings. In Wicca, a Beltane ritual involves fertility symbols, including the Maypole dance. The pole consists of flowers and ribbons that are woven by the dancers. By the end of the dance, the ribbons are intricately woven together to form a pretty pattern. May 1st first represents the endless circle of life bringing birth, growth, death, and rebirth to life.

Litha/Midsummer (Summer Solstice) - Depending on which day the summer solstice begins, this day falls on June 21st or 22nd. Many cultures have celebrated this day as the first day of summer, and it is a celebration to balance the light and dark. Just as winter solstice had begun, the Oak King and the Holly King take battle again. The Oak King is seen as the winter to summer solstice ruler, whereas the Holly King is seen as the summer to winter solstice ruler. Midsummer, or Litha, is a time when Wiccans would light fires on high hilltops to honor the space between heaven and Earth. In other religions, it is a battle between light and dark. On the first day of summer, the Oak King wins the battle for power, but by the end of summer and by the beginning of the winter solstice, the Holly King takes the power back.

Lammas/Lughnasadh - This holiday falls on August 1st, and it is thought to be the celebration of an early harvest. In some religions, this day is used for worshipping Lugh, a Celtic god of craftsmanship. Lammas is the first of three harvest Sabbats and defines the time between late summer and early fall. If you harvested grain before then, it meant a bad coming year for agriculture, because the previous year's harvest had run out early. In modern days, we do not understand the hard work and survival that our ancestors had to undergo. For us, we go to the store to buy bread, and if we run out, we just return to the store. August 1st represents life and death for our ancestors, as they had to make sure that the first grain was cut, and then the wives had to make bread from scratch. A lot of families would starve if the grain was cut too late or too early. This is a day to give thanks and recognition to our ancestors, as they are the reason we have food on our tables today.

Mabon - Mabon is what we call "thanksgiving", and it falls on September 21st or 22nd, depending on the fall equinox. It is a reminder to us that the long days and hot summer weeks are about to end, and the long winter nights are right around the corner. This is a time when there is an equal amount of light and dark, which is why we give thanks to all that we have to our crops and harvest. We celebrate the gifts of nature and Earth, while at the same time coming to an acceptance that the soil is dying as the days get colder. In many Wiccan religions, this ritual consists of giving food and harvest to those less fortunate. This time of year is about the celebration of the harvest and kinship, but also about the balance between light and dark, as the darkness of the moon and the light of the sun are equally balanced.

Samhain - In modern times, we call this day Halloween, and it always falls on October 31st. This holiday goes back thousands of years, and it is known as the witch's new year. Witches will contact spirits through a seance, because the veil between this world and the Otherworld is at its thinnest. The celebrations begin at dusk on the 31st, and the new year of the Celtics begins on November 1st, basically indicating that the old year has passed, and a fresh new year is now beginning.

The Esbats revolve around the moon's cycles, or lunar phases, and in these celebrations, modern Wiccans and Pagans celebrate the festivity with magick and by honoring their gods and goddesses. Covens usually meet once a month on a full moon to do healing magick rituals. All magick ceremonies represent when the moon is at its different stages - for example, full moon, dark moon, last quarter moon, first quarter moon, and so on. If a Wiccan was to begin a project, they would start at the sight of the new moon and continue their process as the moon goes through the stages within the month. Generally speaking, a new moon to a full moon represents the beginning of things, and a full moon to dark moon is used for the death of things, like getting rid of the negative things from your life.

First Quarter Moon - This moon represents growth and to build upon. So, when you see this moon, it is the time to put effort into what is holding you back.

Gibbous Moon Magick - This moon is 10-14 days after the new moon and is the perfect time to make the changes you need from the previous moon phase. It's the time to either relax and take some time to think and regain energy or put forth energy into what you have been working on.

Full Moon Magick - The full moon allows you to predict the future and to protect yourself and the ones you love. Psychic powers are heightened at this time, and goddesses such as Arianrhod, Danu, Isis, Ashera, and Selene are called upon to come help you at this time. Creativity is developed, and chances of success in what you are doing is greatly increased.

Last Quarter - If you want to rid yourself of bad habits, decrease illness, and banish negativity, this moon provides you with the strength to do so. The last quarter moon represents the death of something - to banish something from your life.

5.7 The Wiccan Elements

The elements involved with Wicca include air, fire, water, earth, and aether (which is defined as spirit). The elements are used for spells and are connected to every single thing that involves nature. Each witch or practitioner needs to learn about and completely understand the attributes of these elements, which takes time and patience.

Air - In Wiccan magick and rituals, objects are tossed into the wind, aromatherapy is used, songs are sung, and things are hidden in really high places. The spells associated with air involve travel, instruction, freedom, and knowledge, they and can be used to increase psychic powers. Other things air represents are as follows:

- The mind and intelligence
- Communication
- Telepathy
- Inspiration
- Motivation
- Imagination
- Creativity
- Dreams and passions

The symbols associated with the air element are the sky, the wind, the breeze, clouds, feathers, breath, vibrations, smoke, plants, herbs, trees, and flowers. The goddesses to call upon when doing air spells are Aradia, Arianrhod, Cardea, Nuit, and Urania; the gods are Enlil, Kheoheva, Merawrim, Shu, and Thoth.

Fire - In Wiccan rituals, witches will burn objects, use love spells, bake ingredients, and light a candle. Fire is the element of change, and it is the most physical and spiritual of the five elements. It represents the following:

- Energy
- Inspiration
- Love
- Passion
- Leadership

The symbols associated with fire are flames, lightning, heated objects such as stones, volcanoes, the sun, the stars, lava, and heat. The goddesses to call upon are Brigit, Hestia, Pele, and Vesta; the Gods are Agni, Horus, Prometheus, and Vulcan.

Water - In Wiccan rituals, this is associated with pouring water over objects, making potions, healing spells, bathing, and tossing things into a bucket of water. Water represents the following:

- Emotions
- Absorption
- Subconsciousness
- Purification
- Eternal movement
- Wisdom
- Emotional components of love and femininity

The gods and goddesses to call upon are Aphrodite, Isis, Marianne, Dylan, Ea, Osiris, Neptune, and Poseidon.

Earth - In Wiccan rituals, it is common to bury things in the earth, create herbs, and make things out of nature, such as out of wood and stone. It represents the following:

- Strength
- Abundance
- Stability
- Prosperity
- Wealth
- Femininity

Aether (Spirit) - This element is the glue for all the other elements. It provides balance, space, and connection for the other elements. Aether is connected to our sense of spirit and wellbeing, and it represents joy and union. The goddess to call upon is the Lady, and the god to call upon is the Horned God

Book 9: Paganism

Chapter 1: What Is Paganism

In order to practice a religion, the practitioner must first understand what the religion is and why they are practicing it. Therefore, in this chapter I am going to explain to you the exact definition of paganism and the different forms that exist. So, let's get started with a definition.

Paganism is a polytheistic or pantheistic nature-worshipping religion. There's a lot of poly and pan in that definition, so let's break it down. Polytheistic translates to a belief in more than one God or Goddess. A pantheistic religion is the belief that the universe or nature is the same as the God or Goddess, so the universe is the deity. Of course, most know that religion is a belief system that centers on the idea that one there is a herculean power that either created and/or is in control of everything.

A pagan is someone who is a follower of a polytheistic or pantheistic nature-worshipping religion. That leaves a lot of options about who can be classified as a pagan. There are numerous religions that center on the belief of nature or multiple Gods or Goddesses existing. The following is just a small sampling of those religions, all of which are modern. Paganism is an ancient belief system that began thousands of years ago; therefore, there are a lot to choose from.

Pagans practice the ancient beliefs of their ancestors, and many of their belief systems stem from the prehistoric times. If you were to go down into a caveman dwelling and look at the drawings on the walls of their homes, you would see prayers strewn across the rocks, etched into them or carved there using softer stone.

The drawings of the animals littering their dwellings were not only pictures of the animals they hunted for food, but also pictures of the spirits within the animals. The presence of these animals meant life or death for these people literally, and they understood their importance. In time, these early ancestors understood the cycles of the sun and the moon, and how they related to the changing of the seasons. They also recognized that the animals appeared and disappeared with the different seasons. There as a magic to this cycle and they wanted to be part of it.

They sang and danced to celebrate the wonders of nature and they painted murals on their caves in order to depict them better and perhaps to tell future generations about their findings. They created a language they could communicate through with nature and were the first bearers of the 'Old Religion' of paganism.While most modern religions believe in one God or Goddess that controls every aspect of the human existence, and all existence for that matter, pagans believe there is both a God and Goddess, and this couple are represented in all creations equally. The pagan viewpoint is that of opposites, of yin and yang or light and dark. In most religions, the Gods or Goddesses are in control of nature, but pagans believe nature **is** the God and Goddess.However, in paganism, the Goddess is seen as a more important role. She is Gaia or Mother Earth, and she is seen as the one who creates all. She is worshiped in the form of the Triple Goddess; the Maiden, the Mother, and the Crone. Women were the

Goddess's guardians on Earth and thus were given power within the clan. Unfortunately, pagans had a rough start when other modern day religions came about. The role of landowner used to belong to the woman hundreds of years ago, but it was taken away from women and given to men. The Church of Rome began a crusade to wipe out the pagans and their beliefs, which has brought about the modern belief that Pagans worship Satan and cast spells upon people to cause harm. In the year 447, the Christian Church officially adopted the concept of Satan and Lucifer and the genocide of the pagans began.

Ironically, at the same time, the Christian Church and many other religions adopted a lot of the pagan ways into their scripture in order to convert pagans to their belief system. For example, the vestment, chalice, and the censer are all part of ancient pagan rituals and the Christmas tree and Easter Bunny are actually pagan beliefs that derived long before the Bible was ever written. This is not to denote any of the Christian beliefs, but it is an example of how paganism is woven into numerous religions around the world.

Paganism does not worship any essence of evil. In fact, pagans do not believe in good or bad, they simply believe in yin and yang or light and dark. Therefore, there isn't an evil God for them to worship. They believe in balance and harmony between male and female, and both opposites are represented equally within the religion. Now that you have a clear understanding of what paganism is, let's look at some of the sub-religions that fall underneath this category: Wicca, Gardnerian Movement, Alexandrian Movement, Feri Movement, Asatru, Cunning Folk, and Druidry. All of these religions are known as Neopaganism and have been modified from the ancient practices of paganism.

1.1 Sub-Religions of Paganism

Most of the ancient pagan religions have morphed into religions classified as Neopaganism. It's rare to find groups that still practice the ancient rituals of paganism due to the genocide that the pagans went through a few hundred years ago. However, there are some that will be discussed later on in the chapter. First, let's look at some Neopaganism belief systems.

1.2 Neopaganism Beliefs

1.2.1 Wicca

One of the most popular of the Neo-Pagan Movements, Wicca was founded by Gerald Gardner in the 1950's. It is a mix of western European folklore, Eastern philosophy, and Qabalistic mysticism. Wicca was originally focused on magical pursuits but switched over to more of the New Age spiritual movement. This religion is organized and focuses on witchcraft and rituals.

1.2.2 Alexandrian Movement

Created by Alexander Sanders in the 1960's, the Alexandrian Movement is very similar to Gardner's movement in the 1950's, except there are a few changes. It is still considered Wicca and is not considered 'Old Religion' by modern day pagans.

1.2.3 Feri Movement

Perhaps its biggest claim to fame is the fact that it uses sexual energy in order to raise 'Feri energy'. This branch of Neopaganism has its own Gods called the Star Goddess, Blue God and the Divine Twins. Created in the 1940's by Victor Anderson, the Feri Movement is not Wicca, but it can be argued that Wicca is an offshoot of Feri.

1.2.4 Asatru

While categorized as a Neopaganism belief system, Asatru is very closely related to the original beliefs of the Norse people. Unfortunately, it was stained by the Nazi regime in Germany due to the fact that they took small parts of Asatru and tried to graft it to their beliefs. However, the religion has nothing to do with Nazi belief systems and should not be associated with it. Asatru is, perhaps, one of the oldest religions that is still practiced today.

1.2.5 Cunning Folk

Also known as wise men, wise women, conjurers, and wizards, the Cunning Folk originated in southern England and appear to have a controversial background. They do not like to be labeled as witches because this is an evil term in their belief system, and it appears that they actually hunted witches back in the day. They perform curses against offenders.

1.2.6 Druidry

Unfortunately, this religion did not write down its belief system and ethics. Therefore, modern Druidism stems from the Romanticism Movement in the eighteenth century. The original religion was practiced by Celts before this time in ancient Britain and Gaul. The most information found about them was discovered in Julius Caesar's 'The Gallic Wars' when he describes the Druids as being the learned, priestly class that were guardians of an unwritten, ancient customary law. They had the power to execute judgment.

1.3 The 'Old Religion' Beliefs

As you've already learned, Paganism is not something that originated recently. There are many ancient practices that are classified as paganism, some of which are very interesting. While the doctrines of these religions are rarely practiced today, a lot of them have a foothold in modern religion. Remember that Paganism is the oldest known religion.

1.3.1 Finnish Paganism

This belief system actually doesn't have a name because it is so ancient and so little information was recorded of this religion. It evolved from shamanism and has features such as ancestor worship and numerous Gods and Goddesses. Finnish Paganism followers believed that every object, whether living or inanimate, had a soul and they believed the world was created from the egg of a diving duck.

Their man God was Ukko, a sky and thunder God, and he was celebrated on April 4. He closely resembles the Norse God Thor because he is the God of thunder and has a hammer.

1.3.2 Minoan Paganism

Another polytheistic religion that is nameless, this religion was followed by the natives of Crete. Most of the information about this religion has been derived from cave paintings and archeological discoveries. An interesting fact about it is that they chased down bulls and attempted to ride them. Their main deity was a Goddess, making them one of the rare matriarchal religions.

1.3.3 Vedism

Practiced from 1500 B.C. to 500 B.C., Vedism is the origin of the modern Hindu belief system. However, this religion was polytheistic in nature and had two different God categories. There were Gods of nature known as the Devas, and Gods of moral concepts, known as the Asuras. Milk and grain were used much more frequently than animal sacrifice, but the unsavory practice was a ritual.

1.3.4 Olmec Religion

The Olmec Religion was practiced from 1400 B.C. to 400 B.C., the time of their destruction. Unfortunately, due to volcanic activity and environmental changes, there are no recording of this religion except for relics found. These relics have been compared to the Mayan and Aztec religions in order to find similarities, and a few facts have been revealed.

The Mesoamerican Olmec people followed a religion that was close to Shamanism and it was polytheistic. The most popular God seemed to be a Jaguar God of rain and fertility, but there were eight separate Gods that were viewed as equal. There were blood sacrifices and jade figures that were made to depict the Gods, and there were Olmec priests that communicated with the spirits. Because of its early rise, the Olmec religion is thought to be the base for numerous other Mesoamerican religions.As you can see, there are numerous similarities between these pagan religions; however, a lot of the more unsavory practice such as human sacrifice and animal sacrifice are not used in modern day pagan religions. However, all of these religions do have several things in common.

Chapter 2: Pagan Symbols

The study of symbolism is a fascinating pursuit and one that can help you to find spiritual elements you might not otherwise discover. If you find yourself powerfully drawn to a symbol inscribed on an amulet or a piece of jewelry, investigate why the image is reaching out to you.

Long before I became a pagan, I was deeply drawn to Celtic imagery especially that connected with Scottish mythology. Now, having done past life work and spending time in the highlands of Scotland, I understand that in a past life, those mountains were my home.

The Celtic symbols with their elegant knots and intricate meanings continue to speak to me more eloquently than any other pagan symbols and I have many fine examples of Celtic amulets in my home.

Symbolic jewelry allows pagans to infuse their daily lives with subtle magic. To the casual observer, the ring on your hand may be nothing more than an attractive piece of jewelry. To you, it symbolizes a powerful bridge between the material and spiritual worlds.

The following symbols are some of the most common in pagan spirituality, but they barely scratch the surface of the wealth of emblems employed by the various faiths. In this regard, the Internet is a wonderful resource for the beginning pagan. Search for phrases like "Pagan amulets" or "Celtic charms." You will find not only beautiful items for purchase, but useful explanations of the symbols.

2.1 Pentagram

The five-pointed star or pentacle is one of the most widely recognized of all pagan symbols. This emblem has nothing to do with Satanic worship and it is not a symbol of the devil.

The four points of the star represent the traditional elements of earth, water, air, and fire with the fifth honoring spirit.

The circle connecting the points denotes the reciprocal relationship of the elements as they are embodied in nature.

Pentacles are used in magical work and are placed on altars in various traditions. Since the emblem is one of protection, pentacles are also popular as amulets and other pieces of jewelry.

2.2 Triquatra

Both Christians and pagans use the triquatra or "trinity knot." The symbol dates to the 7th century A.D. and in neo-paganism is specific to The Morrigan, a triple goddess associated with war.

In some traditions, especially in modern times, the triquatra is a symbol of the intimate connection of mind, body, and soul. It is popular with many Celtic pagan groups who use it as an emblem of the earth, sea, and sky

The triquatra is one of the simplest of the Celtic knots, which may account for its popularity. The graceful lines and balance of the symbol are appealing, and its triple nature lends itself to multiple interpretations.

2.3 Chalice

The cup or chalice is both a symbol and a tool in pagan ritual. It represents water and the feminine aspects of intuition, psychic ability, emotions, and the subconscious. The cup also depicts fertility and gestation and is an emblem of the womb of the Goddess. Like other pagan symbols, the chalice also has strong Christian associations, especially those associated with the Holy Grail – the cup used at the Last Supper, which then caught the blood of Jesus spilled from the cross. Interestingly enough, the Grail myth is believed to have been adapted from older Celtic tails of maidens who guarded sacred wells.

2.4 Triskele

The triskele, which can be found carved in Neolithic stones in Ireland and Western Europe, is an emblem of the realms of the earth, sea, and sky.

Although its origins pre-date the Celtic peoples, the triskele is popular with Celtic neo-pagans as well as some Germanic groups. Like the triquatra, this symbol is useful to depict any triple concepts.

The symbol is so common it appears in such incongruous places as the seal of the United States Department of Transportation and (in roundel form) on the emblem of the Irish Air Corps. Many Christian churches incorporate the triskele in carvings and stained glass windows.

2.5 Four Elements

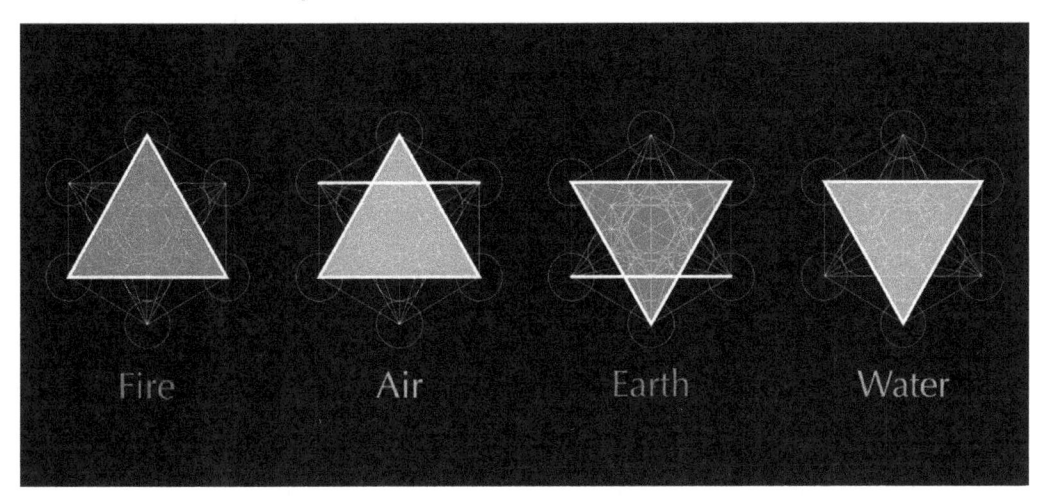

Fire Air Earth Water

Each of the four classical elements of earth, water, air, and fire has a representative symbol used in pagan ritual and adornment. The air symbol, for instance, is an emblem of the connection between the breath of life and the soul. The triangles are simple to work into jewelry designs and are often used in concert with other symbols as bounding devices.

2.6 Triple Moon

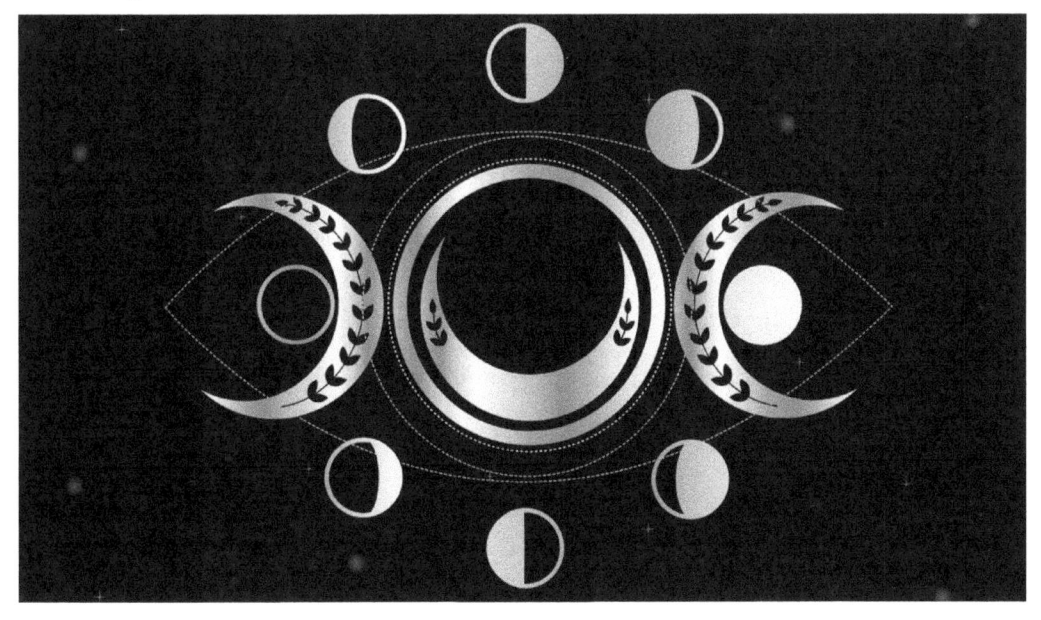

The triple moon symbol depicts the three phases of the moon (waxing, full, waning). It is sometimes referred to as the triple goddess symbol, reflecting the three phases of a woman's life (maiden, mother, crone.)

The waxing moon represents new life, new beginnings, and rejuvenation. The full moon is the manifestation of magic at its most powerful point. The waning moon represents the sending away or removal of things in your life or the need to finish something left incomplete.

2.7 Caring for Your Pagan Symbols

When you wear symbols of your pagan faith on your body, the jewelry absorbs the energies moving through your system.

In a sense of "attunement" this is a good thing. There are times, however, when your own energy needs to be "re-charged." Once this is accomplished, you don't want to then be exposed to any stored negativity in your symbolic objects.

I like to take my amulets and energetically cleanse them at least once a month, especially it it's during a period when I have been grappling with numerous problems and challenges in my life.

If the symbol is strongly associated with female energy, I place the items in the light of the full moon. If their energy is more masculine, they go into a warm, energizing puddle of sunlight.

With new jewelry, it's best to first cleanse the pieces under running water before wearing them. This removes any negative energy that has entered the items through casual content

While the jewelry is submerged in the water, offer a cleansing prayer. After a minute or so, take the items out and gently pat them dry.

To charge the jewelry and make it your own, wear it against your skin for 7-9 days. This binds the piece to you. Avoid letting anyone else touch or handle the item.

If this is unavoidable, immediately cleanse the piece in moonlight or sunlight.

Personally, I also have an attraction to antique jewelry. I often find that these pieces "speak" to me in powerful ways. If you do acquire any item of jewelry, especially one with symbolic significance that has been worn by another person, take the time to cleanse and recharge the item.

This will not lessen your psychic connection to the piece, but it will protect you from any stored, latent energies that might affect you in a negative way.

Chapter 3: Simple Rituals for Starters

Rituals represent a very important aspect of spiritual practice when it comes to Paganism. Through those rituals, pagans can tune their minds to the rhythm of nature, celebrate life, create communities, and use magic. Moreover, through a ritual, the pagan folk can strengthen their relationship with the divine, regardless of their sacred form.

These rituals allow pagans to flourish and evolve until they have reached their ideal self.

3.1 Understanding the Pagan Ritual

Pagan rituals can be quite diverse, depending on the pagan community that you ask – as well as who performs them. They may be performed by one person or they may have more people within the circle. Some rituals take a lot of planning – sometimes even months before – while others have a more spontaneous nature. A pagan rite can be done with a script – in a theatrical manner – or it can be done through improvisation. Depending on the pagan ritual, some may only need one performance while others need to be repeated time after time – having a standardized form. Other pagan rituals will be evolving over time and will be modified continuously in order to be kept fresh.

A pagan may perform a ritual with a specific purpose in mind – or they may perform it for general reasons. Some pagan rituals may take no more than a few minutes – while others may even last a few days. However, the average ritual will last around one or two hours. Depending on the pagan ritual, it may be predominantly quiet or performed in silence. On the other hand, it can be exuberant and noisy, with a lot of drumming and chanting. Most pagan rituals will have their fair share of volumes and sounds, as well as some silent meditation. These rituals are generally visually powerful, and they include a fair number of tools for rituals – such as incense, wands, chalices, crystals, pentacles and so on. Depending on the ritual, some pagans may even choose to dress up; to wear specific robes and jewelry.

A pagan ritual can have different goals or purposes. Some may only have one purpose – while others may have more of them. Most of the rituals have the purpose of worshiping a deity. However, you can also come across healing rituals or celebratory ones. Some pagan rituals are so big that they might require their own event – and this is actually how most pagan gatherings today came to be.

There's not really a specific time and place for pagan rituals, as they can be performed wherever is most convenient for the caster. Such a ritual can take place indoors – or they can be moved outdoors, for the benefit of the one that had cast the spell. Generally, most pagans will perform their rituals indoors, where they already have their own altar put in place. However, some pagans also choose to take their rituals outside to be closer to nature – the actual thing that gives them power. Pagan rituals do not necessarily have to be held on a particular day. For example, simple rituals such as healing ones can take place at day or at night, without any issues. Some rituals, however, are pertaining to certain holidays or cycles – such as the Pagan Sabbat, Samhain, or even the full moon. If you were to compare it with something, the pagan ritual is exactly like a church service – only instead of listening to the preaching of a priest about God, you are celebrating your own gods. The purpose of a ritual is to raise awareness, energy – and overall, to provide a feeling of blessing.

Such a ritual is the pagan's way of communicating with their deity – acting as a spiritual focal point for a group or an individual. These rituals can have both spiritual and physical gain – and they can be performed for both the caster and someone else. For example, the one who performs the ritual may be praying for him and his family's wealth. They can also be performed as a healing aid for a friend or an individual living somewhere else.

You will just need to have the tools in order to perform the rituals. By doing so, you will be able to enrich your life and aid your spiritual development.

3.2 Pagan Rites of Passage

Among the most important rituals and ceremonies is the pagan rite of passage. This ritual has the purpose of marking a pagan's passage from one stage of life to the next. These rites of passage will ease up the pagan's existence from one phase to another, making it easier to pass over the threshold. Some people believe that the rite of passage only concerns someone's passing away – but these rituals are even more than that. They spread over every stage of being a pagan, including baby-naming, marriage, initiations, and so on. Each rite of passage is special in its own way, offering a sense of strength and empowerment.

3.2.1 Baby Naming

Each culture and religious group will have their own ceremony for naming a baby – and pagans do too. However, Pagans believe that children should be able to choose whether they want to follow in the religion of their parents or not.

As a result, a pagan baby-naming ceremony will not also include a pledge that the baby will be brought up pagan. They may, however, include a desire for instilling those values, familiarizing the child with the religion. This way, the children will be able to choose for themselves whether they want to be initiated in this religion or not.

3.2.2 Coming Out

Coming out "of the closet" as an LGTB is certainly a rite of passage – and definitely a liberating one for those concerned. It signifies that an individual no longer needs to remain hidden – and can be accepted within a society and culture. These rituals can be found in a variety of pagan religions, from the polytheist people to the druids, heathens, and Wiccans.

3.2.3 Coming of Age

In Western culture, coming of age is when a person goes from childhood to adulthood. Most of the time, that age is 18 years old – but sometimes, these passages can take place at 15, 16, 22, or 24. It mainly depends on the customs that they have been brought up in. Aside from the occasional expensive parties that parents throw their children, Western culture doesn't have any rituals when the little ones have come of age. Judaism is the only one that has a close ritual, called "bat mitzvah" or "bar mitzvah." In pagan culture, people are going into celebration when their daughters have their first menstruation. For them, it is a sign that she has become fertile – and has, therefore, become a full-fledged woman. The only condition is that the daughters should **want** to be celebrated as well.

Indigenous cults also have their own coming of age rituals; however, these are found in the form of a vision quest. These children are sent into the wilderness where they can learn how to survive and come to terms with their inner self. They may or may not have to return home with a "trophy" to prove that their quest was completed.

3.2.4 Initiation

Most pagan and religious traditions have their own initiation rite of passage, in which they fully become part of the culture that they have grown up in or simply wish to join. Depending on the religion, the initiation can take part when the child is only a newborn – or it may happen when the child has already come of age. In pagan culture, there is still some controversy around the true meaning of initiation. Some believe in the value of selfinitiation while others believe you need to be initiated in a group or a coven. However, there are pagans that believe self-initiation is one and the same with coven initiations.

Initiation can cover various aspects. For example, when it comes to self-initiations, you are finding your connection with the gods – discovering the mystery of the religion and going through your inner transformation process. Coven initiation, on the other hand, can be given when the secrets of an initiating group are revealed. This happens when a person is joining a tradition and lineage to which he/she had no access before.

3.2.5 Marriage

Practically every religion has its own marriage rite of passage. In Paganism, this rite of passage is called "handfasting," and can be contracted for different periods: a day, a year, a lifetime – and even all the lifetimes that are to come. Pagans are generally polyamorous, and they recognize both opposite-sex and same-sex marriages.

In the United States and Canada, pagan marriages have legal validity if you are registered with a religious body that is recognized. The same thing applies to

Scotland if you are a celebrant that has been registered. However, England and Wales do not offer legal validation – at least not yet.

The ritual of handfasting involves wrapping a cord or a ribbon around the couple's clasped hand, "tying the knot," so to speak. It symbolizes a declaration of unity, symbolically binding their fate. In ancient times, this was also considered the ceremony for betrothals.

3.2.6 Divorce

Pagans have always been liberal in nature – which is why they also have a ritual for divorce. This is exactly why handfasting also permits for a "trial marriage" where the couple accepts the possibility that a marriage may not work out.

There is no exact ritual for divorce in Paganism, but many individual pagans may have crafted their own ritual for "untying the knots" and asking for better luck in the future.

3.2.7 Croning

Just like coming of age is a ritual that celebrates menopause, croning is one that recognizes menopause. It signifies the moment when a woman is no longer menstruating – and has become a "crone." Pagans use the word "crone" with a deepest of respect, signifying an "old and wise woman."

3.2.8 Death

Pagan funerals are rites of passage where the focus of the ritual is to celebrate the life of the one who has passed away. Various liturgies and chants are used during these rites, and their purpose is to guide the person into the afterlife.

3.3 Pagan Prayers

When it comes to pagan rituals, prayer plays a very important role. Not only are they practiced in beliefs such as Christianity or Islam, but they are also a part of pagan daily rituals. The prayers have been documented as far as the ancient Egyptian times, where the tombs of the Egyptian pharaohs have been adorned with inscriptions and carvings designating ancient prayers.

Most prayers have been lost once Christianity has settled in - but some of them still survive. However, their means of passage is not in the written form; they are documented orally. Folktales, legends, songs - these are the mediums that take the prayer from one generation to another. In Paganism, a prayer is the pagan's way of saying to the gods that they are unable to do this alone and that they could use some help. A prayer is a plea for strength, both spiritual and corporeal - a plea so that they can escape the hardships that they have encountered.

3.3.1 Altars and Offerings

In most pagan religions, it is a tradition to provide an offering to a celestial being, a god. This offering is simply a gift, a token of good faith - and by no means a trade-off. It's a way of showing the gods some respect, regardless of what the answer of the prayer would be. In Wicca, the dedication and time spent on the ritual or ceremony are just as important as the tangible offering.

Many of these offerings are left either on a shrine or an altar created for the gods - a practice which is very common in many faiths. Catholic faiths practice the same thing - for example, candles and flowers seen in front of a statue of the Virgin Mary or any other god.

3.3.2 Prayers Vs. Spells

When it comes to Paganism, many non-pagan people believe the prayers are just spells; however, they are wrong. A player is a request in which you ask for guidance from your god. It is the person's way of saying "please help me," without any guarantees that your prayer will be listened to. A spell, on the other hand, is a command. Through this spell, the caster is redirecting the energy and causing a change so that your wish becomes a reality. During spells, one may ask the gods for a bit of help - but that is not always necessary. Spells take power from the caster, whereas the prayer takes power from the gods. There are countless pagan prayers to be offered - some of them being custom-made while others are "standard" for a certain god. You have everything from hymns to the Egyptian god Amun-Ra to prayers for Celtic spirits or the Earth itself.

Depending on the god that you want to reach, you might want to use the right offerings and tools. Certain spirits require particular foods and drinks, while other spiritual entities answer better to certain incenses and tools. However, this is not set in stone anywhere – and is generally adapted from one pagan to another.

Chapter 4: Myths About Paganism

The word 'Pagan' can arouse prejudice and fear and there is much misunderstanding of what Paganism represents. Let us examine some of the myths.

4.1 Paganism Does Not Mean Materialism.

A British Catholic bishop recently wrote in a Catholic newspaper that to open stores on Sundays was 'Pagan'.

This is not Paganism but **secularism** and **consumerism.**

Pagans believe that it is good for all of us to have days that are focused on worship and leisure rather than on working and earning money. The only difference is that Pagans may not think that these days have to be Sundays.

4.2 Paganism Does Not Advocate Black Magic or Animal Sacrifice.

Anyone seeking to use magic to gain power over others or for material ends would be better advised to apply elsewhere! Most Pagans believe that the human mind has powers that are as yet little understood. These are the power to transmit thought, the power to see the future, and the power to effect change by the use of love and will. These powers can only, however, be used in ways that are acceptable to the Gods; that is, in ways that benefit humankind and other forms of creation, not in ways which cause harm.

As briefly stated above, Wiccans can choose to be a Pagan, though others do not consider themselves to be as such. It is hard to identify exactly what Paganism is because, over time, it has been defined as many things; essentially, it is an umbrella term. The Latin word **paganus** is where the word "paga" comes from. In Latin, it refers to someone who comes from or resides in a rural country as opposed to a big city. Pagans were considered anyone who lived outside of Rome, as this was the primary city of the Roman Empire and where the word originated from.

Once Rome introduced Christianity as the primary religion, Paganism started to evolve into something of a different meaning. Anyone who did not worship the gods or goddesses from Christianity was thought to be a Paganist. If they did not convert to the Christian ways, they were referred to as morally deficient and were in need of saving. The reason Paganism is thought of negatively is that anyone who wasn't a Christian in the older centuries were thought to have worshipped the devil. The word became more and more condemned. This is the reason that some Wiccans resist being called a Pagan to this day.

Nowadays, "Paganism" refers to any religion that is not one of the three primary religions of Judaism, Christianity, and Islam. Therefore, it falls under Buddhism, Hinduism, and Wicca. Depending on one's belief and how comfortable they feel with the word, it can be insulting, neutral, or a non-matter issue. In other words, being referred to as a Neopagan feels insulting to many because it implies that their practices are dismissible and nongenuine. However, in reality, it refers to the difference between modern Pagans and older Pagans. Some Wiccans are willing to use the label "contemporary Pagan", and others feel no need to make any distinction to the Pagan term, whether it is neo or contemporary, because they are not ashamed of the history and know what the word represents.

4.3 What Do Wiccans Believe?

The Wiccan belief system is actually quite complex in the fact that Wiccans have a certain way of thinking and living their lives. Similar to other religions, Wiccans like balance and peace of all things. They are very in tune with nature and the Earth making all things whole and a sense of oneness with all living things. They go by a guilt-free morality. What this means is that there is no jealous or vindictive God in Wicca.

The mother goddess is mainly loving, nurturing, generous, and wise. Whereas the gods are protective, playful, assertive, and strong without punishment or violence. Wiccans live vicariously through their gods and goddesses and implement all that is pure in the Wiccan form. Wicca Spirituality says "No guilt, no shame, no violence, no judgment... Wicca is a religion of life, freedom, celebration, responsibility, and growth."

Wicca is a guilt-free religion. A lot of people may think that guilt suggests you have regret, remorse, and act in a righteous manner. However, guilt and shame have nothing to do with any of that. Virtuous behavior does not come from the regret of what you have done in the past but from learning from your mistakes and choosing the right choices for your future. It is only when we learn from our actions and mistakes that motivation to become and do better is when you can love a virtuous life.

The main difference between religion and spirituality is that in most religions, righteousness and morality are forced. Spirituality helps people find their own morality and righteousness within themselves and then try to live up to their own expectations. Wicca is a spiritual religion, which is to say that it is not just based upon religion or that it is purely spiritual. It is not about morality or virtuousness, it is more about the guidance that comes from the gods and goddesses and holding that within your beliefs as a Wiccan.

The spiritual truths in Wicca are as follows:

- Be your authentic true self.
- Harm nothing and no one (living things such as plants, animals, and humans).
- Whatever you put out into the universe you will get three times over (the Rule of Three).
- What you push away will continue to haunt you.
- How you think and feel creates your reality and what you go through.
- We are all equal and one.

These principles in Wicca are the source of their morality. They respect all life forms and take full responsibility for all their actions. Unlike most religions, Wiccans do not create rules, because rules can easily be broken and are hard to follow at most. So the purity of just accepting yourself is what a Wiccan stands for - learning from your mistakes and striving to always do better than you did before. They focus on seeing people as who they are and who want to be rather than focusing on who they were or used to be.

4.4 Gods and Goddesses

Wiccans worship their gods and goddesses through critical awareness. They are aware of the following:

There is only one "source".

All gods and goddesses represent a variety of faces from the source.

All living things on Earth are elements of the source.

The Wiccans' deepest loyalty is to their gods and goddesses which is the "one" behind the mask. The one is the thing you form all your devotion to. The most important thing in Wicca is that you **do** worship your gods and goddesses. The first rule in Wicca and the way of your life is in devoting and dedicating all your actions and your awareness to the creator - whatever that may be for you.

In any religion, they all have one thing in common which is to worship their one divine source. In Christianity, it is a higher power, and in Hinduism, they have many gods. In China, they worship the Jade Emperor. The gods and goddesses are the ones who share their lives with you and with whom you choose to share your journey.

In Wicca, the deity is a transformational spiritual practice to perceive the divine as something that lives in every being as every being:

- Your Mother - the Goddess
- Your brother - The God
- Your baby - The Divine
- Your friend - The Source
- Your enemy - The One
- Your cat/pet - All that is
- Your self - The Eternal Light

The list explains that everything around you is your gods and goddesses. When you truly understand that the divinity is none above others is when you can fully begin to worship all that surrounds you. The list above is what the Wiccan deities are.

4.5 Wiccan Holidays and Rituals

Wiccans have what is called the "Wheel of the Year", and it is used to mark down all the major solar and lunar events, which are what their holidays are based on. For example, the Sabbats are for celebrating the sun's influence on Earth, which is the seasonal growing cycle. Wiccan Esbats celebrate the moon phases, especially the full moon.

Here is a list of the Wiccan Wheel Year:

Name	Holiday	Earth Event	Date	Occasion
Samhain	Halloween	Fifteen' Scorpio	October 31st	Cleansing releasing. Celebrating the dead. The Pagan new year.
Yule	Christmas	Winter Solstice	December 22nd	Rebirth.
Bridgid	Candlemas	Fifteen' Aquarius	February 2nd	Purification, allegiance, and initiation
Eostara	Easter	Spring Equinox	March 21st	Innovation, revitalization, and new beginnings.

Beltane	May Day	Fifteen' Taurus	May 1st	Fertility, happiness, and passion that fuels life.
Lithia		Summer Solstice	June 21st	Passage, and planning
Lammas	First Harvest	Fifteen' Leo	August 1st	Appreciation, abundance, and fruition.
Mabon	Thanksgiving	Autumn Equinox	September 21st	Giving thanks, thoughtfulness, and expression.

On all these holidays and events, it is essential for the Wiccan to do traditional rituals. Whether you do it in a group setting, in a quiet get-together, or a full-on drama ritual routine, the point is that you do worship and do the ritual. The rituals consist of:

Honoring the divine in all the elements of life

Recharging or regenerate your spiritual batteries

Centering and balancing yourself with Earth's shifting energies. The Wiccan dates are confusing, but to start a holiday or a "new day", the Wiccan dates start on the previous day at dusk once the sun has gone down. Each coven or witch will have their own way of doing things, but most of the time, the holiday starts at sunrise on the date.

Book 10: Tarots for Beginners

Chapter 1: What Is Tarot

A popular, widespread belief is that the tarot deck we use today was based on a standard deck of playing cards, originally created and used in the late 1300s, brought to Europe through trade with Middle Eastern countries.

This may be a myth, as there is no mention of anything related to the tarot until a century later. The mysterious etymology of the word "tarot" is unclear. Some speculate that it might have originated from the Arabic word "taraha", meaning to put aside, or discard, though that connection is obscure at best. One Swiss philosopher believed that the word "tarot" originally came from the Egyptian words "royal road", and he posited that the tarot cards were a sort of divine road towards enlightenment.

While we do get our numeric system from Islamic culture, it wasn't until the late 1400s that an alternate take on standard playing cards, called the "Triumph" cards, spread like wildfire throughout the Italian society. Wealthy families often commissioned artists to create luxurious decks of triumph cards, a complete set of which included the four suits of standard cards as well as the court cards or "face cards", but it also contained an additional suite of imagery cards. These additional imagery cards were created with heavy symbolism, archetypes, and iconic pictures, and were used as trump cards. The new triumph deck was a great success, and a game called **tarocchi appropriati** originated from it, adored by aristocratic society. In a game of tarocchi, players drew random cards and constructed lyrical verses based on what they interpreted from the card's imagery.

Tarocchi was later shortened to "**tarot**", the French word from which **tarocchi** was adapted, and the tarot deck was born. Draws pulled during tarocchi were nicknamed "sortes", or destinies.

French and English occultists helped the tarot deck rise to popularity in the 1700s. Soon, instead of tarot being a mere parlor game, it began to be recognized as a valuable, powerful tool of cartomancy—the practice of divining one's future through the use of cards.

In 1909, the world's most instantly recognizable tarot deck, the Rider-Waite tarot, was invented. In the 70s, an author named Stuart Kaplan published a book on tarot and the ancient practice of tarot card reading was suddenly catapulted into the 20th century.

1.1 Other Theories

There are still questions as to where the original images and image-related definitions came from so suddenly to traverse the wealthy societies of Italy. One theory suggests that the ideas came from a book that was lost when the Egyptian library at Alexandria burned down. Trade and conquest between the Roman Empire and Upper Egypt was a regular occurrence, and many occultists believe that the tarot was one of the many treasures lost in Alexandria's catastrophic, world history-altering fire.

Another Egypt-centric theory was that the images and meanings were based on a holy book written in Egypt, and then brought by peoples who would become

Romani tribes in Europe and Britain. The presence of triumph cards predated the first appearance of the Romani in European countries, so this theory doesn't stand up as well to the others, but it is an interesting thought.

In the late 17oos, a teacher and author named Jean-Baptiste Alliette wrote a book in which he described the game of "Piquet". He introduced a special card called an "Etteilla", which he also used as his nom de plume, or pen-name, created by reversing the letters of his last name. The etteilla card would symbolize the subject or querent in a game of piquet, and we can see this same practice used in many modern tarot spreads, including the popular Celtic cross spread.

A fascinating detail is that Etteilla himself claimed to see Egyptian symbolism in the tarot cards. He did not yet know that some of those were Egyptian hieroglyphs, because it would not be until the year 1799 that archeologists discovered the Rosetta Stone—the key to cracking the code of ancient Egyptian lettering. Etteilla believed that the tarot deck was originally designed by priests of Thoth, the Egyptian god of wisdom, and then went on to design what is known as "The Egyptian tarot". In the Egyptian tarot, we can instantly recognize much of the same symbolism that exists in the Rider-Waite tarot deck, but with Etteilla's attention to Egyptian details.

1.2 Archetypes and Their Effect on Culture and Society

Archetypes are symbols that are recognized across our world, regardless of what society we were raised in, what our background is, or what our culture or class might be. An archetype's meaning will inspire instant emotion and connection, depending on the viewer. Here are a few classic archetypes for reference:

- The elder (wisdom, experience, patience)
- The mother (nurturing, abundance, fertility)
- The child (discovery, enthusiasm, naïveté. We can see this archetype in the Fool tarot card, as well as in the pages of the four minor arcana suits).
- The trickster (a universal archetype found anywhere from the Coyote folktales of Native American cultures to the Norse God Loki. We can see traces of this archetype both in the Fool as well as the Magician.)

There are more archetypes that are echoed throughout the tarot, such as the animal-soul, the dark goddess that we see in the High Priestess, and the outlaw.

Archetypes become a universal way to connect to the world, through self-reflection, storytelling, and creations of literature and art. The tarot uses archetypes to enable the reader and querent to step into the shoes of a character, and thus come into a selfrealization that they may have never otherwise imagined.

Carl Jung was the psychologist who made "archetypes" a household word. He believed that, by the subject embodying an archetype for a moment, the subject would learn invaluable lessons about themselves. So, too, does the tarot help us look within, and see answers within our own subconscious minds that we might not have been able to otherwise make rise to the surface. Working with archetypes is not always a walk in the park, however—self-discovery often comes with a price. Powerful emotions may become unleashed when certain aspects of the self are unlocked. It is important to proceed at a cautious pace when engaging in any practice of self-reflection. This includes the tarot.

Archetypes can also help us learn about what motivates us. The archetype of the outlaw, for instance, is motivated by freedom, and its opposite is the pope or hierophant, who is motivated by the law.

Another school of thought concerning archetypes is that by actively seeking to embody them, we become them, gaining access to their remarkable power and abilities. This ties in with exercises mentioned in the final chapter of this book—how to meditate and manifest your goals and dreams through the powerful tool of the tarot.

Chapter 2: Tarot Mechanics

2.1 Quantum Physics, Synchronicity, and the Tarot

Just about everybody who's ever read tarot and worried about its accuracy asked, "Why does it work?" The solution to that problem is primarily based on our interest in morality, religion, and how the universe operates, so there are several potential hypotheses. At one end of the gamut, many tarotists assume that a conscious entity directs their reading, be it God / Dess, the lord, the divine leader, or the higher self. On the other end of the continuum are therapeutic school tarotists that assume that tarot cards should only represent predictions of everything that the client (and the reader) feels and who have a more immersive reading approach comparable to therapy.

And there are the two possibilities which shape the focus of this article - those who do not assume that a conscious power drives any reading, but who think that there is more happening than a psychological interpretation. In this middle field, I confess to slipping.

Since most of my readings are done by text, without the customer seeing the cards until after translation is completed, I cannot probably find any implicit corporeal hints that allow me to interpret the cards. Nonetheless, except with those who are informative and precise, I get such highly supportive reviews that I cannot accept that the decline in cards is not in any manner relevant to the real situation of the consumer. Unless I didn't think it was, I couldn't start reading this kind of tarot ethically.

As a scientist at heart, I must ask myself, "How does it work?" It has to meet specific basic parameters, whatever it is:

- Distance does not affect it. The consumer can be anywhere in the world
- There is no clear energy connection between the reader and consumer
- It may reflect on the situation of a particular client
- it may influence the actual structure of the cards

I don't find myself telepathic or neurological, so I tentatively rule such processes out, but I don't ignore the likelihood of tarot cards or other devices making these capacities possible for people who don't already learn them. Now let's look at some intriguing theories – quantum mechanics and Jung's synchronicity hypothesis – of which the conditions mentioned above may be met.

While some argue that it has not yet been proved that these processes can reliably affect real objects such as tarot cards, they are investigating what could happen further and, if not, are fascinating to know about them than any other hypothesis I have seen.

2.1.1 Quantum Physics

Quantum mechanics is a physics division that was initially created to describe how extremely tiny particles, such as photons or electrons, acted in the same manner as more significant artefacts. Large bodies obey some simple physics principles, which were previously established, called Newtonian mechanics.

For, e.g., if you push a ball with a certain energy, it goes in a particular direction at an individual pace. You will tell just what is going to happen because you know something about the scenario, including the weight of the ball and the degree of energy you use.

The event must act in keeping with the unchanging rules of cause and effect whether you watch it or not. We now know that all artefacts, irrespective of scale, are susceptible to quantum mechanics; nevertheless, these results will usually only be seen in large objects, so Newtonian mechanics are still ideal for explaining their behaviour.

As physicists began studies of tiny particles, they found that Newtonian mechanics was no longer valid. Issues will no longer provide a trigger for the result —atomic contaminants, for example, degrade without a transparent excuse.

If their activity has been evaluated in the past, we can estimate the probability of radioactive decay for a given amount of time. Still, we can't say whether or why it would happen. Nor would we be willing to, because particles of this scale are consistent with probability and not with unique action and reaction chains.

Another reason is that it cannot be known where very tiny objects are positioned precisely. We live then in a sort of "probability space" – there is a distinct possibility of getting there, and a distinct possibility of being there. Not just that, they're not here or there, but here and there at the same moment! Also, science researchers recently split an atom into two of its wave-functions effectively generating a condition in which the whole bit was in one position and the other simultaneously.

It's all pretty mind-boggling, but it has some essential elements. One is that particles are related to each other at a fundamental level and often appear to "learn" what condition other particles are in, even though the gap is too large for them to transfer energy or knowledge back and forth. The farther we go, the more issues are intertwined in areas that don't involve energy transfer. When items should be linked in this manner, a link could be created between a tarot reading in one location and the knowledge condition in another position (client environment).

Second, events at this point all function as expectations, not as fixed-behaviour artefacts. And if we obtain knowledge through these simple intertwined channels, we generally operate for probability rather than set outcomes. Much of the time, we'll provide the possible facts regarding the situation - but occasionally, we may obtain unexpected details.

When we take enough readings, the chances are that in our research, we'll finally find something impossible to happen. We've also felt that – a passage that, at random times, either doesn't seem to work or appears wrong.

The odd things concerning quantum particles are in probability space before we gaze at them. When we encounter them, we cannot resist influencing the system in such a way that their wave-forms fail, so they "choose" one condition or another to be in. And afterwards, they remain in that territory. It's almost as if, as long as we're not looking, everything is fluid, and anything is possible.

If we agree to look, any possibility is selected as a fixed truth. It is unusual as it implies that the condition of the universe is not independent of our conscious perception of it, a notion that goes against conventional science on a fundamental basis.

An important question to ask is, will this alter the situation? The response is most definitely yes, it does. We should at least have noticed a condition according to quantum mechanics and modified certain things by reading it. It is just set at this moment, though, and subsequent acts alter the state again. The fascinating thing about quantum mechanics is: the more you get down to abstract reality, the more the universe appears to be intertwined, and the less defined truth seems to get. Particular encounters are no longer restricted to time and place, so the "laws" of the cause so effect break on the lane. In truth, our understanding or interpretation of nature itself seems to be disturbed. This opens the door to the possibility that certain aspects just aren't the way the modern community has believed for many decades. In comparison, there is presently no proof that quantum influences may be found on the actions of large items such as tarot cards or that the entangled trajectories are adequately precise to relay the sort of knowledge that occurs in a tarot reading. What is the definition of synchronicity?

2.1.2 Synchronicity

Carl Jung, the respected psychologist and scholar, found that several of his patients and he had encounters in which "coincidence" appeared to play a significant part but also were too impossible to arise spontaneously. For, e.g., a patient might dream about a particular butterfly only to find a real butterfly during a therapy session the following day, the patient mentioned the vision. Under his view, such incidents were more likely to take place while the individual wanted the knowledge to create a breakthrough.

Jung identified a potential interpretation of the phenomena he found, dubbed "synchronicity," in the concepts of quantum mechanics. He postulated that there is, in addition to the causes and results we are acquainted with, another "link theory" that is acoustic. In other terms, two events may be linked without any clear association of cause and effect.

While Jung was not particularly acquainted with tarot, he was intrigued by I Ching and indicated that synchronicity was responsible for the functioning of the divination with I Ching. He also performed astrological studies to check theories of synchronicity. Still, he was not wholly confident whether the celestial cycles necessarily have no causal connection to our identities and incidents in our lives.

Jung describes several ESP studies in his treatise on synchronicity, which demonstrates that a relationship may occur between real artefacts (e.g., visual cards) and the visions that one experiences in one's head, even though it may not be causal. In an indication of this occurrence, he also addresses precognitive dreaming. One of the more fascinating features of this research is that these different "psychical" powers have not been influenced by time or space, close to how quantum particles can be associated irrespective of the gap between them. Indeed, many of the precognitive dreams he recorded for his patients were not in time, but only in a matter of days.

Because these synchronous events typically include specific objects, tarot lectures and other divination methods may be explained. Jung argues that our work has been so high in the concepts of cause and effect in recent years that no case that does not fit the trend has been ignored or ridiculed. Because these structures have been seen to occur at the very foundation of our observable universe, and on the broader environment, synchronistic anomalies can gain more confidence. Synchronous activities are, sadly, perhaps by nature, virtually challenging to research since the experimental process is focused on repeatable cause and effect. Because they do not arise with any predetermined regularity, their presence is challenging even to confirm. It leads to a possible issue with this principle as a foundation in tarot reading. This process operates again and again in fair confidence any time a tarot reader needs to learn.

One aspect that Jung found regarding ESP and astrology was that the findings relied on the frame of mind of the topic. For starters, if a person was depressed or disbelieving, he or she might not perform well in an ESP test relative to an ESP enthusiast. Similarly, if a professional astrologer were to randomly pick the charts of participants for an experiment on astrological conjunctions before marriage, a higher percentage of respondents would synchronize with the appropriate collaborations without having even looked at the tables. On the other side, a computer-generated match will select just an average number of individuals with the correct relations. This was unforeseen and was not part of the initial astrological research.

Such findings indicate that even though the fundamental processes work, it relies on the own state of mind and perception to use synchronistic strategies. Tarot writers learn that to a degree indirectly. Our tests are higher if we feel confident and responsive and do not question our ability. This can also mean that we will guide our thinking along the right lines to produce the best outcomes. When all is linked to a fundamental point, we will attain some result because we do not switch our attention to a single individual and his related circumstances and resources. It may also be the case for long-distance or email readings in which the consumer is not present.

While ESP and astrological tests indicate that the predictive association is far higher than randomly stated, it is necessary to remember that it is still too weak to be called "reliable." In other words, while it seems to be a correlation, like a gambler or a mentalist, you can't make a living off it as your forecasts will always be wrought. Even tarot readers have found that the outcome of activities such as athletics or democratic rivalry is impossible to foresee. Tarot could operate much better with certain forms of knowledge, such as energies and dynamics, than with conclusive details. Quantum mechanics and synchronicity, in particular, include principles that may clarify how tarot reading works, in the massive centrepiece of divine guidance and mere psychology. Although the actual state of one of these principles is not well advanced to demonstrate plainly, it offers at least some logical explanations and suggestions associated with our observations as tarot readers. So, it's enjoyable to talk about them.

Chapter 3: Introduction to Cards

While tarot cards can pale to play a normal deck, enjoying a whopping seventy-eight different cards, any beginner can get a pack and start practicing if they understand the fundamentals.

The cards in the tarot pack can be divided into several categories:

- Adapt
- Main and smaller Arcanes
- Pip Card
- Court Documents

Once you understand the different characteristics of any category, reading tarot cards is simply a matter of mixing and matching information.

The most basic distribution of Tarot Cards is between the twentytwo main Arcanes, forty pip cards, and sixteen Court cards. The best way to begin to understand the meaning of each card is to arrange each of the 22 main Arcana in a circle, with the first card in position twelve. From there, looking through the map clockwise, you will be able to follow the path of the soul inevitably passes during its existence.

Around the first circle, then place forty pip cards. It begins with a Pentacles suit, the first twelve-position map depicting the winter solstice. In the position of three, follow the Pentacles suit with a sword suit, indicating the spring equinox. Then place the wand suit in a six-hour position, which means the summer solstice. Finally, it ends with a suite of Cups, starting with the position of the nine and marking the autumn equinox. Just as the rotation of the main Arcana represents a cycle, the rotation of the PIP map demonstrates the movement of the Earth around the sun through the seasons.Finally, between these two circles, evenly distribute the remaining sixteen Court cards, working from the princess to the king in the seeds that correspond to the outer circle. These maps show different important personalities and how we grow over the years.

In this exercise, it is important to note that just because one card fell into the upper circle or the lower part is not more important than the other. Each card, whether it's major arcana or Minor Arcana, has a very special place in tarot reading.

Each seed in a smaller Arcane has very specific meanings that play an integral role in reading.

Cups: the cups are connected to the water element. Just as water can flow smoothly, be stopped by the dam, or boil and anger in the storm, as well as our emotions. When reading the cards that fall under the cups, it is important to read the procedure from one to ten in an emotional way.

Chopsticks: the chopsticks are attached to the fire element. Fire full of rhythm and movement; it can create and destroy. Therefore, chopsticks are the germ of change and action. Reading this dress, you will see cards that represent the first steps in a new beginning, the creation of our destiny, and cards that tell us that we acted too quickly, without thinking about the future.

Pentacle: Pentacles are associated with the element earth. The Earth is stable, solid, grounded. This is where we build our homes, feed ourselves and support ourselves. Similarly, these dresses focus on the body and our senses. Whether it's creating a family environment where you feel safe, getting financial security, or taking care of yourself and building a family, all this will be found, if you read the pentacles

Swords: swords are connected to the air element. We can't live without air, and we can't breathe. However, the air can also take your breath away in an instant. Just as the air can be sharp and pungent, so can the sword. This dress focuses on the intellect. It was said that there is no greater weapon than words, so beware of the warning that this seed can carry in terms of communication with others. It also explores the need for mental clarity and new ideas.

It also takes into account the personalities represented in the court's documents. These cards are incredibly important in reading because they can be directly related to you or someone who is closely related to your situation. Sometimes, it can help us understand who we can turn to for help, or who could hinder our progress.

Princesses: princesses and pages are interchangeable, and your deck will certainly be one or the other, but never both. When you draw a princess, you read about someone who is somehow young. Perhaps they have unfulfilled and unrecognized potential or are, in fact, a child. A princess can mean a student or someone who has just started a new adventure in her life.

Princes: princes are synonymous with Knights in a tarot reading, <u>and again the bridge will have one or the other, but never both.</u>
The principles symbolize movement and action; they thirst for progress in life and can often be naively idealistic. People who are read like a prince are warned about actions without thinking because they often jump the gun and assume that everything will work out in the best case. Princes are considered eager in all things and are a generous type of person who is always eager to help others.

Queens are considered caring and intuitive people. They are highly respected and admired and lead inspiration rather than command. The Queen can represent a man or a woman if it is someone who illustrates the above aspects. Often, they are a mature person or a relative-someone with life experience to draw on when offering advice.

Kings represent a person who grew up in his life and is now wise and perfect. Often the person who is represented by this card will feel a great duty and responsibility towards others, placing the needs of friends and family before their own.

After examining the classifications of court cards, seeds, and how to arrange a set of tarot cards in order to trace its history, the meaning of each card should begin to become clear. At this time, a beginner could choose a deck card and give it at least a very simple definition. Once you feel comfortable with this information, consider the numbers from one to ten and finally go through all the main mysterious cards one by one. When you have an understanding of what each number represents, and what the titles of the major arcanes represent, you can then read tarot de Marseille. It will take practice, and sometimes, you may need to refer to the reference table, but slowly and surely understand the concepts that go into the divisions of tarot cards, and everyone can pick up and be a simple and basic tarot reader.

Chapter 4: The Minor Arcana

The minor arcana cards as you already know reflect on the happenings from your everyday life and how that affects you. These practical cards symbolize your routine experiences, interactions, events, feelings and emotions as you experience them in your daily routine.

Let us take a deeper look into these cards and figure out the meanings associated with the four suits in the minor arcana cards.

4.1 Reading with Minor Arcana Cards

If your reading shows more of the minor arcana cards, it reflects on your daily issues and how you deal with them. For instance, you may be having trouble adjusting to a new colleague in the office or you may have started a new workout practice that makes you feel awkward at times. Such day-to-day experiences do not leave a very lasting and strong impact on you and your life, but it is nonetheless important to reflect on them.

When you reflect on your everyday experiences, you get better insight into how you react and respond to routine life situations and occurrences. Reacting refers to impulsively acting to something whereas responding refers to thinking through the situation and then taking a more rational and informed action or decision. It is important to ponder on your daily interactions and how you think, feel, behave and act so you become more aware of your attitude in life and can get an understanding of it to make decisions that are more informed.

The minor arcana cards are divided into 4 suits, each of which has further 14 cards starting from ace going up to king. Let us take a deeper look at the four suits and delve into the meaning associated with each of the 4 suits.

4.1.1 Suit of Cups

The suit of cups has the element water and signifies your emotions, creativity, intuition and feelings. The cup cards are likely to turn up in a reading about your emotional intelligence, emotional connection with oneself and others, love, happiness and relationships.

Water is agile, fluid and flows easily, but also holds a lot of power within itself. It can be gentle and harsh at the same time and knows how to make its way between things.

This is symbolic of our feelings and emotions because they too can be extremely tender, but immensely strong and volatile at times. Since water is the element of the suit of cups, when any cup card turns up in a tarot reading, it is likely to signify your emotions and feelings about a particular issue.

Cup cards in a reading are indicative of your ability to think from your heart instead of from your head and reflect your impulsive responses as well as your habitual reactions to different experiences and situations in life.

They are also associated with romanticism, imagination, fantasy and creativity; therefore, if your reading is about an intimate relationship, the cup cards could refer to the different fantasies and feelings of romanticism you have associated with that relationship.

The suit of cups also represents your overly emotional or irrational feelings when you can set unrealistic expectations from others or fantasize about things to the extent that you tend to make life difficult for others and even yourself. Tarot cards are also related to the astrological signs and in that sense, cups mostly related to those with Scorpio, Pisces and Cancer star signs.

If your reading shows predominantly cards from suit of cups, it is likely to indicate that you are in search of solutions to conflicts related to your personal interactions with others, matters of the heart and personal emotional issues.

4.1.2 The Suit of Swords

The suit of swords deals with your conscious mind and your level of consciousness centered around your intellect. Swords are mostly double-edged and in this aspect the suit of swords signifies the beautiful balance between your power and intellect and how the two elements can be employed for both, good and bad things. The suit of swords is linked with the 'air' element. Air is unseen and intangible, but it is in complete constant movement always. It is usually unnoticed and still but has the power to wreak havoc if it turns into a ferocious wind or tycoon and can instantly make you feel pleasant when it takes the shape of a breeze. It is cleansing, refreshing and powerful at the same time. It is indicative of your actions, knowledge, ability to change and power within. Air is a masculine energy that can be led by power and force. The sword cards in a tarot reading reflect your routine actions, power, forceful or influential decisions and how you adjust to changes and bring changes within yourself. They also symbolize your courage, ambition, any oppression you inflict upon someone or suffer from yourself and the conflicts you experience in routine life. They also signify your guilt, anger, lack of empathy, harsh judgments and any type of abuse you inflict or suffer from.

If the sword cards show up in a reading, they represent those with zodiac signs Gemini, Libra and Aquarius. When a tarot reading comprises of largely sword card, you are looking for solutions to your mental conflicts and struggles, and want to reach a decision soon.

You may also be going through some sort of abusive or traumatic experience that needs to be dealt with firmly. Sword cards also warn you to be more cautious in life and alert you of some unforeseen and undesirable situations approaching you fast.

4.1.3 The Suit of Pentacles

The suit of pentacles symbolizes your material possessions, work life and finances, and these cards are likely to show up in a reading concerning your professional life and finances or financial struggles. These cards deal with external and physical level of consciousness, and mirror our outer situations related to our work, creativity, finances and health. They are pertinent to how we perceive our external environment and how we form it, shape and influence it and make it grow. On an esoteric level, the suit of pentacles is also linked with your self-image, self-acceptance, self-esteem and ego. This suit is associated with the 'earth' element, which is tangible, tactile and is perceived as a symbol of being grounded and humble. Earth is fertile, supportive and stable, supports all the life forms in this world, and nurtures them to grow. It is a feminine element like water and helps grow, nourish and sustain life.

In a tarot card reading, if you get pentacles, it means you are focusing on events and problems related to your business, work, property, trade, money and other financial and career related matters.

Pentacles are also associated with prosperity, realization and manifestation as well as being greedy, overly materialistic, possessive and over-indulging. If your tarot reading reflects that you are over-indulging, being greedy and not focused on your finances, you need to ground yourself, figure out the things that truly matter to you and realign your focus on them.

Pentacles mostly correspond to people with the zodiac signs Virgo, Capricorn and Taurus. If your reading comprises of predominantly pentacle tarot cards, it means you seek solutions to conflicts pertinent to materialistic possessions, property, financial issues and work-related problems.

4.1.4 The Suit of Wands

The suit of wands is associated with your spirituality, primal energy, strength, determination, creativity, intuition, thoughts, expansion and ambition. It basically refers to the personal assets, elements and tools you need to move forward in life. It is associated with the 'fire' element, which is unpredictable, full of energy and extremely hot. It also symbolizes enthusiasm, vitality, sexuality and passion and is a masculine element that reflects the willpower and drive of the masculine energy. Fire is a helpful element in helping us unlock our creative side, pushing ourselves forward, finding new talents, becoming enthusiastic about our work and adding vitality into our lives.

Suit of wards in a reading signify that you are focusing on things that form the core of your existence and are related to your spirituality. They also address issues that make your ego, personality, enthusiasm, energy and self-concept tick.

The suit of wands is also associated with egotistical behavior, illusion, lacking purpose and direction in life, feeling meaningless and acting impulsively. The suit of wands mostly corresponds to people with Leo, Aries and Sagittarius zodiac signs. If your tarot reading comprises of mainly wand tarot cards, it is likely you are in search of solutions pertinent to problems related to the different stages of the development of an idea or those related to your realm of thought. You may also be looking to find greater sense of direction in life and clarity on your purpose in life. You need to go through the meanings and associations of all the suits in detail before starting your tarot reading. You can also keep this book by your side when conducting a reading and refer to it as you flip a card.

Now let us move on to the next chapter and learn about some different kinds of tarot spreads.

4.2 Tarot Spreads

There are different kinds of spreads you can use to carry out a tarot reading and gain better insight into a problem you are going through in your life. Here are some easy to practice spreads for beginners.

4.2.1 Single Card Spread

This is the simplest of all spreads you will ever come across and is extremely suitable for beginners who do not wish to get into any complications and those who have trouble focusing on several cards or things at the same time. Here is how to do it:

- Think about any problem or aspect of life you would like to explore and get clarity on and then pick your deck of cards thinking about that question. This step is important for all types of spreads that you carry out and is a must-do before and during every tarot reading you ever conduct.
- Shuffle the deck of cards and then pull out a single card from it.
- Put the card down and focus on the question you asked. Make sure the question is a simple one that does not have too many options attached to it.
- Focus on the meaning of the card and explore it from different aspects to get more clarity on it. It is better to write down the aspects you explore and the answers that come to you when analyzing the card.
- Keep thinking about the answers you discover in light of the problem to get a more meaningful answer and conclusion.

You can use only the major arcana cards if your query is related to a major life event such as marrying your partner or accepting a new job offer that requires you to move to another state. If your problem is related to routine events and is not too intense, but you wish to get a deeper understanding of it, you can use all the cards or just the minor arcana cards as well.

4.2.2 The 3 Card Spread

This simple, self-explanatory tarot spread has been around for a very long time. It is easy to carry out and read, and gives you a good understanding of the problem you are trying to explore. In addition, it works well for big and more impactful problems as well as routine issues, and a mixture of these two problems as well.

Here is how to do it:

- Shuffle the deck and focus on the problem at hand.
- Now pick out three cards from the deck and put them down on the table. Remember the order in which you pulled them out.
- The first card represents your past, the second reflects your present and the third signifies your future.
- You need to analyze them one at a time to figure out how they represent the specific period and what the card is trying to convey to you. For example, if you are focusing on your career and trying to figure out what suits you best, seeing your past card may make you realize that you should pursue your passion and viewing the present card may make you feel that your current career does not feel thriving and exciting to you, and your future card may speak to you about how good things come from following your ambitions. If you take it as a whole, the reading is likely trying to tell you to believe in yourself and follow your passion of becoming a singer and songwriter like you always wanted to do.

After you have conducted the reading, write down the findings and go through them a few times. It is best to reflect on a reading for a few days preferably a couple of weeks before carrying out another one on the same issue. You need time to think through the answers you have discovered and analyze them in detail. With many responsibilities to tend to, this cannot happen in a day so take your time.

The 3 card spread is a great reading that helps you understand the lessons you have gained over time and how things were, are right now and can be regarding a certain problem.

4.2.3 Mind, Body and Spirit Spread

This is another brilliant spread for beginners especially because it is simple to carry out. It is similar to the previous spread because this too involves three cards, but different in the manner that the three cards in this spread refer to your mind, body and spirit.

This spread gives you better insight into how your mind, body and spirit are working individually and as a whole, and whether you are going through a conflict between any two or all of them. Here is how you can practice it

- Pick out any three cards from the deck after shuffling it
- and lay them down.
- The first card points to your mind and how you are feeling about things from conscious and unconscious perspectives. You need to focus on whether you feel good about something from your mind and whether your head feels aligned to an issue or not.
- The second card symbolizes your physical state regarding a matter.
- The third card reflects the matters of your heart and whether or not you have a spiritual connection with an issue or matter.
- After you have picked out the three cards, analyze them individually one by one. As you explore the reading of a card, understand it in the light of the query you had in mind and write down the findings. For instance, you may be worrying about your deteriorating health and why you keep falling sick, and may be concerned that it is because you feel stressed because of your marriage. In that case, you need to see what each card in the spread says to you and then analyze it as a whole.
- Once you have assessed the cards individually, take them as a whole and read them collectively. If you are deeply upset about something, the 3 cards are likely to show trouble in all the 3 aspects: mind, body and spirituality. However, this may not be the case every time. You may

sometimes encounter a situation where there exists conflict between your heart and mind. You may feel more convinced about something if you see it from your heart, but your mind may try to pull you away constantly from it. When using this spread, you need to see the entire matter very objectively and be clear on how you feel about an issue from the perspective of your heart/ spirituality, body and mind.

This spread works well for you when you are trying to deal with an inner conflict regarding an important decision. Also, it is a spread you can carry out as a weekly ritual just to make sure all three aspects of your being; your mind, body and heart are well connected to what you are doing in life so you live with harmony.

4.2.4 Horseshoe Spread

If you are concerned about a matter from different angles, and would like to get a clearer idea of how things would work out for you regarding that issue in the end, the horseshoe is the right spread to practice.

This spread enables you to understand how things may unfold and gives you a bigger picture regarding a certain matter so you become more aware of the problem at hand and how things are likely to pan out in the near future and the long-term. Here is how you to do it:

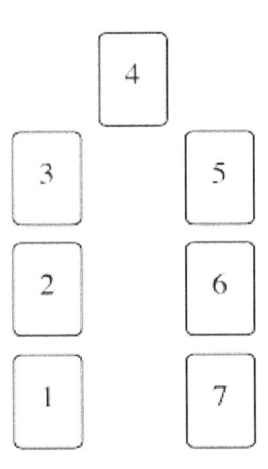

- Shuffle the deck and then draw one card at a time.

- You need to start placing the cards from your bottom left and keep putting down one card after another until you reach your bottom right and end up creating an upsidedown U shape of sorts.

- You should end up having seven cards in total.

- When reading the horseshoe that you have spread in front of you, you need to analyze the situation from how it was in the past to how it is now in your present to how things will unfold in the future while moving from the left side to the right.

- The bottom left cards reflect the past events while the cards in the middle speak about your present, and the ones on the far right symbolize possible outcomes. So if you are wondering about a certain relationship or want to get more insight into why you feel depressed, the cards on the far left will tell you how you felt in the past or point to a specific event in the past that may have triggered your depression, the ones in the center will reflect your current situation, and the series of cards on the bottom right will show you how things are likely to unfold for you.

Like with other spreads, write down the findings of the reading and go through them several times to make better sense of the entire reading. This is a nice spread to practice when you have some lingering questions about a certain issue.

4.2.5 The Celtic Cross Spread

This complex spread gives you a more detailed understanding of a specific issue. It is a more detailed version of the horseshoe which is also referred to as the 'more modified and modern' version of the Celtic cross.

If you are a more detailed oriented person who loves to understand and get into the details of an issue, this spread is right for you. However, it will take you a few tries to get the hang of it and understand what each card is trying to tell you, but if you are persistent and keep practicing it, you will become an expert at it soon. Here is how you can practice it:

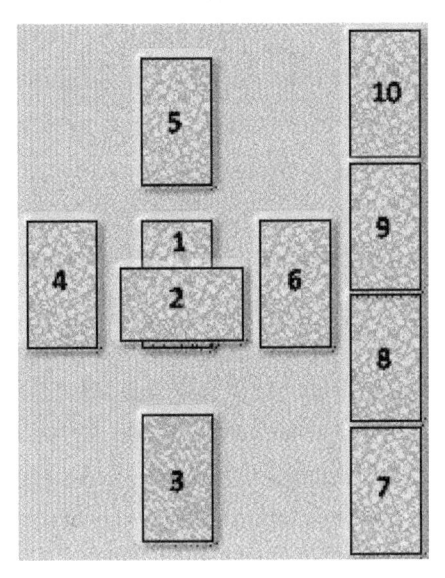

- Shuffle the deck of your tarot cards. This is a 10-card spread.
- Pull out a card and put it in the center.
- Pull out another card and place it on the top of the first card.
- The third card needs to go at the bottom of the first card; the fourth card should be laid on its right side, which makes it your left; the fifth card on the top of it and the sixth card towards your right, which makes it the left of the first card.
- You need to pull out four more cards and they should be placed parallel to the cards number 1, 3 and 5 in a manner that the 7th card is on the bottom and the 10th card on the top adjacent to the 5th card just like shown in the image above.
- If you cannot memorize the order of the cards, you can mark them from 1 to 10 with a soft lead pencil that can be easily erased afterwards.
- Now it is time to read the spread and analyze the answers.
- The 1st card signifies the 'querent' which in this case is you; the person asking the question. You need to carefully analyze the first card and check its meaning from the descriptions shared in the previous chapters to understand what it means. Probably it is trying to point out your state of mind or any character trait or how you feel at this point of time, or what you want from life right now or in general. Sometimes, this card

can also refer to someone in your life. For instance, it may point out to someone you share a close bond with or maybe someone you are on conflicting terms with, but would like to improve the relationship with.

- The second card reflects the situation you are going through in your present. Depending on the question you asked, it could point to the matters of the heart, a financial crunch you are going through, emotional issues, relationship problems or tensions in your professional life. Sometimes, the card may not seem relevant to the query you have in mind. That is because it is pointing to the actual query, the one you should focus on. For example, you may want to know about whether or not to marry your partner, but the card may be suggesting that you are not fulfilled and content from within. This can mean that you first need to be happy from within and then find a partner accordingly because that is how you will be able to find the right partner for yourself.
- The 3rd card represents the foundation of the problem at hand. It helps you understand the different factors and elements that have produced the issue you are suffering from and are mostly related to your past. For instance, when trying to figure out why you have developed a controlling and manipulative attitude towards your loved ones, you may figure out that is because your parents treated you like this when you were younger. Remember, the cards are not going to tell you everything plain and simple, and out loud. They will obviously present many things to you, but it is you who has to make sense of the meanings and for that, you need to really dig deeper into things.
- The 4th card symbolizes your recent past, something that is associated with your past as shown by the 3rd card, but something that happened only recently. For example, if your third card reflects emotional problems, the fourth card is likely to point out the loss of a loved one or the end of an important relationship. If the reading is a positive, happy one, the fourth card is likely to symbolize happy, bright events.
- The 5th card shows the different episodes or events you will experience in the next few months or maybe a couple of years. This is from where things start to move towards the future and you get a clearer idea of how

things will pan out for you. If you are going through a financial crunch, you may foresee better things coming up for you or maybe the situation may worsen.

- The 6th card indicates your current state and gives you an understanding of whether or not your problem will resolve soon enough. You get an idea of your relationship with the prospective future outcome. Continuing with the previous example of a financial struggle, the card may show more emotional problems coming up if the 5th card shows your financial crunch will continue for another year.
- The 7th card symbolizes the different outside influences you are surrounded with regarding the issue at hand. You may become aware of those supporting you or those who do not back you up, and makes you aware of how different people in your social circle influence you regarding that problem.
- The 8th card is indicative of the internal influences you experience which are basically your feelings about the situation or problem you are trying to get a better understanding of. It speaks directly to you about how you feel regarding the situation you are in and the feelings could be positive, negative or a mixture of the two kinds. If the overall reading is a happy one, you may feel good, confident, peaceful, cheerful and excited, or just any one of these feelings or any other positive feeling. If the overall reading is about a grave issue, your feelings may lean more towards frustration, stress, anger, sadness or even jealousy. This obviously depends on the problem you are trying to explore.
- The ninth card represents the hopes, fears and apprehensions you nurture. While it is similar to the previous card, it is more related to the different concerns you have regarding the problem you are engulfed in.
- The final card of the spread points to the long-term situation and outcomes you are likely to experience in the next six to twelve months. It is more like the conclusion of the nine cards you have read prior to this one. It talks to you about how things will unfold in another few months and prepares you for the outcomes beforehand. For example, if you get the death card as the tenth card and you are thinking about your business

and the problems you are facing in it, it may mean that your business is likely to end in another few months and it is not a lucrative option for you so it is a good time to think about another option and explore it. Sometimes, the tenth card may not make any sense at all. If that happens, pull out another card or maybe two cards and place them next to the 10th card or even replace the 10th card with them. You need to then read the new cards or the 10th card along with the new card and explore the other nine cards in reference to it. You are likely to comprehend the situation and reading better then.

Do jot down the meanings and answers you find and take time to reflect on them. A single Celtic cross reading can provide you with a number of points and ideas to ponder on and it can take you anywhere from a couple of hours to even a few weeks to fully comprehend the lessons reflected in a Celtic cross reading.

You can also conduct a Celtic cross reading as a continuation of a single or three card spread. For instance, if you just conducted a single card spread about an important issue or even a routine matter but something you feel strongly about, and would like to explore it further, continue with that in a Celtic cross reading. After conducting a one card spread, explore the meaning you found out for some time and then conduct a Celtic cross reading after a couple of hours or even a few minutes after that first reading. However, it is best you take at least a day's gap between two readings to get better comprehension of its meaning and the results.

4.2.6 Relationship Spread

This is a nice spread to practice when you wish to explore a relationship you share with someone. The best thing about this spread is that it applies to all sorts of relationships. Here is how you can carry it out:

- After shuffling the deck, pull out three cards and put them on the left side. These cards reflect you and your feelings pertinent to that person and the relationship you share with him/her.
- Pull out another three cards and put them on the right side. These cards are indicative of that other person you wish to explore your relationship

further with. The cards may also show his/her feelings related to you and how the relationship is going forward from their perspective.
- Pull out one more card and place it in the middle of the two sets. This is the advice card which points to the outcome or future of the relationship you are trying to understand, and may provide tips on how to better the bond and strengthen it.

You need to first read the cards individually and then as a whole to better understand how you feel about that person, how he/she feels about the relationship and whether or not the relationship is going somewhere, and if it is, what you can do to make it a successful venture together.

All these spreads are really helpful and can provide you with valuable insight into the different experiences and problems you are going through in life. Try your hand with each one of them depending on the issues you are experiencing and see how each works out for you. You may find yourself inclining towards a certain type of spread after you have had a good experience with it.

Now that you know the different kinds of spreads you can practice, let me share with you some tips to prepare yourself for a tarot reading and cleanse afterwards for effective results.

Conclusion

Unlike most other Western religions, Wicca is highly decentralized—there is no official sacred text, no central governing body, and this means there is no one way to practice the religion.

With this in mind, it is very difficult to create a truly encompassing beginner's guide to the topic, simply because different Wiccans will interpret the many facets of the religion differently—in some cases, **very** differently.

There is no right or wrong. As long as you keep the Wiccan principles at heart, and never intentionally seek to harm others, you can practice Wicca in any way you see fit. In fact, I would actively **encourage** you to seek out your own path.

One of the best things about Wicca is that your interpretations, views, and beliefs are highly flexible. When you are just starting out, you are encouraged to read and learn as much as possible, and so your initial beliefs are bound to be shaped by the guides you read.

Over time, when you begin to embrace Wicca in your daily life, you might have certain epiphanies that re-shape your approach to the practicing this religion. What you believe on day one, might be **very** different to your beliefs on day 100, which could be a world apart from your views on day 1,000. It can be a lifelong journey, and even after decades you will still find yourself learning new things. This is one of the many benefits of keeping your own Book of Shadows—you can literally track how your Wiccan journey has evolved over time.

Remember: nobody can tell you how to practice Wicca, and the religion can mean anything you want it to mean to you. While I have presented the information in this guide as "correct", I am in no way suggesting that it is the only way to practice Wicca. If you read other guides, there may be conflicting information. And when you read another guide to the topic, you will likely come across even more conflicting information!

That's just the way Wicca is. Even if you encounter some different opinions— even those completely opposed to what you have read in this guide! -it doesn't mean one guide is right, and another is wrong: it just means the many different authors have interpreted different aspects of the religion differently.

I will leave you with that thought, as it is now time for you to start your own journey, and interpret the information presented to you in your own way. I have included a number of tables of correspondence at the end of this guide, which you should find helpful at some point in time. I have also included a number of suggested sources for further reading, as in the early days it is important for you to absorb as much information as possible on the subject.

I sincerely hoped you enjoyed learning about Wicca with me, as it is a topic close to my heart. It would mean a great deal to me if you continued on your path towards Wicca, but if you choose not to, I hope I have educated you on the belief system of the wonderful people who choose to practice Wicca.

Can I ask you a favor?

Thank you for reading this book, we hope you enjoyed it, and most of all we hope you found it useful!! Please leave an honest review to support our work and future books I'm going to publish.

We thank you again and hope to have you always with us on this wiccan journey.

Best wishes!